States, Firms, and Power

SUNY Series in Global Politics
James N. Rosenau, editor

States, Firms, and Power

Successful Sanctions in United States Foreign Policy

George E. Shambaugh

State University of New York Press

Published by
State University of New York Press, Albany

© 1999 State University of New York

For information, address State University of New York Press
State University Plaza, Albany, New York 12246

Production by Dana Foote
Marketing by Patrick Durocher

Library of Congress Cataloging-in-Publication Data

Shambaugh, George E., 1963–
States, firms, and power : successful sanctions in United States
foreign policy / George E. Shambaugh.
p. cm. — (SUNY series in global politics)
Includes bibliographical references and index.
ISBN 0–7914–4271–3 (hc. : alk. paper). — ISBN 0–7914–4272–1 (pbk.
JK   : alk. paper)
1. Economic sanctions, American. 2. Export controls—United
States. 3. United States—Commercial policy. 4. United States—
Foreign relations. 5. United States—Foreign economic relations.
I. Title. II. Series.

HF1413.5.S53 1999
337.73—dc21   99–28280
                                                              CIP

10 9 8 7 6 5 4 3 2 1

To my mother,
whose life and memory continue to inspire me

CONTENTS

Tables

PREFACE AND ACKNOWLEDGMENTS

Economic sanctions and incentives are often maligned, misused, and misunderstood, yet they are also the policy tools of choice against foe, friend, and firm. Case in point: As of May 1998, the United States was imposing sanctions against 75 countries and more than 335 private companies.[1] However, most studies of these and other sanctions have evaluated only the ability of states to use economic penalties and rewards to alter the behavior of other states. This book differs from these studies in two ways. First, rather than focusing on the effect of economic sanctions or incentives on the policies or behavior of a primary target like a rogue or risky state, it examines the more difficult problem of how to get reluctant but otherwise friendly countries and foreign companies to cooperate with the use of sanctions or incentives against a designated target. Second, this book focuses on the use of sanctions and incentives by states to sway both other states and private companies. Increasing levels of globalization and privatization in the world economy make the judicious use of economic statecraft against firms and other nonstate actors an increasingly important component of foreign policy. Hence, understanding the costs and benefits of using sanctions and incentives against private companies is critical because they—rather than states—are increasingly the producers, merchants, and consumers of sanctioned goods and technology.

The arguments developed in this volume contribute to the broader study of international politics and international political economy by increasing our ability to evaluate, explain, and predict power relations between states and firms in world politics by analyzing the sources and limitations of this form of state power via the effects of economic dependence on state and nonstate actors. It is thus intended to supplement existing studies of economic statecraft by extending the analysis and pragmatic use of sanctions and incentives beyond the traditional realm of these policy tools. In the final analysis, it concludes that economic incentives and threats can be effective tools of statecraft when applied judiciously under the conditions specified in this book. Guidelines for policymakers seeking to apply economic incentives and threats in a productive manner, or, conversely, to minimize their vulnerability to them, are also included.

I am indebted to many colleagues, friends, and family members who helped me to bring this book to fruition. My colleagues and friends at

Columbia University, Smith College, and Georgetown University deserve credit for their comments, as well as their willingness to repeatedly discuss and read portions of this project. Professors David Baldwin and Helen Milner from Columbia University, David Spiro from the University of Arizona, Eve Sandberg from Oberlin College, and Margee Ensign from the University of the Pacific all saw promise in my initial attempts to formulate my arguments and all provided guidance throughout the writing process. Professors Patricia Weitsman, Joseph Lepgold, and Luan Troxel provided significant insights, criticisms, and support without which this project would have been far more daunting. My graduate student assistants and colleagues Scott Bowden, Renae Ditmer, and Mira Sucharov provided indispensable editorial comments and research support. My father, brothers, and sister were constant sources of motivation to pursue and complete this project. And, most importantly, my wife Jacqui deserves special recognition for her tireless support and tolerance for endless proofreading, short weekends, and my general preoccupation with this project. I thank the editor and reviewers at *International Studies Quarterly* for their comments and suggestions on an article that explored some of the ideas that grew into this book. I also thank the editor, reviewers, and production team at the State University of New York Press for their assistance with the final manuscript. Finally, this project could not have been completed without financial support from the Eisenhower Foundation, the MacArthur Foundation, the Oberlin College Alumni Foundation, the Smith College Faculty Development Fund and the Georgetown University Graduate School of Arts and Sciences Competitive Grant-in-Aid. I alone, however, accept full responsibility for any errors of commission or omission.

Note

1. Richard Haass, "Sanctions Almost Never Work," *The Wall Street Journal* (19 June 1998). A current Denied Persons List is available on the World Wide Web at http://www.bxa.doc.gov/.

1

The Puzzle and Argument:
Dominance, Dependence, and Political Power

> Washington takes aim at its foe and shoots its friend.
> —Canadian Foreign Trade
> Minister Arthur Eggleton[1]

THE POWER AND INFAMY OF SANCTIONS

Economic sanctions present a stark intellectual puzzle to students of international politics. Though often maligned, misused, and misunderstood, they stand as the policy tool of choice against foe, friend, and firm. Indeed, the United States has imposed sanctions against other countries nearly seventy-five times in the past five years—more than half the total instances in which sanctions have been imposed against other countries since World War II.[2] The stated purposes for imposing these sanctions have varied widely. They include discouraging the proliferation of weapons and strategic goods, as well as punishing countries for perceived violations of human rights and religious freedom, terrorism, drug trafficking, and violations against the environment.

In May of 1998, the United States continued this pattern by joining numerous other countries in imposing economic sanctions on India and Pakistan to penalize them for testing nuclear weapons and building missiles that could deliver their bombs into each other's territories. Curiously, though there is little doubt that those imposing the sanctions deplore and fear India and Pakistan's nuclear activities, soon after the sanctions were announced, the Clinton administration and others considered toning them down, this in response to growing opposition from business lobbies like the Industry Coalition on Technology Transfer and others who argued that imposing sanctions would hurt American business. The irony is that private companies from the United States and other countries imposing the sanctions are the most likely sources of the materials and technology

1

that enabled India and Pakistan to build their nuclear weapons and delivery systems in the first place.[3] A similar situation developed during the Gulf War of 1991 when private companies from the United States, Germany, France, and other members of the Desert Storm coalition were linked to the sale of weapons systems and related technology to the Iraqi military.[4] The repercussions of corporate activity prior to the Gulf War and the South Asian nuclear crisis suggest that while private companies are among the most ardent critics of economic sanctions, they may also be prime targets of American and multilateral efforts to stop the proliferation of strategic goods and technology.

Recent legislation passed by the U.S. Congress demonstrates that the United States government is not afraid to impose sanctions against private companies[5]—as of May 1998, the United States is currently imposing sanctions against more than 335 private companies[6]—yet it has done so without fully understanding when sanctions are likely to be effective or what the political, economic, and strategic implications of their use will be. For example, as of August 1, 1996, foreign firms conducting business with Cuba may be sanctioned by the United States in accordance with the restrictions specified in the Helms-Burton Act.[7] Similarly, under the Iran and Libya Sanctions Act, sanctions may be imposed against foreign companies conducting certain types of business in Iran and Libya.[8] The explicit goal of these so-called secondary sanctions is to entice or coerce foreign governments and firms to adopt practices consistent with U.S. restrictions against these and other potentially threatening countries. The U.S. Congress has steadfastly maintained these sanctions despite increasing international, domestic, and presidential opposition, and against a growing belief that, as former Secretary of State Lawrence Eagleburger argued, "[S]econdary boycotts are nuts. . . . Sanctions against foreign businesses are an exercise of American imperialism. . . . *They never work.* All they do is get our allies mad at us."[9] And while Congressional resolve to maintain the sanctions remains high, even supporters of the policy such as Lee Hamilton, the ranking Democrat on the International Relations Committee at the time, admitted that, "[W]e do not know whether we are going to achieve our goal."[10] These comments reflect a disturbing lack of understanding among policymakers about economic statecraft and the benefits and limitations of using economic means to achieve political objectives.[11]

This combination of resolve and uncertainty presents a challenge to both policymakers and scholars. Economic leadership in the United States has come to realize the importance of finding a way to improve how we make sanctions decisions, to ensure that their use derives from a coherent strategy, to accurately measure the costs and benefits of sanctions measures, to seek multilateral support where possible, and to improve the coordination between the administration and Congress.[12] This book responds to this challenge by providing guidelines for the effective use and analysis of economic statecraft against states and firms. Most important, it shows that economic sanctions and incentives can be effective tools of statecraft. If such measures are applied judiciously and under appropriate conditions, they can be used to extend political control over actors beyond a state's legal and political borders. Furthermore, in addition to providing guidelines for policymakers seeking to use economic statecraft (and for those seeking to minimize their vulnerability to it), the arguments developed in this book explain when and why economic statecraft will be effective. Taken together they thereby contribute to the broader study of international politics and international political economy by increasing our ability to evaluate, explain, and predict power relations between states, firms, and individuals in world politics.

The primary objective of this book is to analyze the capability and costs of using secondary sanctions and incentives to alter the behavior of foreign companies. Most studies of economic statecraft focus on the use of sanctions or incentives by states against other states. These studies have debated the qualified effectiveness of these tools at length.[13] This book differs from this literature in two significant ways. First, rather than focusing on the effect of economic sanctions or incentives on the policies or behavior of a primary target, it examines the more difficult problem of getting reluctant, but otherwise friendly, countries and foreign companies to cooperate with the use of sanctions or incentives against the primary target. Second, this book focuses on the use of sanctions and incentives by states to influence both other states and private companies. Understanding the costs and benefits of using sanctions and incentives against private companies is critical because they—rather than states—are increasingly the producers, merchants, and consumers of sanctioned goods and technology. Increasing levels of globalization and privatization in the world economy make the judicious use of economic statecraft against firms and other nonstate actors an increasingly important component of foreign policy. This study is thus intended to supplement existing studies of economic statecraft by extending the analysis and pragmatic use of sanctions and incentives beyond the traditional realm of these policy tools.

Can Sanctions Work?

The first step in responding to the challenge of economic statecraft is to determine if and when economic sanctions or incentives can be used effectively as instruments of foreign policy. Economic sanctions and incentives can take a variety of forms and serve a variety of substantive and symbolic purposes.[14] However, for the purposes of this book, an economic sanction will be defined as an economic penalty or cost that is imposed by a sender on a designated target, regardless of the particular form that it takes or the ends that it serves. In parallel, an economic incentive (also known as a positive sanction)[15] will be defined as an economic reward or benefit that is bestowed by the sender to the target.[16] The "sender" is the principal author of the sanction or incentive, while the "target" is the immediate actor against whom the sanctions are imposed or upon whom incentives are bestowed.[17] Secondary sanctions and secondary incentives differ from other sanctions or incentives in that they are not directed toward the primary target, but rather are directed against third parties in an attempt to their behavior or their policies regarding the primary target. For example, the sanctions specified in the Helms-Burton legislation may be referred to as secondary sanctions because they are directed against foreign companies conducting business in Cuba rather than the Cuban regime itself.

While scholars and policy analysts disagree about the types of goals that economic sanctions and incentives can be expected to achieve and, consequently, the criteria against which to evaluate their effectiveness, there is a general consensus that their overall success rate is low.[18] In one of the most extensive and widely cited empirical studies of sanctions to date, Gary Hufbauer, Jeffrey Schott, and Kimberly Elliot analyzed the use of sanctions against countries between 1914 and 1984 and found them to be successful only 36 percent of the time.[19] Using an even narrower definition of effectiveness, Robert Pape argued that only five percent of the cases evaluated by Hufbauer, Schott, and Elliot successfully achieved their goals.[20] These findings imply a dismal record for sanctions, however it is critical to note that they do not tell us whether sanctions can be effective policy tools because they don't tell us why the sanctions succeeded or failed. The results do not tell us, for example, whether the failure was inherent to the instrument itself or the result of mistakes made by policymakers who attempted to use sanctions under inappropriate circumstances or to achieve unrealistic goals. In short, much of the empirical research on this topic is underspecified.

An effective theoretical argument must, however, precede any attempt at hypotheses testing. Trying to assess whether sanctions can succeed in achieving major policy goals without considering a theory of economic statecraft that specifies exactly what sanctions can be expected to achieve and under what conditions these achievements can be expected is akin to assessing the utility of nuclear weapons as policy instruments without examining deterrence theory. Pape's assessment is bleaker than the findings of Hufbauer, Schott, and Elliot in part because he evaluates only cases where sanctions were the sole means used to achieve a major political goal. This restriction severely reduces the likelihood of finding a successful case because sanctions, like nuclear weapons and most other tools of statecraft, are rarely used in the absence of other policy tools.[21] Sanctions are also least likely to be effective when used alone and they are less likely to be effective against states than against other actors, such as private companies or individuals. Pape's criterion, therefore, has the effect of eliminating a large number of instances in which sanctions may have played an important role in U.S. foreign policy, thereby leaving the impression that they are largely useless policy instruments. While we rarely can be certain that deterrence could have succeeded in averting a nuclear exchange with the Soviet Union in the absence of diplomacy and other policy tools, this uncertainty does not tell us that nuclear weapons did not play an important policy role. To avoid a similar spurious interpretation of failure and to assess the effectiveness of sanctions as foreign policy tools, it is necessary to center the debate around competing arguments about why and when sanctions can be expected to work.

For various reasons, including the unpopularity of the use of military force, sanctions are a popular tool of foreign policy and they are being used with increasing frequency to achieve a wide variety of objectives. In the following chapters, I analyze sixty-six cases in which the U.S. government used economic statecraft—primarily in the form of secondary sanctions—as the exclusive or primary means of compelling foreign firms to refrain from trafficking in strategic goods and technology to countries targeted by U.S. export control policy. From this, I find that U.S. secondary sanctions were successful in stopping foreign firms from exporting strategic goods and technology only about 50 percent of the time. This result does not, however, mean that sanctions cannot be used as effective tools of statecraft as sanction critics have argued. Rather, it means that if they are to be used effectively, it is essential that policy decisions be guided by a theory of economic statecraft that specifies the conditions under which they are likely to achieve particular policy objectives.

Given the low success rate against states and the fifty-fifty success rate against firms, it is critical to determine the conditions under which sanctions are likely to succeed and when they are likely to fail. To do so, this book develops a theory of power and economic statecraft based on trade dominance and trade dependence. Hypotheses deduced form this theory predict the success and failure of secondary sanctions used to alter international corporate behavior correctly over 75 percent of the time. The ability to predict success and failure with such a high degree of accuracy suggests that sanctions may be effective when used under appropriate conditions. These include, but are not limited to, the trade dominance of the sender, the target's dependence on the sender, the sender's dependence on the target, and the opportunity costs associated with sending and responding to the sanction.

The ability to identify and manipulate the factors necessary to achieve this high degree of success has important policy implications for the analysis and use of sanctions. At the same time, the use of sanctions, and secondary sanctions in particular, can be costly in economic, political, and military terms. Given these costs, it is crucial to understand precisely when they are likely to be effective, and what the repercussions of using them are likely to be before applying sanctions against otherwise friendly foreign companies conducting business in Cuba, Iran, Libya, India, Pakistan, or elsewhere.

Power, Wealth, and Why Secondary Sanctions Matter

The second step in responding to the challenge of using economic statecraft judiciously is to analyze the implications of using economic means to achieve foreign policy goals. To understand how economic means can be used to achieve political objectives and what the consequences of using them will be, we need to understand the nature of economic statecraft. Economic statecraft is about more than the effectiveness of economic rewards or penalties. It is fundamentally about the exercise of power and the relationship between power and wealth.[22] The exercise of power—defined as getting someone to do something they would not otherwise do—is one of the most fundamental issues in world politics.[23] Economic statecraft, and economic sanctions in particular, are tools that can be used to get others to do something they would not otherwise do. Understanding when and why economic statecraft works, therefore, provides insight into the nature and exercise of power in world politics. Secondary sanctions are particularly important because they are often used to exercise power over trading partners and firms against whom more coercive instruments of statecraft are of limited practical value. Using economic statecraft to influence foreign firms is particularly provocative because, when used properly, sanctions can provide a means of extending political control across national and legal boundaries.

Increasing levels of globalization and privatization in the world economy make the use of economic sanctions against firms an increasingly potent tool of statecraft. Critics who argue that increased economic interdependence minimizes the effectiveness and, therefore, the importance of economic statecraft misinterpret the significance of these global changes on the power of the state.[24] On the one hand, increased globalization and privatization of the world economy have given individuals, firms, and other nonstate actors new incentives, capabilities, and opportunities to pursue wealth on a global scale. In the 1980s, for example, Japan joined other advanced industrialized countries in liberalizing its financial regulations, thus making it easier to use its currency abroad. This liberalization of capital flows represents the last in a series of changes (including the return to currency convertibility in the 1950s, the growth of multilateral production and banking in the 1960s and 1970s, and the rise of Eurocurrencies and the Eurodollar market in the 1970s and 1980s) that marked the genuine globalization of the world economy. In combination with the liberalization of trade, the free flow of capital means that investors are no longer restricted to opportunities at home. They can move quickly to seek out new clients, consumers, and investment opportunities around the globe. In a way that Adam Smith and David Ricardo never fully anticipated, the global forces of supply and demand largely drive the world economy with only minimal interference from national governments.

On the other hand, while potentially extremely profitable for states as well as firms, changes in the nature of wealth creation have profound implications for the nature and exercise of power. At a minimum, private companies and individuals—rather than states—are increasingly the primary producers, merchants, and consumers of strategic goods and technology. As discussed above, U.S. companies including DEC, IBM, and Viewlogic provided computers and related technology that facilitated the development of Indian and Pakistani nuclear weapons and their delivery systems.[25] Similarly, during the Gulf War of 1991, companies from the United States, Great Britain, and Germany were linked to the sale of computers to the Iraqi military and atomic energy agency, ballistic missile and chemical weapon technology to its defense department, personal security equipment to the Iraqi president, and components of SCUD missiles used against Desert Storm troops.[26] Thus, private actors can play a significant and potentially dangerous role in redistributing economic and military capabilities to otherwise weaker states.

At the same time, the globalization of the production, markets, and distribution networks for strategic goods makes them much more difficult than before for governments to monitor and regulate. Even when possible, the extension of legal authority over individuals or firms may not be sufficient to guarantee de facto oversight or control of their activities. Indeed, one of the most common problems with the implementation of multilateral intergovernmental agreements to reduce weapons proliferation or limit the sale of strategic technology is the inability of national governments to stop firms within their countries from financing, producing, and distributing these goods in the global marketplace. This can result in "involuntary defections" from multilateral agreements. In the context of this study, an involuntary defection occurs when a national government supports and agrees to abide by a multilateral accord, but is either unaware that actors operating in its territory are violating the agreement or is unable to stop them from doing so.[27] One of the most highly publicized cases of involuntary defection took place in 1987, when, without the knowledge of the Japanese or Norwegian governments, Toshiba Machine Company of Japan and Kongsberg-Vapanfabrik of Norway sold computerized milling equipment to the Soviet Union that was capable of producing highly sophisticated propellers for submarines.[28] These sales had dramatic military significance and were in direct violation of multilateral agreements restricting the sale of sensitive technologies to the Soviet Union (see chapter 5).

Economic statecraft, in the form of secondary sanctions or incentives, provides a potent tool for minimizing "involuntary defection" and extending control over private actors across national boundaries more generally. When used under appropriate conditions, economic penalties and rewards can be used to coerce or entice individuals and firms operating abroad to alter their behavior. One positive implication of this capability is that secondary sanctions or incentives can be used to assist local governments that concur with multilateral agreements, but are either unwilling or unable (for whatever reason) to enforce them at home. In 1982, for example, the British government actively supported U.S. agents in their efforts to indict and sanction Systime, Ltd., for shipping computers in violation of U.S. export control policy (see chapter 4). This is significant because it suggests that the implementation of multilateral agreements need not rest on the ability of individual signatories to enforce the agreements at home—secondary sanctions and incentives give multilateral institutions a means of doing so themselves.[29] The potential effectiveness of secondary sanctions and incentives, however, exacerbates a second problem. When used without the consent or support of local governments, they may give a foreign government the capability to extend its control over local firms and individuals against the interest of the local government.

For the same reason, secondary sanctions and incentives are likely to engender much opposition from the host government. Autonomous, sovereign control over use of domestic resources is a primary source of state power and wealth. In a drive to maximize their wealth and security, states typically protect resources in their possession while they attempt to acquire relatively more resources than their neighbors. Firms represent a resource which creates both wealth and power. It follows that states will compete to control the activities of multinational firms just as they compete for the control of other resources. The rewards from this competition, however, are exceptionally high. When one state controls the activities of firms within another state's territory it not only decreases the physical resources at that state's disposal, it also undermines its political integrity by challenging its ability to control actors and activities within its territory. Gaining or losing control over local actors, particularly those related to the production or distribution of strategic goods, may have significant implications for economic and military security. This makes the use of economic statecraft by one state to extend de facto control over firms operating outside of its national jurisdiction extremely significant for all states. Thus, rather than representing the "end of the state" and the decline of political power in world politics, increased globalization and interdependence in the world economy have actually expanded competitive relations among states to actors and activities traditionally considered to be beyond the reach of international power politics.

This book analyzes economic statecraft as a means of exploring fundamental questions about the relationship between wealth and power in a global economy. Assuming that while states and firms have different interests and vulnerabilities, they both respond to pressure, I develop a single argument about what constitutes that pressure for both actors. Using this argument as a foundation, I develop a model that accurately identifies and predicts the conditions under which secondary sanctions and incentives can be used by states to compel foreign companies to alter their behavior.

THE THEORY: DOMINANCE, DEPENDENCE, AND THE SUCCESS OF ECONOMIC SANCTIONS

For the past fifty years, the U.S. government has used economic sanctions and incentives to compel reluctant states and foreign firms to comply with its export control policies.[30] The results of these actions are intriguing because the ability of the U.S. government to compel state and firms to change their behavior has varied widely over the past half-century, yet we lack the analytical tools to explain this variation. In general, U.S. efforts to secure compliance with its policies are examples of the phenomenon of "coercive cooperation" in which a dominant state uses persuasion, promises, or threats to secure multilateral cooperation.[31] Structural realism and hegemonic leadership arguments, two of the main frameworks used to explain multilateral economic cooperation and outcomes in world politics more generally, suggest that the ability of the United States to secure extraterritorial compliance should vary as a function of its relative military, economic, and political capabilities. Yet, the changes in the aggregate distribution of these capabilities among the relevant parties cannot explain the wide variation in the United States' ability to secure extraterritorial compliance with its export control policy either in the 1950s at the peak of U.S. hegemony or throughout the Cold War era, and they have particular problems explaining the wide variation evident during the 1980s and 1990s.[32] Furthermore, even if the precise distribution of economic, political, and military capabilities among various states is disputed, structural arguments necessarily imply that American influence should not vary significantly across actors or issue areas.[33] Such predictions, however, expose a striking puzzle: many of the cases discussed below took place at virtually the same time in the same geostrategic environment, yet their outcomes varied dramatically.

The theory of economic statecraft developed in the following section offers two solutions to this puzzle. The first solution is based on the premise that while the outcome of power relations in world politics is likely to reflect the interests of the actor who possesses a preponderance of relevant political, economic, and military resources, the value and utility of particular resources are issue specific and context specific. As a result, one actor will be able to exercise power over another if it possesses a sufficient quantity of those particular resources that are valued by the target. Thus, unlike the structural models, issue- and context-specific models assume that trade dominance in one industrial sector will enable a state to exercise power over foreign companies operating in that sector, but not necessarily in others. The second solution builds on the first. It accepts the premise that the relevance of power resources should be evaluated on an issue- and context-specific basis, but it adds the proposition that the impact of promising or denying access to particular resources is a function of the value of resources exchanged between the sender and the target, as well as the availability of those resources from others. An actor will be dependent on goods it receives (or expects to receive) from others if it places a high value on those goods and they are not readily available elsewhere. Sanctions and incentives are likely to be effective when the targeted actor is dependent upon the particular resources that it is being offered or denied. With little loss of parsimony relative to structural arguments, issue- and context-specific arguments based on trade dominance and trade dependence clarify the link between the ability to exercise control over outcomes and the distribution of resources in international politics.

Dominance and Political Power

As already stated, economic statecraft involves the exercise of power using economic sanctions and incentives. For the purposes of this book, power is defined as the ability of one actor to get another to do something that it would not otherwise do. Building on the work of social power theorists including David Baldwin, Robert Dahl, Abraham Kaplan, Harold Lasswell, and Nelson Polsby, power will be treated as a relational concept based on observable action and an existing conflict of interests or values.[34] The magnitude of power exercised by one actor (the sender) over others is defined by the degree to which the targeted actors alter their policies or behavior as a result of the sender's actions. The view represented by these authors has been described as the "first face" or "one dimensional view" of power.[35] It is described as such because it does not take into account other forms of power, such as power reflected in the ability to keep particular issues on or off an agenda (a "second face" or "two dimensional view" of power),[36] power as reflected in the control or manipulation of ideas or values (a "third face" or "three dimensional view"),[37] power as a reflection of group or "mob" psychology (a "fourth face"), or others.

While the nuances of power reflected in these different faces and views are intriguing, the majority of cases in this study involve overt conflicts between the U.S. government and actors already engaged in the export of strategic goods and technology. The fact that many of the targeted actors were engaged in undesired activity suggests that, if exercised, U.S. power to control various international agendas combined with its ideational and persuasive power were not sufficient to stop them from doing so in the first place. It also suggests that observable changes in their behavior were necessary to achieve the desired outcome. This suggests that the "first face of power" provides the most appropriate framework for analyzing U.S. efforts to use economic incentives and sanctions to secure state and corporate compliance with its export control policies.

The principal insight of the social power school and the "first face of power" is that political, military, and economic resources may not be fungible.[38] That is, the resources that enable you to entice or coerce someone to do something in one area may not enable you to get the same person (or others) to do the same thing in another. This proposition challenges the presumption of structural realist and hegemonic leadership arguments that a preponderance of these resources will enable the dominant actor to influence nearly all others, regardless of the demands placed upon them.[39] This confirms what social power theorists argue: that this presumption is inaccurate because not all actors assign the same value to particular military, economic, or political resources.[40] Given differences in their particular interests and vulnerabilities, this insight suggests that two otherwise similar states may bear different costs from a similar set of economic penalties or rewards and may, therefore, respond to them differently. Furthermore, different types of actors are likely to have even more divergent interests, vulnerabilities, and responses to the same sanctions. For example, given variations in their interests as well as their military and economic vulnerabilities, India and Pakistan are likely to bear different costs from the sanctions that the United States imposed on them in response to their nuclear activities in the Spring of 1998. As a result, they can be expected to respond differently to those sanctions. Yet, while different, India's interests, vulnerabilities and responses are likely to be far more similar to those of Pakistan than they are to those of firms like DEC, IBM, and Viewlogic which are also affected by the sanctions. Economic sanctions can take a wide variety of forms, including financial restrictions such as the reduction, suspension, or cancellation of payments, aid, or other financial transfers, the freezing of assets, unfavorable taxation, and expropriation. They may also take the form of commercial and technical restrictions such as import and export restrictions, license denials, the suspension of contracts, and the blacklisting of companies or individuals doing business with the target. India, Pakistan and Viewlogic would likely respond to any particular combination of these sanctions differently. It is, therefore, crucial to specify the target of the sanctions and identify the value it places on these resources before predicting whether denying of any of them in particular will enable the sender to exercise power over the target.

The social power school's insight that actors may value particular rewards or penalties differently from one another has important implications for the use of economic statecraft. In particular, it suggests that careful targetting and selection of sanctions or incentives will likely increase their effectiveness and reduce the potentially negative spillover effects on non-targeted actors. Sanctions have often been targeted against entire countries and used as "blunt instruments" to decrease their aggregate national economic welfare, the basic premise behind such ambitious strategies being that the targeted country will alter its behavior when losses to the country as a whole are greater than the value of the issues at stake, or when the burdens that the sanctions impose on the target's citizens inspire them to exert popular pressure on their government to alter its behavior (either peacefully or through a popular revolt).[41] This premise is based on the assumption that either policymakers in the target country will place a higher value on aggregate national economic welfare than on maintaining their current behavior or popular protests against the sanctions will be sufficient to alter the government's behavior. Unfortunately, despite the potentially severe negative social and economic impact of sanctions on noncombatants and innocent civilians in the target countries,[42] the history of this strategy in countries like Cuba and Iraq demonstrates that policymakers are often able to protect themselves and their immediate constituents against the negative effects of such sanctions and that the general public often either fails to mobilize or responds to the sanctions by "rallying-around-the-flag," denouncing the sender rather than their local government.[43] Selectively targeting sanctions against the specific actors that the sender wants to influence and selecting the type of sanction to match the target's particular interests and vulnerabilities not only increases their likely effectiveness by focusing the rewards and penalties on the relevant targets, but it also provides a way of minimizing the potentially negative repercussions of the sanctions on non-targeted actors.

According to this intellectual tradition, once a specific target is selected, the type and degree of desired change in the targets' policies or behavior must be determined. Economic statecraft can be used to achieve a variety of substantive, and symbolic objectives.[44] Substantively, at a minimum, it can deter, compel, punish, reward, or assist particular actors or behavior. Symbolically, it can signal support or solidarity, express political rejection, set precedent, demonstrate resolve, warn of future action, or focus world attention on a particular actor or activity.[45] While these substantive and symbolic objectives are not mutually exclusive, they may require different types or degrees of economic penalties or rewards to achieve their goals. As discussed below, the level of penalties or rewards that must be born by the target and sender will vary according to whether the objective is to send a diplomatic signal of revulsion or support of another's policy, or whether it is to achieve a substantive objective such as deterring others from a particular action or compelling them change their behavior. For example, economic sanctions used to signal condemnation of another's actions or policies tend to be more effective when they are expensive to send, regardless of the costs they impose on the target.[46] In contrast, economic sanctions that are intended to bolster military, diplomatic, or other policy tools tend to be more effective when the combined cost or benefits of the sanctions *plus* the other policy instruments on the target are greater than the opportunity cost for the target of complying with the sender's requests. Finally, using economic sanctions or incentives as the sole policy instruments requires that they alone impose sufficient costs or benefits on the target. All else equal, this suggests that the costs or benefits that must be imposed on the target to alter its policies or behavior are greatest when they are used in the absence of other policy instruments. While these various objectives are not mutually exclusive, economic incentives and sanctions are often mistakenly treated as failures because they are evaluated in terms of objectives they were not intended or realistically able to achieve.

Evaluating political power in terms of domain (who is influenced), scope (what they are asked to do), and magnitude (how much change takes place as a result of the action taken) as suggested by the social power theorists is easiest to do in retrospect, after an influence attempt has succeeded or failed. Indeed, several scholars have criticized this approach for its underlying assertion that power cannot be evaluated until observable behavioral change has taken place.[47] Although this can create methodological problems, it does not prevent the principal insights from this approach from being adapted to models of economic statecraft. Specifically, the evidence in this study suggests that the predictive capacity of theories linking the possession of physical resources and the power to exercise control over outcomes can be improved if the distribution of resources among actors is evaluated on an issue-specific and context-specific basis, recognizing the motivations and preferences of the actors involved. This is the case because not all issues or actors are amenable to any given power resource.[48] This specifies a priori two key aspects of power, its intended scope and domain. Based on this proposition, the likelihood of American efforts to secure policy compliance should be evaluated in terms of the specific actors the U.S. sought to influence, what it asked them to do, and which resources that it possessed were valued by, and could be offered or denied to, the actors in question. One would predict, therefore, that the more than U.S. suppliers or markets dominate trade in a particular industrial sector, the more likely that it will be able to use sanctions or incentives regarding access to those suppliers or markets as a means of influencing companies conducting trade in that sector.

A hypothesis predicting outcomes based issue- or sector-specific dominance can be summarized as follows.

$H_{Dominance}$: *Because the outcome of negotiations and bargaining between actors in world politics is likely to reflect the interests of the actor that possesses a preponderance of relevant resources, as an actor's dominance in a particular sector or issue area increases (declines) its ability to entice or coerce others that value those resources into doing its bidding will increase (decline). American attempts to compel foreign companies operating in a particular industrial sector to change their behavior are more (less) likely to succeed as the trade dominance of U.S. firms and/or markets in the relevant sector increases (declines).*

Dependence and Political Power

Dominance, however, is only one aspect of a power relationship involving economic exchange. The power of one actor over another is more than a reflection of the distribution of resources between them, it is also a function of the degree to which the target and sender are dependent upon one another. Building on insights from Albert Hirschman, Kenneth Waltz, David Baldwin, Robert Keohane, and Joseph Nye, dependence can be defined in terms of the value each actor assigns to a particular relationship.[49] The value each actor assigns to a particular relationship is the net positive utility gained from the relationship plus the costs of adjustment if it is altered.[50] Interdependence, in turn, refers to mutual dependence on a particular relationship where the net utility and the costs of adjustment are high (although not necessarily equal) for both sides. The more costly it is for an actor to forgo or change the terms of a particular relationship, the more dependent it is on that relationship, and thus the more likely it is to alter its behavior to maintain the terms of the relationship.[51] Consequently, all else equal, if a targeted state or firm values goods that the U.S. government threatens to take away (or promises to provide) more than the trade it would forgo by abiding by U.S. export control regulations, then a credible threat by the U.S. government to terminate (or grant) access to its markets or suppliers may be sufficient to secure the firm's compliance with its regulations. The ability of the United States to exploit foreign dependence on it may, however, be mitigated by U.S. dependence on the targeted state or firm. If the sender is dependent on its relationship with the target, then the outcome of interactions involving a threat or reward that would alter the relationship will reflect the target's net dependence on the sender. The target's net dependence on the sender is the target's dependence on the sender minus the sender's dependence on the target.

It follows that the degree of dependence on a trading relationship with another actor, and hence its vulnerability to sanctions that could undermine it, declines as the availability of comparable alternatives increases, regardless of the distribution of resources among actors in a relationship.[52] For instance, even though a hegemon may possess the world's largest consumer market or be the world's largest supplier of a particular set of goods, offering or denying access to these goods may have little effect on the behavior of foreign actors if alternate markets or suppliers can be found, and if the cost of shifting to the alternate sources is lower than the cost of the sanctions. Recognition that the availability of resources outside of a particular relationship can undermine political power resulting from economic or military dominance is the principal insight dependence arguments offer to theories linking the distribution of resources among actors to political power.

The validity of these propositions rests on the assumption that the firms and national governments in question are dependent on foreign rather than domestic markets and suppliers. This assumption, in turn, rests on the premise that firms will act rationally in their quest to maximize profits and that they will do so by systematically seeking out the most efficient and cost-effective sources of supply and the most lucrative markets. The existence of trading relations with foreign suppliers and markets, therefore, suggests that the foreign suppliers and markets are the most cost effective ones available. Where possible, the use of domestic substitutes may diminish the impact of the sanctions. But the domestic alternatives are likely to be less cost-effective, less efficient, and, therefore, less desirable.[53] If this were not the case, then domestic alternates would have been selected initially over their foreign competitors.

The target's dependence on the sender is a function of both the proportion of the target's trade accounted for by the sender country and the availability of alternate trading partners. The availability of alternate trading partners for a sanctioned good is a function of the proportion of world trade of that good accounted for by the sender. The greater the sector-specific dominance of the sender, the lower the availability of alternate trading partners and vice versa. The target's dependence on the sender is summarized in table 1.1.

**Table 1.1   Trade Dependence as a Function of
            Trade Volume and Alternate Partners**

	Proportion of Target's Trade with the Sender*	
	Low	High
Availability of Alternate Trading Partners Low	Low Dependence on Sender, Potential Dependence on Others *Sanctions by Others May Be Successful*	High Dependence on Sender *Sanctions Likely to Be Successful*
High	Low Dependence *Sanctions Not Likely to Change Behavior*	Low Dependence but High Short-Term Costs *Additional Sanctions or Policy Instruments Needed*

*The "sender" is the actor that initiates a sanction.
The "target" is the actor against which a sanction is directed.

All else equal, economic sanctions will be successful when the costs they impose are greater than the costs of altering its behavior.[54] The costs to the target are contingent on both the relative value of trade between actors and the availability of alternate trading partners. Neither factor is sufficient by itself. All else equal, the greater the proportion of the target's trade in a particular sector that is accounted for by the sender, the greater the target's dependence on the sender, and the more likely sanctions from the sender involving goods in that sector will be effective. But, even if the target conducts a relatively large proportion of its trade with the sender, its dependence on the sender will decrease as the availability of alternate sources for the sanctioned goods increase. If alternate trading partners are available, additional sanctions or other policy instruments will be necessary to alter the target's behavior. Finally, it is important to recognize that the same factors that affect the target's dependence on the sender, affect the sender's dependence on the target. If the sender is dependent on the target, then imposing sanctions may be prohibitively expensive for the sender even though they may be sufficient to alter the target's behavior. Thus, the likely success of sanctions in a particular sector is a function of the target's net dependence on its trade with the sender.

An increasing number of scholars are noting the advantages of using economic incentives (also referred to as "positive sanctions") rather than sanctions (also referred to as "negative sanctions") as tools of statecraft.[55] As William Long argues, incentives such as technology transfer, promises of government contracts, or promises to decrease trade barriers may be used to increase the potential gains of trade that, in turn, can be used to entice a targeted actor to change its behavior.[56] For example, in the early 1980s the Reagan administration used the promise of access to Strategic Defense Initiative (SDI) technology and related government contracts to entice Israel, Germany and several European countries to increase their local enforcement of American export control restrictions.[57] Based on the dependence arguments summarized in table 1.1, the utility of economic incentives may be treated as a function of the potential value of exchange between parties, and the availability alternate sources of the incentives from outside of the promised relationship. The offer of incentives (like increased trade or preferential access to a government contract with the sender) may shift the target's baseline of expectations regarding the potential value of its future trading relations with the sender and, if few alternative sources of the incentives are available, its perceived dependence on future relations with the target may increase as a result.[58] This suggests that when the utility of economic sanctions is limited due to the lack of trade between two parties, like the United States and North Korea, the offer of economic incentives by the sender may be used to shift the target's baseline of expectations about the potential benefits from future exchanges, ultimately increasing the target's dependence on the maintenance of the incentives and, thus, giving the sender a source of leverage over its activities. Ironically, despite political motivations to the contrary, the comparatively low volume of trade between adversaries suggests that incentives are more likely to be effective against them than sanctions, while the comparatively high volume of trade among allies and long-term trading partners makes them more vulnerable to the threat of sanctions than the promise of incentives.

The U.S. government has used the promise or denial of access to American suppliers and markets as the primary means of securing extraterritorial compliance with its export control policy. A dependence argument suggests that such sanctions are most likely to be effective when the targeted actor's net dependence on existing or promised trade with the United States is high in the sector in which the sanctions or incentives are imposed. The target's net dependence will be high if it conducts a relatively large proportion of its trade with the United States and few non-U.S. sources of the threatened or promised goods are available *and* the United States, in turn, either conducts a relatively small proportion of its trade with the target or has alternate souces of the resources it will lose by imposing the sanctions (or offering the incentives) available to it.

The argument linking dependence and compliance can be summarized in the following hypothesis:

> H$_{Dependence}$: *The ability of one state to use economic incentives or sanctions to alter a targeted actor's (state, firm, or individual) behavior will increase as the target's dependence on relations with it increases and its dependence on relations with the target decreases. Dependence is defined in terms of two dimensions: the utility that each actor gains from its relationship with the other and its ability to adjust to disruptions in that relationship. American attempts to enforce its export control policy abroad against the interests of other countries and foreign firms are more likely to succeed as their dependence on the United States increases and its dependence on them decreases.*

Sanctions against States and Firms

Critics of economic statecraft argue that market power (which is the result of supply and demand) is not necessarily equivalent to bargaining power (which is the result of the relative political evaluation of the consequences of state action) between states.[59] This criticism suggests that it is important to identify the distinct preferences and motivations of states versus firms. As argued here, specifying the appropriate domain of actors the sender wants to influence, and targeting the sanctions or incentives accordingly, thus has important implications for their effectiveness. National and corporate preferences often diverge, particularly when sanctions involve "dual-use" goods with commercial as well as military significance,[60] and they tend to respond to sanctions and incentives based on their particular preferences and vulnerabilities. While the pluralistic character of American politics makes the U.S. government prone to influence from domestic constituents,[61] the cases below demonstrate that the U.S. government has repeatedly been willing to impose foreign sanctions for political, symbolic, and substantive purposes despite high costs to domestic companies.[62] Despite the increasing success of corporate lobbying efforts to reduce certain export restrictions,[63] national security concerns, rather than corporate interests, have provided the primary motivation behind imposition of export controls by the United States.[64]

Several authors have argued that the lack of multilateral compliance with U.S. export control policy can be explained by the lack of a credible threat of penalizing non-compliance.[65] The evidence in this study supports this contention to some extent, but not entirely. Unfortunately for U.S. companies, the willingness of the U.S. government to impose sanctions against offending foreign actors, despite the costs they impose on American firms, increases the credibility of the threat to use such sanctions in the future.[66] For example, the Clinton administration demonstrated resolve by giving international political concerns priority over those of an American company when it terminated petroleum exploration and production by the American firm Conoco in Iran in the spring of 1995, despite knowledge that French and German oil companies were ready to fulfill the Iranian contract once Conoco's bid was removed, is one of the most recent examples of this phenomenon.[67] At the same time, in contrast to its historic and current willingness to impose sanctions that are costly to local or foreign firms, the U.S. government has often failed to impose sanctions that are costly to itself. The threat of sanctions against offending foreign actors is lease likely to be credible when the costs of imposing the sanctions undercut the sender's government or its security interests.

Given the divergence of corporate and governmental actions, it may be useful to specify the particular preferences, motivations, and vulnerabilities of firms and states, and to focus sanctions as precisely as possible on them.[68] National governments and firms may be dependent on both foreign suppliers and foreign markets and may consequently respond to sanctions involving access to either one, but their priorities tend to be different. National governments may struggle to guarantee foreign market access for their firms, particularly when access to foreign markets is seen as a key factor behind economic wealth and national power. Yet, all other things being equal, national governments are more likely to respond to threats (or promises) regarding sources of supply than market access.

National governments' preference for secured supply over market access may be due to the fact that the supply of specific goods, especially those considered necessary for national defense, have a more immediate and direct effect on national security than do the wealth-seeking aims of particular firms. Sanctions that restrict access to strategic goods vital for national defense impose high costs on states and can be a potent source of leverage. Sweden, for instance, has maintained its neutrality and has generally refused to take part in U.S. or CoCom embargoes. It has also often fought on behalf of its firms when they were threatened by U.S. sanctions. In 1985, however, the Swedish government abruptly changed its policy and forced key Swedish companies to submit to inspection and surveillance by American export control officers.[69] This policy shift was the result of a threat by the United States to terminate the sale of AIM-9 Sidewinder air-to-air missiles as well as other arms and electronic equipment from American firms to Sweden that were not available elsewhere.

Termination of the supply of American goods and technology would have had a direct effect on Swedish military security. As a result, despite strong corporate protests, Prime Minister Olof Palme altered a longstanding Swedish policy. This preference ordering is consistent with classic mercantilist and realist emphases on national security and war preparation over economic or other concerns.[70] It is also consistent with the view of a growing number of international political economists who argue that security concerns and quests for "power" have a profound effect on the strategies states use to pursue their economic interests and the pursuit of "plenty."[71]

As the Swedish example suggests, it is also important to recognize that national decision-making calculations are likely to a include or be linked to a broader range of noneconomic factors than corporate decision-making calculations.[72] In comparison to firms, states are more likely to sacrifice economic gains to achieve noneconomic objectives. This implies that economic factors alone are more likely to influence corporate than national behavior, while political or military concerns may have a more immediate affect on national as opposed to corporate behavior.

Despite economic nationalist arguments to the contrary, local firms do not automatically conform to national interests, nor do they necessarily give preference to national over foreign markets or suppliers. Even "national champions" and corporations that are given preferential treatment by their governments may respond to external economic incentives and sanctions despite domestic political pressure not to do so. For example, enticed by the potential for higher corporate profits abroad, Michelin moved its production sites overseas despite promises of protection and continued financial assistance by the French government.[73] Similarly, despite domestic pressure to keep its production facilities at home, Volkswagen was willing to shift its output at the expense of exports from Germany in order to secure its continued production and market position in Brazil. The responsiveness of firms (including national champions) to selectively targetted rewards and penalties provides the U.S. government with a source of leverage against them even when their local governments are pressuring them to act differently.

In January 1994, Under Secretary of Commerce Jeffrey Garten used a selective targeting strategy to win concessions in extended and often confrontational trade negotiations between the U.S. and Japanese governments. Rather than negotiating solely with the Japanese government—a trade strategy that had produced several months of heightened tension and few results—Garten initiated negotiations directly with Japanese companies in the automobile, construction, and telecommunication industries.[74] Instead of threatening to impose broad sanctions against U.S.-Japanese trade and rely on linkages between the government and corporate decision makers to change Japanese trading practices, the threat of sanctions was targeted specifically against the industries that the U.S. government wanted to influence. Garten justified this strategy by arguing "the fact is, the big issues in the automotive sector are driven by the companies themselves. To think the Government is going to press a button and say, 'We're going to change the trade balance' is a mirage."[75] Despite criticism by some government and corporate officials that this strategy could potentially undermine ongoing negotiations between the U.S. and Japanese governments, it succeeded where broader negotiations, threats, and promises made between the U.S. and Japanese governments had not. As a result of direct meetings between U.S. government and corporate representatives, Nippon Telegraph and Telephone Corporation agreed to buy more foreign equipment, and Toyota, Nissan, and Honda agreed to buy more American parts and allot more research, development, and management jobs to Americans.[76]

In the export control arena, the ability to inflict costs or offer benefits to firms directly means that the United States (or other senders) may be able to sidestep intergovernmental negotiations and entice or coerce foreign firms directly. For example, as discussed above, despite widespread political condemnation of U.S. secondary sanctions by Canadian, Mexican, and European governments, the U.S. government succeeded in compelling private companies in these countries to alter their trading practices with the Soviet Union in the 1980s and with Cuba in the 1990s. Its ability to influence some private companies and not others can be better explained in terms of the targeted firms' interests and vulnerabilities to U.S. sanctions than as a response to actions taken by their host country's government.

Like states, firms that are dependent on foreign suppliers will alter their behavior to maintain access to desired goods. However, firms that are denied access to traditional suppliers also tend to develop substitutes internally. This option is often difficult and may require a large financial and technological capability, but designing out foreign parts is an effective way of minimizing dependence on foreign suppliers.[77] In the early 1960s, for example, the United States forbade the export of radar equipment to Viscount Aircraft because the British company sold planes to communist China. After failing to alter U.S. policy, the company redesigned its planes to avoid using U.S. equipment. It thus avoided U.S. restrictions and the sales went through.[78] Similarly, in 1987, following the grounding of the U.S. space shuttle fleet, General Motors and General Electric requested and were initially refused export licenses that would allow them to launch their communications satellites on Soviet rockets.[79] These restrictions applied to all equipment that possessed American components, whether they were possessed by American or non-American firms. To avoid similar constraints, foreign producers of satellite equipment began designing their equipment to avoid using American parts.

This option is less feasible if the lead time to develop alternatives is long and the costs of doing so are high; however, the global diffusion of technology today increases the likelihood that foreign firms will be able to develop restricted goods domestically more quickly and at a lower cost than in the past. Indeed, their ability to do so undermines both the effectiveness of sanctions and the competitiveness of firms in the sender country by creating new alternate suppliers.[80] The fear that sanctions could give foreign competitors an unfair advantage in emerging markets was one of the principal arguments used by corporate lobbyists in their efforts to change U.S. export control policies in the late 1980s.[81]

For this reason, manipulating foreign dependence on domestic markets may provide a less risky source of political power than manipulating foreign dependence on local suppliers. Gary Hufbauer and Jeffrey Schott's extensive study of embargoes suggests that import (market) restrictions may be even more successful than export (supply) restrictions.[82] Laura d'Andrea Tyson supports this point, arguing that the creation of new export markets tends to be more difficult for firms than is finding or creating alternate sources of supply.[83] Dependence on markets is an important and often overlooked component of political power.

Dependence arguments imply a hypothesis that supersedes issue-specific power analysis: the United States should be able to use sanctions to secure extraterritorial compliance with its export control policy when the target's net dependence on the sender is high, but not otherwise. Furthermore, while both national governments and firms are likely to respond to sanctions or incentives involving market access and supply, national governments will tend to value the supply of goods, particularly goods with strategic value, more than they value market access. Firms, however, will tend to value market access more than the supply of particular goods. Sanctions will be most effective if targeted accordingly.

The hypotheses about government versus corporate responses to sanctions can be summarized as follows:

$H_{FirmGovt}$: *While dependent governments and firms may respond to threats (or promises) regarding access to both foreign suppliers and markets, national governments will tend to weigh threats (or promises) regarding the supply of strategic goods more heavily than market access, relative to firms. In contrast, relative to states, firms will tend to weigh threats (or promises) regarding market access more heavily than the supply of strategic goods. American attempts to secure the extraterritorial compliance of firms is more likely when the sanction involves market access, while its attempts to secure the cooperation of foreign governments is more likely when the sanction involves access to American suppliers.*

If the dependence arguments are correct, then the degree of corporate compliance and intergovernmental cooperation in response to U.S. secondary sanctions and incentives should vary according to whether the sanctions involved access to markets or suppliers. Firm and state reactions as a function of dependence on market access and dependence on supply are summarized in table 1.2.

In addition to the basic distinction between firm and state interests and reactions to economic sanctions, it is important to recognize that corporate interests and actions will tend to be sector specific in nature,

**Table 1.2   Compliance of Noncooperative States and Firms
as a Function of Dependence**

		DEPENDENCE ON MARKETS	
		Low	High
DEPENDENCE ON SUPPLIERS	Low	Corporate Defiance	Corporate Compliance
		Host Government Confrontation	Host Government Undetermined
	High	Corporate Actions Undetermined	Corporate Compliance
		Host Government Compliance	Host Government Compliance

while governments are more likely to think in terms of, and engage in, issue-linkage strategies. While firms in one sector tend to act independently from those operating in unrelated sectors, national policymakers are more likely to assume and respond to a high degree of linkage across issue areas. Consequently, issue linkage is likely to be less effective with firms than with states. This has two policy implications. First, it implies that national governments are likely to be susceptible to a comparatively broad range of sanctions or incentives that are perceived to affect the "national interest," while corporate actors will tend to be relatively unresponsive to sanctions or incentives in unrelated industrial sectors; states are more likely than firms to respond to linked threats or promises. Second, governments are likely to retaliate against unwanted sanctions by imposing penalties on the sender in whatever way it can; firms, on the other hand, are likely to retaliate on a sector-specific basis by altering their particular economic activities. One would expect, therefore, that a threat of retaliation from national actors is likely to be broader in scope than the threat of retaliation from individual firms. In the current disputes involving the Helms-Burton Act, for example, corporate actors that are challenging the U.S. legislation are doing so on a narrowly defined, case-by-case basis, while national governments have resorted to issue linkage such as bringing the case before the World Trade Organization (WTO) as a means of strengthening their bargaining position relative to the United States (see chapter 5).

SOVEREIGN AUTHORITY, SOVEREIGN CONTROL, AND SECONDARY SANCTIONS

While the United States has attempted to extend its regulatory power abroad more frequently than other countries, it is not the only country to use secondary sanctions to compel foreign actors to comply with domestic legislation. For example, the Arab boycott against Israel includes a secondary boycott that forbids Arab states from trading with parties that the Arab League Boycott Committee designates to have contributed to Israel's economic and military strength. It also includes a tertiary boycott that forbids the use of materials, equipment, or services of blacklisted firms by Arab countries.[84] Regardless of domestic legislation designed to protect them from foreign regulations, firms that were dependent on the Arab countries—particularly in the banking and energy sectors—often complied with the requests made in conjunction with the Arab boycott. For example, despite the threat of severe penalties imposed by the Office of Anti-Boycott Compliance in the Department of Commerce, 188 U.S. firms and affiliates complied with the Arab League Boycott between 1979 and 1984 and were charged in the United States for violating antiboycott legislation under the Export Administration Act.[85]

The ability of the United States, members of the Arab League, or any country to alter the behavior of foreign firms and individuals operating abroad using economic incentives or sanctions means that the de facto domain of sovereign control of the senders may be much larger than the de jure domain of their sovereign authority. It also means that the de facto domain of sovereign control of the state where the targeted firms or individuals are operating may be much smaller than the de jure domain of its sovereign authority. Gaining or losing control over local actors, particularly those related to the production or distribution of strategic goods, is a matter of high politics. This makes the ability to use economic statecraft as a means of extending sovereign control across national boundaries crucial for all states. In light of this, the following section examines the implications of economic statecraft for sovereign authority and sovereign control over actors and resources at home and abroad.

Sovereign Authority and Sovereign Control

Within the world of sovereign states, each of which possess autonomous legal authority over the actors and activities that take place within its borders, many commercial and business transactions take place across national boundaries. And, as Raymond Vernon argued over a quarter century ago, every international transaction involves a minimum of two national jurisdictions and two potentially competing national interests.[86] The most basic form of these transactions involves the sale or purchase of goods and services across national boundaries. Based on the territoriality principle of international law, legal authority over those resources shifts from country to country when they cross national boundaries. These transactions usually occur without incident. Interstate disputes tend to arise, however, when one state challenges the authority of another over traded goods by asserting the precedence of a competing basis of jurisdiction, such as the nationality principle over the territoriality principle (For a discussion of these legal issues see the Appendix). This has often been the case when the extension of U.S. export control regulations to actors operating overseas clash with the policies and regulations of their host country's government, often undermining its sovereign autonomy.[87]

"Sovereignty" is a legal, political, and social concept that identifies the state as an autonomous entity responsible to no outside authority.[88] Under international law, sovereignty refers to the authority claims of a particular state as linked to international institutions and the practices of other states.[89] Mutual recognition of this authority enables states to interact as legal equals in the international system.[90] Traditional international relations and legal scholars argue that while trade and monetary relations between states can influence decision making within states, these relations in no way supersede state authority.[91] Under this conception, while the pressures resulting from the strategic interdependence of state and nonstate actors in world politics can potentially be used to influence a state's policies, they cannot supplant its authority.[92] All enticement and enforcement actions, including blockades, boycotts, and other economic sanctions or inducements, leave the authority and legal autonomy of the target state intact.[93] The pervasiveness of anarchy does not, however, imply that states have unlimited freedom of action.[94]

Autonomous sovereign authority is not equivalent to complete political independence or autarchy. Sovereign autonomy, dependence, and interdependence coexist in international politics. Simply because states have the legal authority to do something, or a legal basis for refusing to do it, does not mean that they will act accordingly. Rather, the actual interdependence of states in political, economic, military, and technological matters may make it difficult for certain states to pursue independent domestic and foreign policies. At the same time, asymmetries in interdependence may enable a state to extend its control beyond its territorial limits.[95]

The cases analyzed below suggest strongly that sovereign authority does not necessarily translate into sovereign control over actors or resources.[96] In order to preserve their sovereign autonomy, foreign governments have enacted domestic legislation to prohibit firms within their borders from abiding by U.S. or other foreign laws. The most blatant exercise of this authority since the 1958 Eisenhower-Diefenbaker agreement limited the application of U.S. regulations in Canada,[97] came in 1982 when the British, Canadian, French, German, and Italian governments enacted legislation that directly challenged American attempts to enforce its regulations in their territories (see chapter 3). Despite government action on their behalf, however, firms like Ford of Canada and Aluminum Company of Canada (Alcan) in the late 1950s,[98] and Alsthom-Atlantique in the 1980s, chose to abide by U.S. restrictions because of the threat of U.S. sanctions if they failed to do so (see chapter 3).[99]

Historical studies of sovereignty indicate that sovereign control over actors and resources in a particular territory has waxed and waned considerably despite the state's claim of sovereignty over the past three centuries.[100] As Janice Thomson notes, since the recognition of the authority of the sovereign state three centuries ago, "there has never been a time when state control over everything, including violence, was assured or secure."[101] Stephen Krasner takes this one step farther and argues that the Westphalian model of sovereignty based on the convergence of territory and political autonomy has never been an accurate description of the majority of states. There never was, in his words, a "golden age of the Westphalian state."[102] He cites examples ranging from the Catholic Church and Islamic on attitudes of birth control, abortion, and other beliefs, to conditional lending on the part of the International Monetary Fund, to the British Commonwealth and the European Union as examples to support the argument that, while not always obvious, violations of the principle of autonomous sovereign control, in which an external actor can exercise control within the territory of another state, are perhaps more frequent than instances of control based on territoriality.[103]

Authority and control are critical aspects of sovereignty (and international law more generally).[104] Sovereign authority is the claim to an exclusive right to make rules, whereas sovereign control is the capability to enforce that claim.[105] As Anthony Arend argues, "control exists if one determines an actual outcome, irrespective of whether or not it was perceived to be authoritative."[106] In contrast, while sovereign authority is dependent on domestic and international recognition of authoritative jurisdiction, sovereign control rests more on the capability to monitor and enforce compliance with rules that are made as a result of that authority.[107] The absence of a necessary link between de jure authority and de facto control over the activities of domestic actors makes power capabilities critical to sovereign autonomy when preferences of actors are incompatible.[108] The ability of a state to use economic rewards or penalties to manipulate the behavior of foreign actors and the use of other resources across international borders expands the effective domain of its sovereign control, regardless of the jurisdictional or territorial limits of its recognized sovereign authority.

When foreign governments or companies have failed to conform to its export control policy, the U.S. government has attempted to apply and enforce its export control regulations to the full extent of its capabilities. Indeed, in order to bolster its enforcement activities abroad, the U.S. government has attempted to assert its jurisdiction over the international movement of strategic goods and technology as far as possible under accepted principles in international law. It has justified extending its authority abroad based on a variety of legal grounds including the nationality principle, the territoriality principle, the objective territoriality principle, the protective principle, and the universality principle (the legal basis of U.S. export control policy and the legal justifications for extending these regulations abroad are analyzed in the Appendix).[109] The most common justification used to promote the extraterritorial application of U.S. export control policy has been the nationality principle of international law. While the nationality principle is widely accepted under certain circumstances, it often clashes with the territoriality principle, which grants absolute and exclusive jurisdiction to the state over actions, actors, and resources within a specified territory regardless of their national origin (see Appendix).[110] The resulting conflicts of concurrent jurisdiction over property, licensing rights, technical know-how, and the actions of individuals and firms have created an unresolved question of who has sovereign authority over these individuals, firms, and resources.[111]

At the same time, even if the basis of U.S. authority over foreign actors is challenged by other countries and the extent of U.S. jurisdiction over foreign actors is limited, the U.S. government can use secondary incentives or secondary sanctions to entice or compel foreign actors to conform to its restrictions. Secondary incentives may take the form of rewards offered to compliant firms, such as privileged access to U.S. resources including its markets, products, technology or other resources. Alternatively, secondary sanctions may impose penalties on offending firms such as indicting negligent actors in U.S. courts, imposing fines for violating U.S. law, restricting their ability to travel in the United States, terminating their access to government contracts, or fully denying them access to American citizens, markets, products or technology.[112] Such secondary incentives or sanctions imbue domestic legislation with substantial extraterritorial effect, even when its legal impact is minimal. Consequently, as Hans Morgenthau argues in *Politics among Nations*, the concept of sovereignty in legal theory cannot be divorced from "the political reality to which the concept is supposed to give legal expression."[113] Regardless of the letter of the law or international agreements made on the legal boundaries and limits of state action, states can and will extend their authority as far as other states will permit.

In sum, the important point here is that even when the legal basis of extending national authority across international borders is disputed, the degree of dependence between firms operating abroad and those local firms over which a national government has de jure control may provide that government with a source of de facto enforcement capability over firms operating abroad. Sanctions may enable the assertion of extraterritorial control, regardless of legal barriers to the contrary. The U.S. government has, for example, exerted influence over the activities of foreign firms regarding their relations with Arab countries, Cuba, the People's Republic of China, South Africa, and the Soviet Union, among others.[114]

The hypotheses developed above can be used to predict when these efforts are likely to succeed and when they are likely to fail. The availability of alternate markets or suppliers means that the costs of adjustment to a potential target will be low, and the threat to its sovereign authority or sovereign control will be minimal. The target's sovereign autonomy will be preserved. As Theodore Moran argues, this is true even if "[t]he last domestic-owned firm is acquired by a foreigner or driven out of business by a superior foreign-owned rival" because states can find alternatives and compensate for the costs of sanctions from any one foreign supplier or market.[115]

In contrast, local dependence on foreign suppliers or markets means that sovereign autonomy may be undermined, and that sanctions may enable foreign actors to compel domestic actors to comply with their policies, regardless of domestic legal barriers to the contrary. If markets or suppliers are concentrated in a few states or firms, then governments in those monopolistic or oligopolistic states can use promises of access or threats of denial to extend their control across jurisdictional boundaries. In this way, corporations that are dependent on particular foreign markets or supply networks may be compelled to change their behavior in ways that augment the power of the state(s) that can control access to those markets or suppliers. Under conditions of dependence, Raymond Vernon's dictate that "[t]he network of the multinational enterprise can become a conduit through which the power of one sovereign state is projected into the territory of another" can thus become a reality.[116]

CONCLUSION: DEPENDENCE AS A POSITIVE HEURISTIC

Economic statecraft is fundamentally about the exercise of power and the relationship between power and wealth. Economic sanctions are tools that are particularly well suited for getting corporate as well as national actors to do something they would not otherwise do. Understanding when and why economic sanctions and incentives work, therefore, provides insight into the nature of power and wealth in world politics.

Economic sanctions and incentives are generally considered to be tools used against states.[117] They may, however, be used to entice or coerce firms and individuals directly. Restricting the movement of strategic goods and technology requires the cooperation of all actors (states, firms, and individuals) that possess or can produce the goods in question. In the cases analyzed in the following chapters, when sufficient cooperation was not forthcoming, the United States government used economic incentives and threats to compel others to comply with its export restrictions. The findings below suggest that while intergovernmental cooperation facilitates local enforcement of multilateral agreements, it is sometimes neither necessary nor sufficient to secure extraterritorial compliance by corporate or individual actors. Under appropriate conditions, sanctions may be used to compensate for this inability and the resulting prevalence of involuntary defection.

Statistical analyses of U.S. export control policy since 1949 are presented in chapter 2. They serve as a preliminary test of the hypotheses linking firm and state dependence, economic and military dominance, and the ability to alter firm and state behavior using economic sanctions. The results suggest that foreign dependence on local suppliers increases the likelihood that economic sanctions will be effective. The findings suggested by the statistical analyses are bolstered by a detailed comparative analysis of two sets of cases in chapters 3 and 4. One set of cases, involving American efforts to stop construction of a trans-Siberian Pipeline between 1981 and 1984, involved firms and countries that were not overly dependent on the United States. The other set, including U.S. efforts to control high-technology goods and information from 1981 through 1988, involved firms and states highly dependent on the United States. The statistical overview verifies that the cases chosen for more detailed analysis are representative of other export control cases. Moreover, comparative analysis of these two cases identifies the causal links between firm and state dependence, dominance, and political power.

Exploiting trade dominance or dependence for political purposes may have political and economic costs, and these costs must be weighed against the benefits gained from using these sources of political power. Chapter 5 examines the potential costs of using sanctions that result from a variety of factors including the reciprocal nature of dependence, the effect of sanctions on the reliability and competitiveness of domestic firms, and the motivation sanctions provide for the indigenous development of restricted resources. Understanding these costs and the potential of retaliatory action is crucial before current legislation targeting firms conducting business in Cuba, Iran, and Libya is implemented. This book concludes by assessing the likely effectiveness of sanctions targeted against Cuba under the Helms-Burton Act and sanctions under the Iran and Lybia Sanctions Act targeted against firms conducting business in Iran and Libya.

When used under appropriate circumstances, economic statecraft works. The temptation to use secondary sanctions or incentives must, however, be tempered by recognition of the political, economic, and social costs of using them. Once these costs are understood, the theory of economic statecraft developed in this book can be used judiciously by policymakers to extend political control over firms operating around the globe. At the same time, it may enable intrepid firms to recognize their vulnerabilities and protect themselves from the imprudent use of economic statecraft.

Notes

1. Anne Swardson, "Canada Vows Sanctions against U.S. for Enforcement of Anti-Cuba Trade Law," *Washington Post* (18 June 1996), p. A7.

2. Richard Haass, "Sanctions Almost Never Work," *The Wall Street Journal* (19 June 1998), p. A14.

3. Gary Milhollin, "Made in America? How U.S. Exports Helped Fuel the South Asian Arms Race," *Washington Post* (7 June 1998), pp. C1, C5.

4. David Campbell, *Politics without Principle: Sovereignty, Ethics, and Narratives of the Gulf War* (Boulder, Colo.: Lynne Rienner, 1993), pp. 36, 39, 40; Jochen Hippler, "Iraq's Military Power: The German Connection," *Middle-East Report* 21 (January/February 1991): 27–31; Kenneth Timmerman, *The Death Lobby: How the West Armed Iraq* (Boston: Houghton Mifflin, 1991); United States House Committee on Foreign Affairs, Subcommittee on International Economic Policy and Trade, *United States Exports of Sensitive Technology to Iraq: Hearings* (8 April and 22 May 1991); David Albright, "Iraq's Shop-Till-You-Drop Nuclear Program: IAEA Inspectors Found German Fingerprints on Much of Iraq's Nuclear Weapons Technology," *Bulletin of the Atomic Scientists* 48 (April 1992): 26–37.

5. In fiscal year 1995 alone, thirty-one firms and individuals were denied export privileges under the Export Administration Act and the Export Administration Regulations. U.S. Department of Commerce, Bureau of Export Administration, *Export Administration Annual Report 1995 and 1996 Report on Foreign Policy Export Controls* (Washington, D.C.: GOP 1997), pp. 11–54.

6. A current Denied Persons List is available from the Bureau of Export Administration in the U.S. Department of Commerce. The list is also available on the World Wide Web at http://www.bxa.doc.gov/.

7. The "Helms-Burton Act" is formally known as the Cuban Liberty and Democratic Solidarity Act of 1996, 22 USC 6021, Public Law 104–114, 110 Stat. 785 (12 March 1996). The Gilman Act, targeted against Iran and Libya, is H.R. 3107, Report No. 104–623, Parts I and II, 104th Congress, 2d Session, Union Callander No. 308, (14 June 1996). The act was approved unanimously by the House of Representatives on 19 June 1996.

8. Eric Pianin, "Clinton Approves Sanctions for Investors in Iran, Libya," *Washington Post* (6 August 1996), p. A8.

9. Emphasis added. Clay Chandler, "U.S. Expects Furor over Trade Sanctions at Summit," *Washington Post* (27 June 1996), p. A20.

10. Alissa Rubin, "House Passes Curbs on Trade with Iran," *Congressional Quarterly* (22 June 1976): 1775.

11. Uncertainty about the nature and impact of economic statecraft also plagued the implementation of sanctions against India and Pakistan. Thomas Lippman, "U.S. Limits Scope of Sanctions on India, Pakistan to Minimize Hardships," *The Washington Post* (June 19, 1988), p. A29.

12. Thomas W. Lippman, "U.S. Rethinking Economic Sanctions," *The Washington Post* (January 26, 1998), p. A6.

13. See for example, Kenneth Abbott, "Collective Goods, Mobile Resources, and Extraterritorial Trade Controls," *Law and Contemporary Problems* 50 (1987): 117–152; David A. Baldwin, *Economic Statecraft* (Princeton: Princeton University Press, 1985); David Cortright and George A. Lopez, editors. *Economic Sanctions: Panacea or Peacebuilding in a Post-Cold War World?* (Boulder: Westview Press, 1995); M. S. Daoudi and M. S. Dajani, *Economic Sanctions: Ideals and Experience* (Boston: Routledge & Kegan Paul, 1983); Garry C. Hufbauer, and Jeffrey J. Schott, *Economic Sanctions Reconsidered* (Washington, D.C.: Institute for International Economics, 1985, 1990); Stephen Kobrin, "Enforcing Export Embargoes Through Multinational Corporations: Why Doesn't It Work Anymore?" *Business in the Contemporary World* 1:2 (1989): 31–42; Donald Losman, *International Economic Sanctions: The Cases of Cuba, Israel, and Rhodesia* (Albuquerque: University of New Mexico Press, 1979); Andreas Lowenfeld, *International Economic Law: Trade Controls for Political Ends* (New York: Matthew Bender, 1983); Lisa Martin, *Coercive Cooperation* (Princeton: Princeton University Press, 1992); and Michael Mastanduno, *Economic Containment: CoCom and the Politics of East-West Trade* (Ithaca: Cornell University Press, 1992).

14. For examples of different forms of statecraft, see Baldwin (1985), pp. 44–50; Barry Carter, *International Economic Sanctions: Improving the Haphazard U.S. International Legal Regime* (New York: Cambridge University Press, 1988), p. 24; and Margaret Doxey, *International Sanctions in Contemporary Perspective, 2nd edition,* (New York: St. Martin's Press, 1996), pp. 14–15.

15. David Baldwin, "The Power of Positive Sanctions," *World Politics* 24 (1971c): 145–55; David Cortright, editor, *The Price of Peace: Incentives and International Conflict Prevention* (New York: Rowman & Littlefield Publishers, Inc., 1997); and William Long, *Economic Incentives and Bilateral Cooperation* (Ann Arbor: University of Michigan Press, 1996), pp. 19–24.

16. Whether a particular exchange constitutes a penalty or a reward may be a matter of interpretation based on what each actor expected to receive from the other. For example, an offer of aid or financial assistance that is less than anticipated may be interpreted by the recipient as a penalty, while the imposition of a trade restriction or fine that is lower than anticipated may be interpreted by the recipient as a reward. For further discussion see Baldwin (1971c).

17. For further discussion of the terms sender and target, see Hufbauer, Schott and Elliot (1985), p. 27.

18. Daoudi and Dajani provide an extensive set of commentaries from pessimistic scholars and practitioners regarding the ineffectiveness of sanctions. Daoudi and Dajani (1983), pp. 43–50.

19. Hufbauer and Schott (1985), p. 80.

20. Robert Pape, "Why Economic Sanctions Still Don't Work," *International Security* 22,2 (fall 1997): 90–136. See also David Baldwin and Robert Pape, "Evaluating Economic Sanctions," *International Security* 23,2 (1998): 189–98.

21. Hufbauer and Schott (1985), p. 89.

22. See Baldwin (1985).

23. David Baldwin, "Power Analysis and World Politics: New Trends Versus Old Tendencies." *World Politics* 31:2 (1979): 161–94.

24. Kimberly Ann Elliot, "Factors Affecting the Success of Sanctions," in David Cortright and George Lopez, eds. *Economic Sanctions: Panacea or Peacebuilding in a Post–Cold War World?* (Boulder, Colo.: Westview Press, 1995), pp. 54–59.

25. Focusing on the impact of corporate activities in the 1990s is not intended to underplay the role in the transfer of nuclear materials and technology played by the U.S. and Canadian governments under the "Atoms for Peace" agreements in the 1960s. Milhollin (7 June 1998), pp. C1, C5.

26. David Campbell, *Politics without Principle: Sovereignty, Ethics, and Narratives of the Gulf War* (Boulder, Colo.: Lynne Rienner, 1993), pp. 36, 39, 40; Jochen Hippler, "Iraq's Military Power: The German Connection," *Middle-East Report* 21 (January/February 1991): 27–31; Kenneth Timmerman, *The Death Lobby: How the West Armed Iraq* (Boston: Houghton Mifflin, 1991); United States House Committee on Foreign Affairs, Subcommittee on International Economic Policy and Trade, *United States Exports of Sensitive Technology to Iraq: Hearings* (8 April and 22 May 1991); David Albright, "Iraq's Shop-Till-You-Drop Nuclear Program: IAEA Inspectors Found German Fingerprints on Much of Iraq's Nuclear Weapons Technology," *Bulletin of the Atomic Scientists* 48 (April 1992): 26–37.

27. See Robert Putnam, "Diplomacy and Domestic Politics," *International Organization* 42:3 (summer 1988): 427–60; and Stephen Haggard and Beth Simmons, "Theories of International Regimes," *International Organization* 41:3 (summer 1987): 491–517.

28. Beverly Crawford, *Economic Vulnerability in International Relations: East-West Trade, Investment, and Finance* (New York: Columbia University Press, 1993), pp. 139–50.

29. This could be done through the United Nations as well as other multilateral bodies. James Ngobi, "The United Nations Experience with Sanctions," in Cortright and Lopez, eds. (1995), p. 24.

30. For an earlier version of these arguments, see George E. Shambaugh IV, "Dominance, Dependence, and Political Power: Tethering Technology in the 1980s and Today," *International Studies Quarterly* 40, 4 (1996): 559–88.

31. Martin (1992), p. 4.

32. Even near the height of American hegemony in 1953, American military and economic dominance did not enable it to secure European cooperation with its export-control policy towards the Soviet Union and China. See Gunnar Adler-Karlsson, *Western Economic Warfare, 1947–1967* (Stockholm: Almquist and Wiksell, 1968); Michael Mastanduno, "Strategies of Economic Containment: United States Trade Relations with the Soviet Union." *World Politics* 37:4 (1985): 503–31; George Shambaugh, "Sanctions and Sovereignty in the Cold War Era and Today," Panel Presentation, Annual Meeting of the American Political Science Association, Washington, D.C. (1993).

33. See Joseph Grieco, "Understanding the Problem of International Cooperation: The Limits of Neoliberal Institutionalism and the Future of Realist Theory," in David Baldwin, ed., *Neorealism and Neoliberalism: The Contemporary Debate* (New York: Columbia University Press, 1993); and Kenneth Waltz, *Theory of International Politics* (Reading: Addison-Wesley, 1979).

34. See Baldwin, (1979); Robert Dahl, "The Concept of Power," *Behavioral Science* 52 (1958): 205–15, *Who Governs? Democracy and Power in an American City* (New Haven, Conn.: Yale University Press, 1961), and *Modern Political Analysis*. 4th ed. (Englewood, N.J.: Prentice-Hall, 1984); Harold Lasswell, and Abraham Kaplan, *Power and Society* (New Haven, Conn.: Yale University Press, 1986); and Nelson Polsby, *Community Power and Political Theory* (New Haven, Conn.: Yale University Press, 1963).

35. Peter Bachrach and Morton Baratz, "The Two Faces of Power," *American Political Science Review* 56 (1962); Steven Lukes, *Power: A Radical View* (New York: Macmillan, 1974), pp. 11–15.

36. Bachrach and Baratz (1962), and "Decisions and Nondecisions: An Analytical Framework," *American Political Science Review* 57 (1963): 632–42; William Riker, "Some Ambiguities in the Notion of Power," *American Political Science Review* 58 (1964): 341–49, and *The Art of Political Manipulation* (New Haven, Conn.: Yale University Press, 1986).

37. Lukes (1974).

38. See Baldwin (1979), and (1985); Dahl (1958); Klaus Knorr, *The Power of Nations* (New York: Basic Books, 1975); and Lasswell and Kaplan (1986).

39. Logically, the reasoning behind this assumption does not stand up to careful scrutiny. Not all contentious negotiations, particularly those among allies or between states and firms, are likely to be solved on the battlefield, as realists have argued. See Robert Gilpin, *War and Change in World Politics* (New York: Cambridge University Press, 1981), p. 31; Grieco (1993); Robert Keohane, "Institutionalist Theory and the Realist Challenge after the Cold War," in Baldwin (1993); and J. March, "The Power of Power," in David Easton, ed., *Varieties of Political Theory* (Englewood Cliffs, N.J.: Prentice Hall, 1966).

40. See Baldwin (1979), (1985); Dahl (1968); Knorr (1975); and Lasswell and Kaplan (1986); March (1966).

41. Pape (1997), pp. 93–94 and Baldwin and Pape (1988), p. 197.

42. See chapters by David Cortright and George Lopez, Chris Joyner, Jack Patterson, Drew Christiansen, and Gerald Powers in David Cortright and George A. Lopez, *Economic Sanctions: Panacea or Peacebuilding in a Post-Cold War World* (Boulder: Westview Press, 1995).

43. Ivan Eland, "Economic Sanctions as Tools of Foreign Policy," in David Cortright and George Lopez (1995), pp. 31–35, and Juhan Galtung, "On the Effects of International Economic Sanctions, with Examples from the Case of Rhodesia," *World Politics* 19, 3 (1967), pp. 26–28, 31, 47–48.

44. See, for example, Doxey (1986), pp. 55–58.

45. Baldwin (1985), pp. 96–101; Kobrin (1989), pp. 33–34.

46. Baldwin (1985); Renwick (1981); Schelling (1976), (1980), p. 86. The relationship between costs to the sender and the political weight of an action is similar to Robert Jervis's (1970) distinction between signals versus indices. The latter are taken more seriously in international relations because the costs of the costs of imposing them are higher. In contrast, James Marrow argues that resolve requires that some targets respond negatively to a particular signal or that other senders do not offer it. Without such variation, it is difficult for the target to judge the credibility of the sanction. James Morrow, "Signaling Difficulties with Linkage in Crisis Bargaining," *International Studies Quarterly* 36 (1992): 166–67.

47. Karl Deutsch, *The Analysis of International Relations*, 2d ed. (Englewood Cliffs, N.J.: Prentice Hall, 1978); Lukes, (1974).

48. See Baldwin (1979); Robert Keohane, *Neorealism and Its Critics* (New York: Columbia University Press, 1986), p. 187.

49. Albert Hirschman, *National Power and the Structure of Foreign Trade.* (Berkeley: University of California Press, 1980); Kenneth Waltz, "The Myth of Interdependence," in Charles Kindleberger, ed., *The International Corporation* (Cambridge: Harvard University Press, 1970); and David Baldwin, "Interdependence and Power: A Conceptual Analysis," *International Organization* 34:4 (1979), and Baldwin (1980);

Robert Keohane and Joseph, *Power and Interdependence* (Boston: Little Brown, 1977).

50. Hirschman emphasizes power resulting from the termination of trading relations as a function of the target's net gain from trade, its adjustment costs in the event of termination, and its vested interest in the trading relationship. My approach expands on Hirschman's by allowing for mutual dependence on a trading relationship, and the use of positive incentives—like the offer of special or expanded trade—as well as threats. Hirschman (1980), chapter 1.

51. See P. T. Hopmann, "Asymmetrical Bargaining in the Conference on Security and Cooperation in Europe," *International Organization* 32:1 (1978): 141–78; Hirschman (1980); and Anatol Rapoport, *Two-Person Game Theory: The Essential Ideas* (Ann Arbor: University of Michigan Press, 1969).

52. The use of the term *dependence* in this book is similar to Keohane and Nye's concept of vulnerability interdependence. Robert O. Keohane and Joseph Nye, *Power and Interdependence*. (Boston: Little Brown, 1977).

53. Losman, (1979), pp. 18–19.

54. If sanctions are used to send a political signal, the costs born by the target of the sanctions are far less important than if the sanctions are intended to change the target's behavior. Symbolic sanctions are discussed in chapter 5.

55. Baldwin (1971c); Cortright (1997); Long (1996).

56. Long (1996), pp. 20–21.

57. *Financial Times* (21 April 1986). Continued access to SDI technology required these countries to control the technology in a manner acceptable to the United States. See Stuart Macdonald, *Technology and the Tyranny of Export Controls* (London: Macmillan Press, 1990), p. 133.

58. Baldwin (1971c).

59. Harrison Wagner, "Economic Interdependence, Bargaining Power, and Political Influence," *International Organization* 42:3 (1988): 461–84. For a detailed analysis of Wagner's critique, see William Long, *Economic Incentives and Bilateral Cooperation*. (Ann Arbor: University of Michigan Press, 1996), pp. 19–24.

60. Helen Milner argues, for example, that multinational and trade dependent firms are put at risk by government interference in international trade due to the possibility of retaliation by foreign governments, general adverse international economic effects, and adverse consequences for their domestic market positions. See Helen Milner, *Resisting Protectionism* (Princeton, N.J.: Princeton University Press, 1988), pp. 21–24.

61. Theories of state-society relations tend to confuse rather than clarify motivations behind national policy and corporate actions in the export control arena. Counter to predictions of popular state-societal approaches, foreign firms were more likely to get national support in their fight against U.S. export controls from so-called strong states like France than in "weaker" states like Great Britain, and domestically oriented firms were more likely than internationally oriented firms to

secure the support of their governments. See Peter Gourevitch, *Politics in Hard Times* (Ithaca, N.Y.: Cornell University Press, 1986); Peter Katzenstein, *Between Power and Plenty* (Madison: University of Wisconsin Press, 1978), and *Small States in World Markets* (Ithaca, N.Y.: Cornell University Press, 1985), pp. 20–21; Stephen Krasner, *Defending the National Interest* (Princeton, N.J.: Princeton University Press, 1978); Milner (1988); and Ronald Rogowski, *Commerce and Coalitions: How Trade Affects Domestic Alignments* (Princeton, N.J.: Princeton University Press, 1989).

62. The relative isolation of the Executive branch in this issue area has enabled it to act relatively unencumbered by Congress and the electorate. At the same time, interdepartmental rivalry over export-control policy remains a problem. See Gary Bertsch, *Controlling East-West Trade and Technology Transfer.* (Durham, N.C.: Duke University Press, 1988); Mastanduno (1985), (1992); National Academy of Sciences, Panel on the Future Design and Implementation of U.S. National Security Export Controls, Committee on Science, Engineering, and Public Policy, *Finding Common Ground: U.S. Export Controls in a Changed Global Environment* (Washington, D.C.: National Academy Press, 1991); and U.S. Congress, Panel on the Impact of National Security Controls on International Technology Transfer, Committee on Science, Engineering, and Public Policy, National Academy of Sciences, *Balancing the National Interest: U.S. National Security Export Controls and Global Competition* (Washington, D.C.: National Academy Press, 1987).

63. The most vivid example of current lobbying efforts is USA*Engage. USA*Engage is a broad-based coalition, launched on April 16, 1997, representing American business and agriculture. The coalition currently includes 674 members including 40 National and State Associations and organizations from major sectors of the US economy. It maintains an active World Wide Web page (http://usaengage.org/index.html) that provides information on current sanctions activity and lobbying efforts against it.

64. Mastanduno (1992).

65. Mastanduno and Martin, for example, each argue that the resulting lack of credibility behind American sanctions explains a variety of American failures to implement its export control policy abroad since 1949. See Martin (1992); and Mastanduno (1985).

66. Christopher Joyner, "Sanctions, Compliance and International Law: Reflections on the United Nations Experience against Iraq," *Virginia Journal of International Law* 32:1 (1991): 3; Robin Renwick, *Economic Sanctions* (Cambridge: Center for International Affairs, Harvard University, 1981), p. 86.

67. David Buchan, "Total Wins Iran Contract, *Financial Times* (14 July 1995): 3.

68. Focusing sanctions against specific actors within particular countries has the added benefit of minimizing the negative impact of the sanctions on unrelated or "innocent" third parties. For a discussion of the ethical and moral implications of targeting sanctions, see Cortright and Lopez, eds. (1995), pp. 89–120.

69. R. Stainbridge, "Sweden Awaits American Wrath," *The Guardian* (19 October 1985): 6.

70. See E. M. Earle, "Adam Smith, Alexander Hamilton, Friedrich List: The Economic Foundations of Military Power," in Earle, ed., *Makers of Modern Strategy: Military Thought from Machiavelli to Hitler* (Princeton, N.J.: Princeton University Press, 1943), pp. 118–19; Robert Gilpin, *The Political Economy of International Relations.* (Princeton, N.J.: Princeton University Press, 1987); and Jacob Viner "Power versus Plenty as Objectives of Foreign Policy in the Seventeenth and Eighteenth Centuries," *World Politics* 1,1 (1948): 1–29.

71. See Joanne Gowa, *Allies, Adversaries, and International Trade* (Princeton, N.J.: Princeton University Press, 1994); Edward Mansfield, *Power, Trade* and War (Princeton, N.J.: Princeton University Press, 1994); Theodore Moran, "Grand Strategy: The Pursuit of Power and the Pursuit of Plenty," *International Organization* 50, 1 (winter 1996), pp. 175–205; Brian Pollins, "Does Trade Still Follow the Flag? *American Political Science Review* 83 (1989): 465–80; and Viner (1948).

72. Stephen Krasner, *Defending the National Interest* (Princeton, N.J.: Princeton University Press, 1978).

73. C. Fred Bergsten, Thomas Horst, and Theodore Moran, *American Multinationals and American Interests* (Washington, D.C.: Brookings, 1978), ch. 11; Theodore Moran, "The Globalization of America's Defense Industries: Managing the Threat of Foreign Dependence," *International Security* 15, 1 (summer 1990); p. 65; Raymond Vernon, *Big Business and the States: Changes Relations in Western Europe* (Cambridge: Harvard University Press, 1974).

74. Andrew Pollack, "Japan's Companies Hear U.S. Trade Appeals," *New York Times* (10 January 1994), p. D1, D16.

75. Ibid.

76. Ibid.

77. W. J. Broad, "Industries Fight Ban on Using Soviet Rockets," *New York Times* (13 December 1987), p. 2; Crawford (1993), pp. 33–34; and Mastanduno (1990), (1992).

78. Jack N. Behrman, *National Interests and Multinational Enterprises* (Englewood Cliffs, N.J.: Prentice Hall, 1970), p. 102.

79. Broad (1987); Crawford (1993), pp. 33–34.

80. Mastanduno (1990); Shambaugh (1993).

81. Kevin Cahill, *Trade Wars: High-Technology Scandals of the 1980s* (London: W. H. Allen, 1986), p. 177; Mastanduno (1992), p. 298; and A. Ramirez, "Move to Liberalize U.S. High-Tech Exports Gains," *New York Times* (21 September 1993), p. D3.

82. Hufbauer and Schott (1985), p. 89.

83. Laura d'Andrea Tyson. *Who's Bashing Whom? Trade Conflict in High-Technology Industries* (Washington, D.C.: Institute for International Economics, 1992).

84. Sarna (1986), pp. 3–36; M. S. Daoudi S. and M. S. Dajani, *Economic Sanctions: Ideals and Experience* (Boston: Routledge & Kegan Paul, 1983), p. 102.

85. Sarna (1986), pp. 210–19.

86. Raymond Vernon, *Sovereignty at Bay* (New York: Basic Books, 1971), p. 232.

87. U.S. Export Administration Act, 50 U.S.C. app.§§ 2401–20; Export Administration Regulations, 15 C.F.R. pts. 768–99 (1989). See Dallmeyer (1989), pp. 565–66.

88. There is an increasingly rich political science literature on sovereignty from realist, institutionalist, regime theory, and constructivist perspectives. James Alan, *Sovereign Statehood: The Basis of International Society* (London: Allen and Unwin, 1986); Richard Ashley, "The Poverty of Neorealism," *International Organization* 38 (1984): 225–86; J. Samuel Barkin and Bruce Cronin, "The State and the Nation: Changing Norms and the Rules of Sovereignty in International Relations," *International Organization* 48, 1 (winter 1994): 107–30; Hedley Bull, *The Anarchical Society* (New York: Columbia University Press, 1977); Richard Cooper, *The Economics of Interdependence: Economic Policy in the Atlantic Community* (New York: McGraw-Hill 1968); Robert Gilpin, *War and Change in World Politics* (Cambridge: Cambridge University Press, 1981), p. 17; Stephen Krasner, *Defending the National Interest* (Princeton, N.J.: Princeton University Press, 1978); "Sovereignty: An Institutional Perspective," *Comparative Political Studies* 21:1 (April 1988): 66–94, and "Compromising Westphalia," *International Security* 20, 3 (September 1995/96): 115–51; Friedrich Kratochwil, *Rules, Norms, and Decisions* (New York: Cambridge University Press, 1989); Hans Morgenthau, *Politics among Nations: The Struggle for Power and Peace* (New York: Alfred Knopf, 1985); J. Rosenberg, "A Neo-Realist Theory of Sovereignty? Giddens's *The Nation-State and Violence*," *Millennium* 19 (1991): 249–59; John G. Ruggie, "Continuity and Transformation in the World Polity: Toward a Neorealist Synthesis," in Robert O. Keohane, ed., *Neorealism and Its Critics* (New York: Columbia University Press, 1986), p. 143; Hendrik Spruyt, *The Sovereign State and Its Competitors: An Analysis of Systems Change* (Princeton, N.J.: Princeton University Press, 1994); Janice E. Thomson, "State Sovereignty in International Relations: Bridging the Gap between Theory and Empirical Research," *International Studies Quarterly* 39:2 (1995): 213–33; Janice E. Thomson and Stephen Krasner, "Global Transactions and the Consolidation of Sovereignty," in Ernst-Otto Czempiel and James N. Rosenau, eds., *Global Challenges: Approaches to World Politics in the 1990s* (Lexington, Ky.: Lexington Books, 1989), pp. 195–219; and Kenneth Waltz, *Theory of International Politics* (Reading, Mass.: Addison-Wesley, 1979), chapter 5.

89. Robert L. Bledsoe and Bloeslaw A. Boczek, *The International Law Dictionary* (Oxford: Clio Press, 1987), pp. 55–56.

90. Stephen Krasner, Robert Jackson, and Carl Rosberg have each argued that the recognition of juridical sovereignty by other states in the international system is an extremely important source of political power, particularly if they lack domestic economic or military resources. Stephen Krasner, *Structural Conflict* (Berkeley: University of California Press, 1985); Robert Jackson and Carl Rosberg, "Why Africa's Weak States Persist: The Empirical and Juridical in Statehood," *World Politics* 35 (October 1982): 1–24.

The traditional positivist approach to international law places particular emphasis on the significance of state practice in determining the nature of law.

International laws, such as those related to sovereignty, are a function of what states have created and recognize. Positivist legal scholars include Georg Schwarzenberger, Lassa Oppenheim, C. Wilfred Jenks, and Propser Weill. George Schwarzenberger, *The Inductive Approach to International Law* (Ferry, N.Y., Oceana Publications, 1965); Clarence Wilfred Jenks, *Law in the World Community* (New York: D. McKay, 1967); Meyers S. McDougal, Harold D. Lasswell, and W. Michael Reisman, "Theories about International Law: Prologue to a Configurative Jurisprudence," reprinted in Myres S. McDougal and W. Michael Reisman, *International Law Essays* (Mineola, N.Y. : Foundation Press, 1981); Prosper Weill, *The Law of Maritime Delimitation: Reflections* (Cambridge: Grotius, 1989).

91. This reflects what Krasner refers to as the "Westphalian model" based on territory and autonomy. Krasner argues, however, that while useful, this view of sovereignty is not entirely accurate given frequent violations to both territory and autonomy in international relations. Krasner (1995/96), pp. 115–51. For a discussion of different sets of criteria for international recognition of sovereign authority, and whose recognition is required see: Ashley (1984); Hedley Bull (1977); Hedley Bull and Adam Watson, eds., *The Expansion of International Society* (Oxford: Clarendon Press 1984); J. Samuel Barkin and Bruce Cronin, (1994); Stephen Krasner and Janice Thomson, "Global Transactions and the Consolidation of Sovereignty," in E. Cziempiel and J. Rosenau (1989); Thomson (1995), pp. 219–20; Waltz (1970); and Alexander Wendt, "Anarchy Is What States Make of It: The Social Construction of State Politics," *International Organization* 46, 2 (spring 1992): 391–425.

92. See Helen Milner, "The Assumption of Anarchy in International Relations Theory," *Review of International Studies* (1991), p. 82. This argument about strategic interdependence ties in nicely with Baldwin's definition of interdependence and is similar to the propositions of systems theorists concerning the intended and unintended consequences of state action within the international system. See Robert Jervis, "Systems Theory," in Paul Lauren, ed. *Diplomacy: New Approaches in History, Theory and Policy* (New York: Free Press, 1979); and chapter 1 in Jervis, *Perception and Misperception in International Politics* (Princeton, N.J.: Princeton University Press, 1976).

93. With the exception of military conflict, as Hans Morgenthau notes, "on a given territory only one nation can have sovereignty—supreme authority— and . . . no other state has the right to perform governmental acts on its territory without its consent." Morgenthau (1966), p. 301.

94. "Anarchy" refers to the absence of a centralized authority in international relations. See Milner (1991) and Waltz (1979).

95. See Keohane and Nye (1977).

96. Stephen Krasner argues that in the midst of a trend towards increased multilateralism in world politics, lesser developed countries repeatedly seek to confirm and strengthen international respect for sovereign authority and sovereign autonomy as a means of maximizing their power in international politics. Krasner (1985).

97. Statement of 9 July 1958, 39 *U.S. Department of State Bulletin* 309 (4 August 1958); Behrman (1970), pp. 105–106; Dallmeyer (1989), p. 567; de Mestral and Gruchalla-Wesierski (1990), pp. 99, 157–58.

98. Based on the Eisenhower-Diefenbaker understanding, it was precisely under these conditions that consultations should be held and U.S. policy negotiated. Yet the presence of the agreement did not alter Alcan's decision not to proceed with the sale. The Eisenhower-Diefenbaker agreement was limited to the extent that it only came into play when the Canadian government intervened on behalf of a company that had already decided to go ahead with a sale and was awaiting export licenses before it did so. Alcan did not challenge the policy because it relied on the U.S. market for the vast majority of its sales. It officially rejected the offer because it feared losing business from its American customers if it proceeded with the sale. House of Commons Debates (1959), vol. I, pp. 274–75. Also cited in de Mestral and Gruchalla-Wesierski (1990), p. 158.

99. Paradoxically, despite all of the measures to block U.S. initiatives in 1982 and those threatened in response to current U.S. legislation regarding Cuba, Iran, and Libya, the allies did not challenge similar restrictions during Operation Exodus throughout the 1980s. Their compliance in the 1980s, in spite of their ability to protest the restrictions, reflects the partial convergence of interest on the goals of Operation Exodus's export restrictions in addition to the use of economic sanctions by the United States to entice and coerce cooperation with its policy.

100. Thomson (1995), p. 214.

101. Thomson (1995), p. 217; Krasner and Thomson, in Cziempiel and Rosenau (1989), pp. 194–219.

102. Krasner argues that there are four primary ways in which sovereign autonomy of the Westphalian state tends to be undermined—through contracts, conventions, coercion, and imposition. While useful as a descriptive categorization of events, examining sanctions as examples of instruments that can be used to extend control across international borders highlights how this list can be refined and expanded. Krasner (1995/96), pp. 115–16.

103. Krasner (1995/96), p. 116. Unlike Thomson, Krasner does not differentiate between sovereign authority and sovereign control. Instead, he tends to address situations where the two converge and uses the more general term *authoritative control.*

104. The link between authority and control is central to the New Haven School of international law as represented by the writings of Myres McDougal and Harold Laswell, McDougal, Lasswell, and Reisman in McDougal and Reisman (1981); John Norton Moore, "Prolegomenon to the Jurisprudence of Myres McDougal and Harold Lasswell," *Virginia Law Review* 54, 4 (1968): 662–88. While this approach has been discredited by some, it has influenced a substantial number of legal scholars. Anthony Clark Arend, *Legal Rules and International Society* (Oxford: Oxford University Press, 1999), chapter 3.

105. Thomson (1995), p. 223. The New Haven School of International Law defines authority more precisely as "the structure of expectation concerning who, with what qualifications and mode of selection, is competent to make which decisions by what criteria and what procedures." It defines control as "an effective voice in decision, whether authorized or not." Myres McDougal and Harold Lasswell, "The Identification and Appraisal of Diverse Systems of Public Order," in McDougal and Reisman (1981), p. 22.

106. Arend (1996), pp. 17–18.

107. Control and authority may converge, as in the case of a sovereign state with absolute authority and absolute control over its subjects. From the New Haven perspective, international law and legal norms exist when they are both authoritative and controlling. At the opposite end of the spectrum, control and authority may diverge completely, as in the case of "pretended power" where a disposed monarch vainly claims authority over his former country or in the case of "naked power" where an imperial state assumes control over a weaker neighbor. Arend (1996), chapter 3, p. 18; McDougal and Reisman (1981), pp. 191–92.

108. Waltz emphasizes the importance of capabilities by arguing that a state recognizes another's sovereignty when the latter has the capability to defend its authority against domestic and international challengers. Waltz (1979), p. 96. Krasner adds to this debate by focusing on the importance of distributional issues. Stephen Krasner, "Global Communications and National Power: Life on the Pareto Frontier," *World Politics* 43, 3 (April 1991): 336–67. See also P. M. Blau, "Critical Remarks on Weber's Theory of Authority," *American Political Science Review* 57 (1963): 313; Thomson, (1995), p. 220.

109. While similar issues have been debated in a variety of issue areas including anti-trust and extradition policy, the following sources provide a general background of the debate regarding the extraterritorial control of strategic goods and technology. Kenneth Abbot, "Defining the Extraterritorial Reach of American Export Controls: Congress as Catalyst," *Cornell International Law Journal* 79 (winter 1984): 79–158; Linda Andros, "Chemical Weapons Proliferation: Extraterritorial Controls: When Too Much Is Not Enough," *New York Law School Journal of International and Comparative* Law 13, 3 (1992): 257–314; David Matthews, "Controlling the Exportation of Strategically Sensitive Technology: The Extraterritorial Jurisdiction of the Multilateral Export Control Enhancement Amendments Act of 1988," *Columbia Journal of Transnational Law*, 28, 3 (1990): 747–74; Armand L. C. de Mestral, T. Gruchalla-Wesierski, *Extraterritorial Application of Export Control Legislation: Canada and the U.S.A.* (London: Martinus Nijhoff, 1990); Dorinda G. Dallmeyer, "Foreign Policy and Export Controls: How Will the Canada-United States Free Trade Agreement Accommodate the Extraterritorial Application of United States Laws to Canadian Exports of Goods and Technology?" *Georgia Journal of International and Comparative Law* 19, 3 (1989): 565–88; David Koplow, "Long Arms and Chemical Arm: Extraterritoriality and the Draft Chemical Weapons Convention,"

Yale Journal of International Law, 15, 1 (winter 1990): 1–83; Homer E. Moyer and Linda A. Mabry, *Export Controls as Instruments of Foreign Policy: The History, Legal Issues, and Policy Lessons of Three Recent Cases* (Washington, D.C.: University of America Press, 1983); Harold Maier, "Resolving Extraterritorial Conflicts, or 'There and Back Again,' " *Virginia Journal of International Law* 25, 1 (1984): 7–48; Neale and Stephens (1988); Cecil J. Olmstead, ed., *Extraterritorial Application of Laws and Responses Thereto* (Oxford: ESC Publishing, 1984); Philip Oettinger, "National Discretion: Choosing CoCom's Successor," *The American University Journal of International Law and Policy* 9, 2 (winter 1994): 559–95; Thomas Schoenbaum and Dorinda Dallmeyer, "The Extraterritorial Application of United States Laws Affecting Trade between Nations," in *Dynamics of Japanese-United States Trade Relations,* Thomas Schoenbaum, Mitsuo Matsushita, and Dorinda Dallmeyer, eds. (Athens: Dean Rusk Center for International and Comparative Law, University of Georgia School of Law, 1986); and Jay L. Westbrook, "Extraterritoriality, Conflict of Laws, and the Regulation of Transnational Business," *Texas International Law Journal* 25, 1 (winter 1990): 71–97. For a summary of U.S. and E.C. policies regarding extraterritoriality and antitrust policy, see Joseph P. Griffin, "E.C. and U.S. Extraterritoriality: Activism and Cooperation," *Fordham International Law Journal* 17:2 (1994): 353–88.

110. Robert Bledsoe and Bloeslaw Boczek, *The International Law Dictionary* (Oxford: Clio Press, 1987): 105–106.

111. Conflicts of jurisdiction also commonly arise over issues involving the ownership and control of various aspects of a transnational corporation. See Alan D. Neale and M. L. Stephens, *International Business and National Jurisdiction* (Oxford: Clarendon Press, 1988), pp. 4–5, 12–14.

112. The Bureau of Export Administration in the Department of Commerce maintains a "Denied Persons List" containing all of the companies and individuals currently penalized for violating U.S. Export Administration Regulations (EAR) as well as a list of penalties and restrictions ("Denial Orders") imposed against them. The Denied Persons List and Denial Orders are available on the World Wide Web at http://www.bxa.doc.gov/.

113. Hans J. Morgenthau, *Politics among Nations* (New York: Knopf Press, 1966), pp. 305–306.

114. Thomas N. Gladwin and Ingo Walter, *Multinationals under Fire* (New York: John Wiley, 1980); Moran, (1990), p. 61.

115. Theodore Moran, "Foreign Acquisition of Critical U.S. Industries: Where Should the United States Draw the Line?" *Washington Quarterly* 16, 3 (spring 1993): 62–63.

116. Raymond Vernon, *Storm over Multinationals* (Cambridge: University Press of America, 1977), p. 177.

117. Doxey (1996), pp. 7–11.

2

Restricting the Proliferation of Strategic Goods and Technology since 1949

EXPORT CONTROLS AND U.S. FOREIGN POLICY

The U.S. government first imposed restrictions on the trade of American goods in 1774 when the Continental Congress outlawed British imports and then again, one year later, when it outlawed exports to Great Britain. Today, the U.S. government restricts the import and export of certain goods and technologies in response to matters of national security, foreign policy, and a variety of issues including short supply, human rights, drug trafficking, the environment, and weapons proliferation. While the primary targets of U.S. export controls have shifted with the end of the Cold War from the Soviet Union and the People's Republic of China to states engaged in "risky behavior"[1] like Iran and Libya, restricting the sale of strategic goods and technology to potential adversaries remains a central component of American foreign policy. Limiting the proliferation of strategic goods using the supply-side strategy of restricting exports requires that all foreign and domestic actors who possess or can produce the restricted goods or technology conform to the restrictions. Thus, like the risky states against whom the primary export restrictions are aimed, all potential suppliers of the restricted goods or technology are potential targets of U.S. enforcement efforts.

Given the potentially wide availability of alternate suppliers of certain strategic goods, the effectiveness of U.S. policy is likely to be enhanced if it is broadly supported by bilateral and multilateral fora. Multilateral efforts to restrict the sale of strategic goods and technology were institutionalized informally with the establishment of a gentlemen's agreement among NATO members and a few others, including Japan, known as the Coordinating Committee on East-West Trade (CoCom).[2] CoCom was established in 1949 to create, maintain, and enforce an embargo of items that it identified as having strategic significance or that could contribute directly to the strategic capabilities of the East Bloc. Reflecting the changes that had taken place with the end of the Cold War, CoCom was disbanded and replaced by the New Forum (also known as the Wassenaar Agreement) in March of 1994.[3] The New Forum has a broader mandate than its predecessor and is intended to manage the proliferation of strategic goods to countries engaged in potentially threatening behavior into the next century. The broader objectives of the New Forum are matched by an expanded membership which includes several Newly Industrializing Countries, as well as former members of the East Bloc that CoCom had targeted.[4] Through the New Forum and other multilateral regimes such as the International Atomic Energy Agency (IAEA), the Nuclear Nonproliferation Treaty (NPT), the Missile Technology Control Regime (MTCR), the Australia Group, and the Nuclear Supplier's Group (NSG); the United States and other member countries have succeeded in promoting a national and multilateral consensus on the need to withhold certain products of obvious strategic value from specific risky countries.[5] These organizations have facilitated the coordination of international efforts to manage the proliferation of strategic goods and technology by establishing guidelines for appropriate behavior, by furnishing fora for negotiations and the coordination of decision making, and by providing information about others' actions and intentions.[6]

Intergovernmental collaboration with U.S. export control initiatives has, however, not been fully forthcoming. Despite a consensus on the need to restrict the sale of a limited number of indisputably strategic goods, there have been recurrent disputes among policy makers at the domestic and international levels over both the objectives of the restrictions and the range of "strategic" goods that should be withheld. While most governments agree that military armaments are strategic in nature and should be controlled, the "strategic" nature of other dual-use goods,

Table 2.1   Multilateral Export Control Regimes

Type of Technology Controlled	Regime(s)
Nuclear	Nuclear Nonproliferation Treaty, Nuclear Suppliers' Group
Chemical	Chemical Weapons Convention, Australia Group
Biological	Biological and Toxins Weapons Convention
Missile	Missile Technology Control Regime
Conventional, Other	Formerly CoCom, new controls are emerging in the post–CoCom regime known as the New Forum or the Wassenaar Agreement

Source: Laura Carlson Chen, "Export Licensing Checklist," *Business Laws, Inc.* (June 1994): pp. 1–5, 1–6.

Table 2.2   Members of Multilateral Export Control Regimes as of October 1995

Nuclear Suppliers Group	Australia Group	Missile Technology Control Regime	New Forum
Est. 1974	Est. 1984	Est. 1987	Est. 1995–96
31 Members	29 Members	27 Members	28 Members
Argentina	Argentina	Argentina	—
Australia	Australia	Australia	Australia
Austria	Austria	Austria	Austria
Belgium	Belgium	Belgium	Belgium
Bulgaria	—	—	—
Canada	Canada	Canada	Canada
Czech Republic	Czech Republic	—	Czech Republic
Denmark	Denmark	Denmark	Denmark
Finland	Finland	Finland	Finland
France	France	France	France
Germany	Germany	Germany	Germany
Greece	Greece	Greece	Greece
Hungary	Hungary	Hungary	Hungary
—	Iceland	Iceland	—
Ireland	Ireland	Ireland	Ireland
Italy	Italy	Italy	Italy
Japan	Japan	Japan	Japan
Luxembourg	Luxembourg	Luxembourg	Luxembourg
Netherlands	Netherlands	Netherlands	Netherlands
New Zealand	New Zealand	New Zealand	New Zealand
Norway	Norway	Norway	Norway
Poland	Poland	—	Poland
Portugal	Portugal	Portugal	Portugal
Rumania	Romania	—	—
Russia	—	Russia	Russia
Slovak Republic	Slovak Republic	—	Slovak Republic
South Africa	—	South Africa	—
Spain	Spain	Spain	Spain
Sweden	Sweden	Sweden	Sweden
Switzerland	Switzerland	Switzerland	Switzerland
—	—	—	Turkey
United Kingdom	United Kingdom	United Kingdom	United Kingdom
United States	United States	United States	United States

Source: The Risk Report 1, 8 (October 1995): p. 2.

(that is, goods such as oil and natural gas, computers and telecommunications equipment that have commercial as well as military uses), has been a matter of contention since countries first agreed to form CoCom in 1949. Furthermore, contrary to the conventional wisdom that these sorts of disputes will recede when states are challenged by a common external threat,[7] the resurgence of external threats to CoCom members

Table 2.3   Domestic Export Control Regulations

AGENCY	ITEMS CONTROLLED	STATUTORY AUTHORITY
Department of State	Munitions	Arms Export Control Act (AECA) *22 USC 2751 ff*
Department of Treasury	New Forum-proscribed destinations, embargoes	Trading with the Enemy Act (TWEA) *50 USC App 5* International Emergency Economic Powers Act (IEEPA) *50 USC 1701 ff*
Nuclear Regulatory Commission	Nuclear equipment and materials	Atomic Energy Act (AEA) *42 USC 2011 ff*
Department of Energy	Nuclear weapons restricted data, sensitive nuclear technology	Atomic Energy Act (AEA) *42 USC 2011 ff*
Department of Commerce	Other "dual-use" items	Export Administration Act (EAA) *50 USC app. 2401 ff*

Source: Laura Carlson Chen, "Esporting Licensing Checklist," *Business Laws, Inc.* (June 1994), Supplement, pp. 1–5, 1–6.

during the Cold War often exacerbated disputes within CoCom and other export control regimes over the breadth and appropriate use of export restrictions.[8] Current international disputes over U.S. sanctions against Cuba, Iran, and Libya, for example, result primarily from divergent views about the nature of the threat each of these countries poses to others and how best to respond to it (see chapter 5). The high intensity of U.S.-European disputes in the early 1980s over whether technology transfers that related to the construction of a trans-Siberian pipeline posed a security threat, indicate how destructive such disagreements can become if they are left unchecked (see chapter 3). Finally, as discussed above, even if these disputes are resolved, securing intergovernmental agreement does not guarantee that the guidelines will be enforced or that private companies will conform to the agreed upon multilateral guidelines.

When sufficient cooperation by foreign governments or firms has not been forthcoming, the U.S. government has attempted to apply and enforce its export administration regulations to the full extent of its capabilities. As discussed above, in order to bolster its enforcement activities abroad, the U.S. government has attempted to assert its jurisdiction over the international movement of strategic goods and technology as far as possible under accepted principles in international law. The resulting extraterritorial application of U.S. regulations over property, licensing rights, technical know-how, and the actions of individuals and firms has often created legal and political battles over the question of who has sovereign authority over these individuals, firms, and resources (see the Appendix). Yet, even if the basis of U.S. authority over foreign actors is challenged by other countries, the U.S. government can use secondary sanctions to compel foreign actors to conform to its restrictions. This chapter tests competing hypotheses about the conditions under which secondary sanctions are likely to succeed and fail in compelling foreign firms to comply with domestic legislation. These tests ascertain the predictive capacity and explanatory power gained by models of corporate compliance based on dominance in and dependence on trade in particular goods. Sixty-six confrontational cases involving the extension of U.S. export control policy abroad since 1949 are analyzed. In each case, the U.S. government used sanctions to entice or coerce extraterritorial compliance by firms or individuals operating abroad. The results illuminate the hypothesized relationship between trade dominance, dependence, and political power.

Table 2.4   Proposed Hypothesis

PRINCIPAL HYPOTHESES OF SECTOR-SPECIFIC TRADE DOMINANCE AND DEPENDENCE

$H_{Dominance}$: *Because the outcome of negotiations and bargaining between actors in world politics is likely to reflect the interests of the actor that possesses a preponderance of relevant resources, as an actor's trade dominance in a particular sector or issue-area increases (declines) its ability to entice or coerce others that value those resources into doing its bidding will increase (decline). American attempts to compel foreign companies operating in a particular industrial sector to change their behavior are more (less) likely to succeed as the trade dominance of U.S. firms and/or markets in the relevant sector increases (declines).*

$H_{Dependence}$: *The ability of one state to use economic incentives or sanctions to alter a targeted actor's (state, firm, or individual) behavior will increase as the target's dependence on relations with it increases and its dependence on relations with the target decreases. Dependence is defined in terms of two dimensions: the utility that each actor gains from its relationship with the other and its ability to adjust to disruptions in that relationship. American attempts to enforce its export control policy abroad against the interests of other countries and foreign firms are more likely to succeed as their dependence on the United States increases and its dependence on them decreases.*

PRINCIPAL HYPOTHESIS ABOUT STATE AND FIRM PREFERENCES

$H_{FirmGovt}$: *While dependent governments and firms may respond to threats (or promises) regarding access to both foreign suppliers and markets, national governments will tend to weigh threats (or promises) regarding the supply of strategic goods more heavily than market access, relative to firms. In contrast, relative to states, firms will tend to weigh threats (or promises) regarding market access more heavily than the supply of strategic goods. American attempts to secure the extraterritorial compliance of firms is more likely when the sanction involves market access, while its attempts to secure the cooperation of foreign governments is more likely when the sanction involves access to American suppliers.*

The results from the statistical analysis of these data are consistent with the detailed comparative cases that follow in chapters 3 and 4. The detailed cases include U.S. attempts to stop European firms from shipping goods and technology to Russia for the construction of a trans-Siberian pipeline between 1980 to 1984, and its efforts to stop foreign firms and individuals from shipping computers and other high-technology goods to restricted destinations through a program named Operation Exodus from 1981 through 1988. The statistical results suggest that the cases chosen for comparative analysis are representative of disputes among state and nonstate actors involving the extraterritorial enforcement of national export control policies. The detailed comparative case studies, in turn, clarify the causal links between trade dominance, dependence, and political power suggested by the statistical analyses.

This chapter consists of four parts. Following the introduction, the section on methodology defines and operationalizes the dependent and independent variables, and discusses the criteria used to select cases. The section on statistical analyses evaluates competing hypotheses about political power using LOGIT analyses of U.S. government attempts to secure corporate compliance with its export control policy. The final section concludes with a summary of the findings and general assessment of the ability of competing arguments to explain success and failure of the extraterritorial enforcement of U.S. export control regulations.

METHODOLOGY

Variable Definitions

This section defines and operationalizes the dependent and independent variables evaluated throughout the book.

Corporate compliance. Economic statecraft can be used to achieve a variety of substantive, symbolic, and political objectives. Substantively, it can deter, compel, punish, reward, or bolster particular actors or behavior. Politically, it can signal support or solidarity, express political rejection, set precedent, demonstrate resolve, warn of future action, or focus world attention on a particular actor or activity. As discussed in chapter 1, while these substantive and symbolic objectives are not mutually exclusive, they may require that varying degrees of rewards or penalties to be imposed to be successful. Given this variation, it is important to evaluate the effectiveness of economic statecraft in terms of the goals it is intended to achieve.

The primary objectives of the secondary sanctions analyzed in this book were substantive in nature. They were imposed to punish foreign firms that failed to conform to U.S. export control regulations and reward those that did so, to compel negligent firms to conform to U.S. regulations, and to deter others from failing to conform. For the purposes of this book, secondary sanctions imposed against foreign companies are considered successful if they succeed in either deterring foreign companies from violating U.S. export control restrictions or compelling negligent firms to change their behavior.

Secondary sanctions will be considered successful if foreign companies conform to U.S. policy when they have the opportunity to do otherwise and they explicitly cite warning or guidance letters from the U.S. government, or the previous imposition of U.S. economic threats or promises, as the primary reason for foregoing trade that would not conform to U.S. export controls.

When deterrence fails, the U.S. government has used secondary sanctions to compel negligent firms to alter their behavior. In these cases, secondary sanctions will be considered successful if the company responds to the U.S. incentives or penalties by terminating the restricted sales or accepts a consent agreement regarding future sales or licensing agreements, or if the penalties were removed or reduced as a result of compliant behavior. The secondary sanctions will be considered a failure if target fails to terminate the restricted sales after notification by the Office of Export Enforcement or another U.S. government agency, if it challenges U.S. jurisdiction or fails to pay the imposed penalties, or if the U.S. government imposes additional penalties on the firm. Trade restrictions, fines, and other criminal or administrative penalties may be imposed to punish nonconforming foreign firms, but punishment alone does not further U.S. export control policy unless the offending firm is compelled to change its behavior or others are deterred by the primary punishment.

Based on these criteria, the effectiveness of secondary sanctions against foreign firms will be treated dichotomously as either success or failure. Secondary sanctions will be considered successful (Compliance = 1) if foreign companies were deterred from violating U.S. export control regulations, or if nonconforming firms were compelled to change their behavior. Secondary sanctions will be considered a failure (Compliance = 0) if they fail to deter or compel foreign firms.

Host government cooperation. Under certain conditions, foreign governments may support the United States's use of secondary sanctions against local firms. Ideally, foreign governments will accept both the political objective and appropriateness of U.S. export controls, and enforce them domestically. The Western allies did this before 1953 in embargoing trade with the Soviet Union, and again in 1979 in responding to the seizure of American hostages by Iran. Alternatively, they may support the policy in question but lack the will or ability to enforce it. Faced with these constraints, foreign governments have occasionally relied on and supported the application of American sanctions locally to enforce U.S. or multilateral regulations. The British government, for example, supported U.S. efforts to penalize and prosecute the British company Systime, Ltd. in the early 1980s. In either situation, the foreign government does not act to undermine the effect of U.S. sanctions on firms operating in its territory.

Alternately, a foreign government may reject the application of secondary sanctions against companies operating in its country. A foreign government may sympathize with U.S. policy objectives but disagree with the U.S. government on the appropriate means for implementing the policy. Examples of this include European positions taken after 1953 concerning trade with the Soviet Union and British policy against the Arab boycott in the 1970s. In the former case, the allies disputed the appropriateness of using the embargo to restrain Soviet military development; while in the latter, Britain supported the U.S. antiboycott measures but argued that British companies should be free to make their own commercial judgements on how to react to it. Finally, the foreign government may disagree with both the policy goals and the means to achieve them. For example, the Canadians, Mexicans, and Europeans do not restrict exports to Cuba, and the British and Canadians maintain only minimal restrictions on trade with the People's Republic of China.

If the foreign government rejects the U.S. application of secondary sanctions, it may intervene and challenge the application of the sanctions on behalf of firms operating in its country. For example, on its own initiative or at the request of its constituents, host governments may enact domestic legislation that forbids the enforcement of U.S. policy initiatives. Such legislation represents an assertion of sovereign authority and an overt attempt to undermine U.S. enforcement efforts. Foreign governments may also threaten to retaliate against U.S. actions in other ways, such as imposing retaliatory sanctions against the United States, its firms or its products. These actions may undermine the impact of U.S. sanctions.

Host government intervention will, therefore, be treated as an intervening variable between U.S. actions and corporate behavior. Inaction or active support of U.S. enforcement efforts by foreign governments may enhance the impact of U.S. economic statecraft on corporate activity. For the purposes of this analysis, such actions or inactions will indicate host government cooperation with the United States. In contrast, active intervention to stop or undermine U.S. enforcement efforts though the imposition of domestic legislation, countersanctions or equivalent means may suppress the impact of U.S. secondary sanctions on foreign firms. These actions will indicate host government intervention against U.S. sanctions on behalf of local firms. Finally, the arguments developed in chapter 1 suggest that while influential, host government intervention is neither always necessary nor sufficient for corporate compliance. If this is correct, then host government intervention should not suppress the impact of trade dependence on corporate compliance.

Dominance. The first explanatory variable analyzed in this project is the trade dominance of the sender. Building on the assumption that outcomes in world politics reflect the capabilities of the actor that possesses a preponderance of relevant resources, one would predict that trade dominance in a particular industrial sector should provide the sender with a source of leverage over foreign actors who rely on imports or exports in that sector. Trade dominance is operationalized in terms of the proportion of global trade accounted for by one actor in a particular industrial sector.[9]

In order to test the subsidiary hypothesis that firms and states may respond to sanctions regarding access to markets and suppliers differently, trade dominance is subdivided into market dominance and supply dominance. The dominance of the sender's (in this case American) markets can be estimated in terms of the value of goods in a particular industrial sector that are imported by the sender as a proportion of total imports of those goods for the world during a particular year. Similarly, the dominance of the sender's suppliers in a particular sector is measured in terms of the value of goods in a particular industrial sector that are exported by the sender as a proportion of total world exports of those goods during a particular year.

Chapter 1 argued that issue and context-specific arguments should provide more accurate explanations of one's ability to exercise control over political outcomes than arguments like hegemonic leadership theory that emphasize the aggregate capabilities of the sender country. This proposition will be tested by comparing the impact of sector-specific dominance and hegemony on corporate compliance.[10] For the purposes of this analysis, hegemony will be measured in terms of both the economic and military characteristics traditionally associated with the concept. The economic component of hegemony will be defined as the proportion of world trade in all sectors accounted for by the sender and the relative size of its GNP per capita.[11] Most studies of hegemonic leadership define military hegemony in terms of a combination of the relative number of armed forces, military expenditure, and nature of national weaponry.[12] For the purposes of this analysis, the military component of hegemony will be estimated in terms of the relative size of the sender's military expenditure in comparison to the total military expenditure of all members of its alliance.[13] The military component of American hegemony will, for example, be estimated by measuring U.S. military expenditure as a proportion of total NATO military expenditure.[14]

Dependence. The second explanatory variable analyzed in this project is foreign dependence. Dependence is defined in terms of the net positive utility each actor gains from a relationship plus the costs of adjustment if it is altered. The costs associated with changing the terms of a particular relationship are a function of both the value of the resources each actor gains from a particular relationship in comparison to other sources, and the availability of comparable resources outside of the relationship. The more costly it is for an actor to forgo or change the terms of a particular relationship, the more dependent it is on that relationship, and the more likely it is to alter its behavior to maintain the terms of the relationship. Each country in a relationship is likely to be dependent on the other, though to varying degrees.

The value of imports in a particular sector that each actor gains from their trading relationship with one another in comparison to other sources is estimated in terms of the proportion of the each actor's imports accounted for by exports from its trading partner. In parallel, the value of exports that each actor gains from a their relationship with one another in comparison to other sources is estimated in terms of each actor's total exports in that sector accounted for by imports by the other.

The proportion of each actor's exports or imports accounted for by its trading partner's suppliers or markets may range from zero to 100 percent. If the proportion of trade is low, the cost of altering that relationship will be low, and neither actor will be dependent on the other. In this situation, economic threats to terminate the relationship will have little effect. Economic incentives may, however, still be useful since increasing trade will increase the value of the exchange between trading partners. If the proportion of trade is high (or potentially high based on a promised increase), then each actor may be dependent on the other.

A high proportion of trade is necessary, but not sufficient, to create dependence. If either actor gains a high proportion of its imports or exports from trade with the other, then its dependence on trade with the other becomes a function of its ability to bear the costs of adjustment if the relationship is changed. The cost of adjustment can be estimated in terms of the availability of alternate trading partners or, more specifically, the availability of alternate suppliers or alternate markets. The availability of alternate suppliers and alternate markets for U.S. goods in a particular industrial sector is a function of the proportion of global exports accounted for by U.S. exports, and the proportion of global imports accounted for by U.S. imports, respectively. These indicators are the same as those used to estimate U.S. trade dominance. The interpretation of these values is, however, slightly different. Rather than indicating trade dominance—and suggesting that dominance in a particular sector can be translated into power over actors in that sector—the relative proportion of U.S.

markets or suppliers in particular industrial sectors will be treated as indicators of the availability of alternates. The higher the proportion of world suppliers or markets accounted for by the United States, the fewer the number of alternate, non-U.S. trading partners. Alternatively, the lower the proportion of world suppliers or markets accounted for by the United States, the greater the number of alternate, non-U.S. trading partners.[15]

In sum, a foreign country's dependence on U.S. markets can be estimated by calculating the proportion of the foreign country's exports in a particular industrial sector that are accounted for by U.S. markets, multiplied by the dominance of U.S. markets in that sector. U.S. dependence on suppliers in a foreign country can be estimated by calculating the proportion of American imports in a particular industrial sector that are accounted for by the foreign country's exports, multiplied by the dominance of U.S. markets in that sector. Given the reciprocal nature of dependence, the effectiveness of U.S. sanctions or promises regarding market access in a particular sector will be a function of the target's net dependence onto the U.S. markets. This is equal to the target's dependence on the U.S. markets minus U.S. dependence on the target's suppliers.

In parallel, a foreign country's dependence on U.S. suppliers can be estimated by calculating the proportion of the foreign country's imports in a particular industrial sector that are accounted for by U.S. exports, multiplied by the dominance of U.S. suppliers in that sector. U.S. dependence on markets in a foreign country can be estimated by calculating the proportion of American exports in a particular industrial sector that are accounted for by the foreign country's imports, multiplied by the dominance of U.S. exports in that sector. Given the reciprocal nature of dependence, the effectiveness of U.S. sanctions or promises regarding access to its suppliers in a particular sector will be a function of the target's net dependence on U.S. suppliers. This is equal to the target's dependence on U.S. exports minus U.S. dependence on the target's imports.

The validity of these indicators rests on the assumption that the firms and national governments in question are dependent on foreign rather than domestic markets and suppliers. It is assumed that firms seek to maximize profits and that they do so by systematically seeking out the most efficient and cost-effective sources of supply and the most lucrative markets. Based on this assumption, the existence of trading relations with external suppliers and markets indicates that they are the most cost-effective suppliers and markets available. This assumption does not imply that domestic alternatives cannot be found. Rather, it asserts that the domestic alternatives are likely to be less cost effective and, therefore, less desirable. If this were not the case, then domestic alternates would have been selected initially over foreign competitors. To verify firm dependence on external suppliers and markets, detailed analyses of several cases are included in this study. The cases presented at the end of this chapter and those in chapters 3 and 4 suggest that the actors that were dependent on U.S. suppliers or the American consumer market altered their behavior in response to U.S. sanctions.[16]

The validity of these indicators also rests on the assumption that trade flows between individual firms are similar to those between countries classified by industrial sector. Trade flows are measured using aggregated national trade data broken down by industrial sector using three-digit Standard International Trade Classifications (SITCs), rather than using trade data from individual firms. This is done to maintain data consistency over as wide a range of cases as possible. Many production figures, including the precise value of imports and exports at the corporate level, are held as proprietary information and are not accessible to the public. This is particularly true when the firms are involved in the production of goods or technology that may have implications for national security (as is evident in many of the cases analyzed for this project).

Variable definitions are summarized in table 2.5.

Research Strategy and Case Selection

This book combines two research strategies. First, it uses statistical techniques to test competing hypotheses about the effectiveness of secondary sanctions. In all, sixty-six attempts by the U.S. government to enforce its export control policy abroad since 1949 are examined. Second, chapters 3 and 4 analyze two sets of cases involving conflicts over export control enforcement, the Pipeline Case and Operation Exodus. While the detailed comparative case studies provide a more nuanced understanding of particular events than the statistical analysis, the latter is a useful technique for testing whether the findings from the detailed case studies are generalizable. The purpose of using multiple methods of analysis is to capture insights that would otherwise be concealed. The arguments are made more powerful by using the strength of each type of methodology to offset the weakness of the other. The statistical models are used to demonstrate that the predictions hold across a range of cases, while the detailed comparative case studies are used to clarify the causal links in the processes that the statistical models described. The reader can thus be more confident in the conclusions when both of these approaches are used in tandem.

This study analyzes U.S. efforts to deter foreign companies from violating U.S. export control regulations and to compel wayward firms to conform to them. Domestic companies are excluded from the analysis

Table 2.5 Variable Definitions

Compliance (COMPLY)

Secured compliance by firms and individuals operating abroad with U.S. export control policy. COMPLY is coded dichotomously as Yes (1) or No (0), and has a mean of 0.51.

Host Government Intervention (HGVTCOOP)

Host government cooperation with U.S. enforcement efforts. HGVTCOOP is coded dichotomously as Yes (1) or No (0), and has a mean of 0.57.

Dominance of U.S. Markets (DOMUSM)

Dominance of U.S. markets in a particular sector. DOMUSM ranges from 0 to 1 and has a mean of 0.14.

Dominance of U.S. Suppliers (DOMUSX)

Dominance of U.S. suppliers in a particular sector. DOMUSX ranges from 0 to 1 and has a mean of 0.27.

Proportion of Host Country Imports from U.S. Suppliers (PCTHMFUS)

Proportion of the target country's imports accounted for by U.S. exports in a particular sector. PCTHMFUS ranges from 0 to 1 and has a mean of 0.31.

Proportion of Host Country Exports to U.S. Markets (PCTHX2US)

Proportion of the target country's exports accounted for by imports into the United States in a particular sector. PCTHX2US ranges from 0 to 1 and has a mean of 0.11.

Net Foreign Dependence on U.S. Markets (NETFDUSM)

Foreign dependence on U.S. imports minus U.S. dependence on foreign exports, by sector. NETFDUSM ranges from –1 to 1 and has a mean of –0.02.

Net Foreign Dependence on U.S. Suppliers (NETFDUSX)

Foreign dependence on U.S. exports minus U.S. dependence on foreign imports, by sector. NETFDUSX ranges from –1 to 1 and has a mean of 0.06.

Military Hegemony (MILEXP)

Proportion of U.S. military expenditure in the NATO. MILEXP ranges from .59 to .77 and has a mean of .66.

Economic Hegemony (SIZE and GNPPCP)

The relative size of U.S. trade in terms of U.S. exports plus imports as a proportion of total OECD exports and imports. Relative U.S. productivity in terms of U.S. GNP per capita relative to the average GNP per capita of OECD countries. SIZE and GNPPCP range from 11.8 to 15.4, and 1.20 to 2.37, respectively, with means of 13.4 and 1.27, respectively.

---

because it is assumed that domestic regulations and enforcement efforts, rather than secondary sanctions, are likely to deter or compel these companies to comply. Foreign companies are selected because of the limits of traditional domestic law enforcement to exert control over these actors.

Foreign companies or individuals that violated U.S. export control policy and were cited for administrative or criminal actions in the *Export Administration Annual Reports* from 1974 through 1986 are included in the statistical analysis. U.S. companies and individuals were excluded, as were foreign companies or individuals for whom the outcome of the sanction or incentive was uncertain or other data were incomplete. Data for cases prior to 1974 were gathered from a survey of the literature in international law, business, politics, as well as the general media.

The vast majority of the cases reported in the general media involve an explicit, publicly announced conflict of interest between the targeted company and the U.S. government. A potentially large number of foreign companies that conformed to U.S. regulations without raising a public outcry against them may thus be excluded from this study.[17] It is always important to consider the cases not analyzed.[18] However, the available data should be skewed in a manner which challenges rather than complements the primary hypothesis. In situations where conflicts of interest are part of the public domain, foreign governments will be more likely to challenge U.S. infringements on their sovereignty than when this is not the case. As a result, using these limited data, one would expect to find a larger percentage of cases resulting in failed attempts at U.S. influence than in the general population of export control cases. This proposition is supported by the assumption that most unreported cases are likely to favor the U.S. government, therefore biasing the available data against the success at U.S. sanctions. Consequently, it is assumed that the available cases will tend to underestimate the extent of U.S. influence.

Finally, a robust model of economic sanctions should be able to explain the success and failure of economic sanctions in cases where sanctions are not likely to be effective. This book develops such a test by examining the use of secondary sanctions to control the international movement of strategic goods. A strategic good may be defined as a good that minimizes one's vulnerability to others or allows the actor that possesses it to create or exploit existing vulnerabilities in others.[19] Therefore, conflicts involving strategic goods involve matters of "high politics," such as military security and sovereign autonomy, where economic statecraft is least likely to be effective.[20] These events, therefore, represent hard cases for the use and evaluation of economic sanctions because there are a lot more than simply market preferences riding on the outcomes.[21]

While the international context has continued to change since the end of the Cold War, the theories and models of power relations among states and firms specified here should not. The recent use of sanctions in U.S.-Chinese and U.S.-Cuban relations, and the use of secondary sanctions to secure extraterritorial corporate compliance with U.S. sanctions against Cuba, Iran, and Libya are analyzed in chapter 5 as a means of confirming the validity of these arguments in the post–Cold War era.

STATISTICAL ANALYSES OF U.S. INFLUENCE ATTEMPTS

The primary hypotheses predict that the sender is more likely to be able to compel foreign firms to alter their behavior when it dominates world markets or suppliers in a particular sector, or when the target is dependent on trade with the sender. Dependence can be reciprocal such that the target's dependence on the sender's markets may be mitigated by the sender's dependence on the target's suppliers; while the target's dependence on the sender's suppliers may be mitigated by the sender's dependence on the target's markets. If the arguments presented in chapter 1 are correct, models based on trade dominance and dependence should provide accurate predictions of the U.S. government's ability to secure extraterritorial corporate compliance using secondary sanctions.

The Model

The primary model examines the impact of dependence, dominance, and hegemonic leadership on the ability of the U.S. government to secure extraterritorial corporate compliance. It can be summarized as follows:

(1) **Corporate Compliance** = $a + b_1$ Dependence + b_2 Dominance + b_3 Hegemony + b_4 Host Govt Cooperation + e

For the purposes of this analysis, trade dominance will be subdivided into market (import) dominance and supplier (export) dominance. Trade dependence will also be subdivided into dependence on imports and dependence on exports. In order to account for the reciprocal nature of dependence, trade dependence is estimated in net terms. The target's net dependence on the sender's (U.S. in these analyses) markets is a function of the target's dependence on the sender's markets minus the sender's dependence on the target's suppliers. The target's net dependence on the sender's (U.S.) suppliers is a function of the target's dependence on the sender's suppliers minus the sender's dependence on the target's markets. Finally, since dependence is an interaction term created by the combined impact of the proportion of trade accounted for by each actor and U.S. dominance, the proportion of the target's imports and exports accounted for by the U.S. will be included in the equation.

Based on the arguments present above, one would predict that an increase in the dominance of U.S. markets or suppliers should increase the likelihood of corporate compliance with U.S. policies. Similarly, an increase in the net foreign dependence on U.S. markets or suppliers should increase the likelihood of corporate compliance. In contrast, a decline in the dominance of U.S. markets or suppliers, or a decline in the net foreign dependence on U.S. markets or suppliers should decrease the likelihood of corporate compliance. The effect of economic and military hegemony is expected to be positive but is less important than the sector-specific trade dominance or dependence. Finally, if, as argued, host government cooperation is not necessary nor sufficient to guarantee corporate compliance, then host government cooperation should not suppress the effect of trade dominance or dependence on corporate compliance.

Data Analysis

This section evaluates the data, compares the predictions with the actual outcomes of the cases, and evaluates the proposed and competing hypotheses based on the results. A correlation matrix of all interval-level variables in the equations is presented in table 2.6. Several of the independent variables are highly correlated, but all correlations between the independent variables is less than $r = .70$, suggesting that multicollinearity should not be a problem in the models presented below.[22]

Specification and analysis of the equations. Maximum likelihood estimations using LOGIT analyses are used to estimate the likelihood of successful compliance with U.S. export control policy.[23] LOGIT, rather than ordinary least squared (OLS) regression analysis, is used to evaluate the data because the dependent variable—corporate compliance—is dichotomous.[24]

Three LOGIT models are used to estimate the likelihood of corporate compliance in response to U.S. secondary sanctions. The first model tests the primary hypotheses regarding trade dominance, dependence, and corporate compliance. It estimates the impact of the relative dominance of U.S. markets and suppliers, the target's net dependence on U.S. markets and suppliers, and the proportion of the target's exports and imports accounted for by U.S. trade on corporate compliance. The results are summarized in table 2.7. Three of the independent variables—including the target's net dependence on U.S. markets, the proportion of the target's imports accounted for by U.S. suppliers, and host government cooperation—are statistically significant. The positive value of their coefficients suggest that, as predicted, an increase in the target's net dependence on

Table 2.6 Correlation Coefficients

	HGVTCOOP	DOMUSM	DOMUSX	PCTHMFUS	PCTHX2US	NETFDUSM	NETFDUSX	SIZE	GNPPCP	MILEXP
HGVTCOOP	1.00	.148	-.114	-.016	.049	.107	-.136	.254*	-.136	-.154
DOMUSM	.148	1.00	-.099	-.088	.129	.093	-.133	.450**	-.143	-.075
DOMUSX	-.114	-.099	1.00	.496**	.196*	-.611**	.562	.022	.363**	.299*
PCTHMFUS	-.016	-.088	.496**	1.00	.565**	-.539	.599**	.117	.463**	.531**
PCTHX2US	.049	.129	.296*	.565**	1.00	-.614**	.024	.036	.262*	.439**
NETFDUSM	.107	.093	-.611**	-.539	-.614**	1.00	-.013	.168	-.371**	-.360**
NETFDUSX	-.136	-.133	.562	.599**	.024	-.013	1.00	.075	.468**	.402**
SIZE	.254*	.450**	.022	.117	.036	.168	.075	1.00	-.036	.142
GNPPCP	-.136	-.143	.363**	.463	.262	-.371**	.468**	-.036	1.00	6.97**
MILEXP	-.154	-.075	.299*	.531**	.439**	-.360**	.402**	.142	.697**	1.00

*Significant at the alpha = .05 level.
**Significant at the alpha = .01 level.

U.S. markets will increase the likelihood of corporate compliance. Unexpectedly, the target's net dependence on U.S. suppliers is not statistically significant;[25] however, the proportion of the target's imports accounted for by the United States is. This suggests that while that target's dependence on foreign suppliers may not affect its compliance with secondary sanctions, increasing the proportion of imports in a particular sector accounted for by the sender does increase the likelihood that it will comply. The cooperation of the host country government has a positive and statistically significant effect, suggesting that host government cooperation with U.S. enforcement efforts increases the likelihood of corporate compliance, and vice versa. Finally, counter to initial expectations, neither the sector-specific dominance of U.S. suppliers nor the sector-specific dominance of U.S. markets had a significant impact on corporate compliance. This suggests that sector-specific trade dominance by the sender does not affect the likelihood that secondary sanctions will be successful. This model accurately predicted the outcomes of U.S. secondary sanctions against firms 75.8 percent of the time, predicting twenty-five out of thirty-three failures and twenty-five out of thirty-three successes correctly.

Table 2.7a   LOGIT of Compliance Based on Dominance and Dependence

EXPLANATORY VARIABLE	ESTIMATED COEFFICIENT	SIGNIFICANCE
Constant	–3.2063	.0106*
Dominance of U.S. Markets and Suppliers		
DOMUSM	3.9314	.2661
DOMUSX	3.9916	.3734
Net Foreign Dependence on U.S. Markets and Suppliers		
NETFDUSM	27.5233	.0173*
NETFDUSX	–6.5989	.3854
Proportion of Host Country Imports from U.S. Suppliers		
PCTHMFUS	6.6443	.0325*
Proportion of Host Country Exports to U.S. Markets		
PCTHX2US	–4.1124	.2948
Host Government Corporation		
HGVTCOOP	1.6339	.0108*
Chi Squared	23.790	.0012**
Valid N		66

*Significant to the alpha = .05 level.
**Significant to the alpha = .01 level.

Table 2.7b   Predictive Accuracy of the Dominance and Dependence Model

		PREDICTED			
		No Compliance	Successful Compliance		% Correct
	No Compliance	25	8	33	75.76
OBSERVED	Successful Compliance	8	25	33	75.76
		34	32	66	
			Overall		75.76

The second model is designed to test arguments of hegemonic leadership. The economic and military aspects of hegemony are estimated using the sender's total trade as a proportion of world trade, its relative productivity, and relative military expenditure. The results are presented in table 2.8. Only one independent variable—host government cooperation—is statistically significant. As in the previous model, the positive value of this coefficient suggests that the cooperation by host governments will increase the likelihood of corporate compliance with U.S. policies. Contrary to expectations based on hegemonic leadership arguments, U.S. military hegemony did not have a significant impact on the likelihood of compliance, nor did the overall size or relative productivity of the U.S. economy. The hegemonic leadership model is less accurate than the previous model. It predicts the outcomes of U.S. secondary sanctions accurately 66.7 percent of the time, predicting twenty of thirty-three failed cases, and twenty-four of thirty-three success cases.

The third model combines the independent variables of hegemony with those of dependence in order to control for the effects of each set of variables. The results of the complete model are consistent with the previous two. Three variables—the target's net dependence on U.S. markets, the proportion of imports it received from U.S. suppliers, and host government cooperation—are positive and statistically significant. This suggests that the effects of trade dominance by the sender and the net corporate dependence on the sender remain the same, even when controlling for variations in the sender's aggregate economic size, productivity, and military capacity. This model is accurate 74.2 percent of the time, accurately predicting failure in twenty-five out of thirty-three cases, and accurately predicting success in twenty-four out of thirty-three cases.

Table 2.8a   LOGIT of Compliance Based on Hegemonic Leadership

EXPLANATORY VARIABLE	ESTIMATED COEFFICIENT	SIGNIFICANCE
Constant	−9.0497	.0616
Hegemony		
Economic Component		
SIZE	.3619	.1892
GNPPCP	2.5063	.3972
Military Component		
MILEXP	.1699	.9831
Host Government Cooperation	1.4374	.0129*
Chi Squared	11.78	.0191*
Valid N		66

*Significant to the alpha = .05 level.

Table 2.8b   Predictive Accuracy of the Hegemonic Leadership Model

		PREDICTED			
		No Compliance	Successful Compliance		% Correct
	No Compliance	20	13	33	60.61
OBSERVED					
	Successful Compliance	9	24	33	72.73
		29	37	66	
			Overall		66.67

The combined results of these equations suggest that, counter to expectations, variations in the dominance of U.S. markets or suppliers in a particular industrial sector did not have a generalizable effect on its ability to deter or compel firms operating in those sectors to change their behavior. At the same time, as predicted by the dependence arguments, the target's dependence on U.S. markets (accounting for the potential for U.S. dependence on foreign suppliers in the relevant sector) did have a

Table 2.9a   LOGIT of Compliance Based on Dominance, Dependence, and Hegemony

EXPLANATORY VARIABLE	ESTIMATED COEFFICIENT	SIGNIFICANCE
Constant	−11.2914	.0982
Dominance of U.S. Markets and Suppliers		
DOMUSM	4.4265	.3414
DOMUSX	7.0849	.2009
Net Foreign Dependence on U.S. Markets and Suppliers		
NETFDUSM	6.2641	.0838
NETFDUSX	−9.5831	.3545
Proportion of Host Country Imports from U.S. Suppliers		
PCTHMFUS	6.2641	.0838
Proportion of Host Country Exports to U.S. Markets		
PCTHX2US	−3.7461	.4220
Host Government Corporation		
HGVTCOOP	1.8439	.0085**
Military Hegemony		
MILEXP	2.454	.8283
Economic Hegemony		
SIZE	−0.0927	.8173
GNPPCP	5.5652	.2253
Chi Squared	29.052	.0012**
Valid N		66

*Significant to the alpha = .05 level.
**Significant to the alpha = .01 level.

Table 2.9b   Predictive Accuracy of the Dominance, Dependence, and Hegemony Model

		PREDICTED			% Correct
		No Compliance	Successful Compliance		
OBSERVED	No Compliance	25	8	33	75.76
	Successful Compliance	9	24	33	72.73
		34	32	66	
			Overall		74.24

significant positive effect on the success of secondary sanctions. Furthermore, the results suggest that the proportion of the target's imports coming from the United States had a significant, positive effect on the success of secondary sanctions. This finding supports the premise of social power theory that power is a relational phenomenon and should be interpreted as a function of the value of exchange taking place between actors. Finally, the results suggest that when host governments cooperated with the United States, the likelihood of success increased; and when they failed to do so, the likelihood of success declined.

Given these general findings, it would be helpful to determine the relative importance of the statistically significant variables and to examine how changes in the value of each is likely to affect the success of secondary sanctions. The relative importance of the three statistically significant variables in the full (third) equation can be tested by estimating the probability of securing compliance (the probability that Corporate Compliance = 1) while varying each of the three significant variables individually, and holding all other variables at their means. If all of the variables are held at their means—that is, their average values for all variables given the sixty-six cases of U.S. secondary sanctions in the analysis—then the probability of success is approximately 46.44 percent. Analyzing the change in the probability of success while altering the values of each

Table 2.10   **Probability of Securing Compliance**

VALUE	0	MEAN − 1 s	MEAN	MEAN + 1 s	1.0
NET FOREIGN DEPENDENCE ON U.S. MARKETS (NETFDUSM)	0.0000	0.0443	0.4644	0.9419	1.0000
PROPORTION OF THE TARGET COUNTRY'S IMPORTS ACCOUNTED FOR BY U.S. EXPORTS (PCTHMFUS)	0.1117	0.1459	0.4644	0.8148	0.9851
HOST GOVERNMENT COOPERATION (HGVTCOOP)	0.2326	0.2564	0.4644	0.6855†	0.6571

†This probability of success is higher than it is for HGVTCOOP = 1 because the standard deviation of HGVTCOOP is greater than its mean. This result represents the probability of success for HGVTCOOP > 1 and does not represent a possible outcome.

individual variable while holding the others at their means enables the relative impact of each variable to be tested at a range of different values.

The results provide strong support for the argument that net foreign dependence on U.S. markets has an important impact on the likely success of secondary sanctions. If all other factors are held at their means and the target's net dependence on U.S. markets drops to 0.00 then the probability of corporate compliance will drop to 0.00; in contrast, if the target's net dependence is 1, then the probability of corporate compliance is 100 percent. A *decrease* by one standard deviation unit (s = .0059) from the mean will *reduce* the probability of success to 4.43 percent, while an *increase* in one standard deviation unit from the mean will *increase* the probability of success to 94.2 percent. This suggests that slight changes in the net dependence of targeted firms on access to U.S. markets in a particular sector will have an important impact on the success of secondary sanctions, even if everything else remains the same.

The results also suggest that changes in the proportion of host country imports that are accounted for by U.S. suppliers will effect the likelihood of success. Holding all other variables at their mean values, the results suggest that if the proportion of host country imports accounted for by U.S. suppliers drops to 0.00, then the likelihood of success drops to 11.1 percent; while, if the proportion increases to 100 percent, the likelihood of success increases to 98.5 percent. Furthermore, a decrease of one standard deviation unit (s = .259) from the mean will reduce the probability of success to 14.6 percent, while an increase in one standard deviation unit from the mean will increase the probability of success to 81.5 percent. This suggests that a decline in the relative value of imports that the target receives from the United States will reduce the likelihood that secondary sanctions will be successful, but a complete lack of imports alone will not necessarily lead to failure.

Finally, the results provide support for the proposition that host government cooperation may facilitate or hinder the success of secondary sanctions, but it is not sufficient to guarantee success or failure. Holding the other variables at their mean values, lack of host government cooperation reduces the probability of success to 23.3 percent, while host government cooperation increases the probability of success to 65.7 percent.

CONCLUSION

Statistical analyses of U.S. efforts to secure extraterritorial compliance with its export control policy generally support the argument that sanctions will be most effective when the foreign actors are dependent on the United States. The estimate of corporate compliance based on the sender's trade dominance and the target's net dependence on the sender is statistically significant, as are the coefficients for the target's net dependence on U.S. markets, the proportion of the target's imports accounted for by U.S. suppliers, and host government intervention. Furthermore, the estimate accurately predicts both the success and failure of U.S. sanctions 75.8 percent of the time. The results suggest that the target's net dependence on U.S. markets—defined as the target's dependence on U.S. markets minus U.S. dependence on the target's exports in the same sector—will have significant and positive impact on the likelihood that the secondary sanctions will be successful. All else equal, increasing the target's net dependence on U.S. markets to 1.0 will increase the probability of success to 100 percent, while decreasing it to -1.0 reduces the probability to zero.

The results also suggest that changes in the proportion of a target's imports accounted for by the United States have a significant positive impact on the likelihood of compliance. Holding all other factors constant, increasing this proportion to 100 percent, increases the probability of success to 94.2 percent, while reducing it to 0.00 reduces the probability of success to 11.2 percent. Similarly, the results support the proposition that while host government cooperation with U.S. secondary sanctions is important, it is neither necessary nor sufficient to secure corporate compliance. All else equal, the lack of host government cooperation reduces the probability of success to 23.3 percent, while securing host government cooperation increases the probability of success to 65.7 percent. Finally and unexpectedly, the dominance of U.S. markets and the dominance of U.S. suppliers do not have a significant, generalizable effects on the likely success of secondary sanctions.

These findings warrant a detailed analysis of several cases to analyze the causal links between trade dominance, dependence, and political power. The combination of the broader statistical analyses in this chapter and the detailed comparative case studies in the next two chapters provides a fuller picture of the role of sanctions in securing extraterritorial compliance and the cooperation of foreign governments.

Notes

1. Gerald Schneider and Patricia Weitsman, eds. *Enforcing Cooperation: "Risky" States and the Intergovernmental Management of Conflict* (New York: Macmillan Press, 1996), pp. 4–7.

2. Adler-Karlsson (1968).

3. Marcel Michelson, "Creation of 'Son of COCOM' Set for September," *Reuter European Business Report* (1 June 1995); "Nations Meet to Discuss New Forum for COCOM," *Jane's Defense Weekly* (5 August 1995), p. 5. For a discussion of the shift

in U.S. policy towards risky and so-called rogue states, see Michael Klare, *Rogue States and Nuclear Outlaws: America's Search for a New Foreign Policy* (New York: Hill and Wang,1995).

4. "Four Eastern European Nations to Join post–COCOM Body," *Jiji Ticker Press Service* (28 August 1995): 884.

5. For a discussion of current regimes established by suppliers of strategic weaponry, see Zachary S. Davis, "Nuclear Proliferation and Nonproliferation Policy in the 1990s," in Michael Klare and Daniel Thomas, eds. *World Security: Challenges for a New Century*, 2d ed. (New York: St. Martin's, 1994); Jean-François Rioux, ed., *Limiting the Proliferation of Weapons: The Role of Supply-Side Strategies* (Ottawa, Ont.: Carleton University Press, 1992).

6. This is consistent with the predictions of neoliberal and institutionalist scholars. See Krasner, ed. (1983); and George Shambaugh and Patricia Weitsman, "First, Second and Third Wave Approaches to the Study of Institutions in International Politics: Is Progress Ever Possible without Reinventing the Wheel?" Conference Paper, Annual Meeting of the American Political Science Association (September 1992). Lisa Martin argues that international institutions facilitate cooperation both when common interests among the sanctioners are present as well as when their interests diverge. See Martin (1992), pp. 39–40.

7. See Kenneth Boulding, *Conflict and Defense: A General Theory* (New York: Harper Publishers, 1962); K. J. Holsti, P. Terrence Hopmann, and John Sullivan, *Unity and Disintegration in International Alliances* (New York: John Wiley, 1973); George Liska, *Nations in Alliance: The Limits of Interdependence* (Baltimore, Md.: Johns Hopkins Press, 1962); Stephen Walt, *The Origins of Alliances*. Ithaca, N.Y.: Cornell University Press, 1987) and "Testing Theories of Alliance Formation," *International Organization* 42:2 (1988): 275–316; Arnold Wolfers, *Discord and Collaboration*. (Baltimore, Md.: Johns Hopkins Press, 1962). As Ernst Haas argues, the presence of an external threat is insufficient to maintain multilateral cooperation unless there is agreement on both the goals states seek to accomplish and the means by which states will accomplish them. Ernst Haas, "Why Collaborate: Issue Linkage and International Regimes," *World Politics* 32 (1980): 357–405.

8. For example, it could be argued that even at the height of the Cold War, European and American decision makers could not agree on how to react to the Soviet production and detonation of a hydrogen bomb in 1952. While the threat was agreed upon, the appropriate response to it was not. The United States saw the bomb as an indication that existing export controls were not stringent enough and needed stronger enforcement measures. European states, on the other hand, interpreted it as an indication that the broad export embargo promoted by the United States was ineffective and an inappropriate means of restricting Soviet military development. See Adler-Karlsson (1968), pp. 87–88.

After the Korean conflict, European and American foreign policy goals and economic concerns regarding the East began to diverge further, and allied cooperation with American efforts to maintain its postwar controls diminished dramatically. See for example Adler-Karlsson (1968), Bruce Jentleson, *Pipeline Politics* (Ithaca, N.Y.: Cornell University Press, 1986), Mastanduno (1985).

9. In each case, the sector corresponds to the goods that are restricted using the Standard International Trade Classification (SITC).

10. The measurement and operationalization of hegemony have been criticized and debated almost as much as the definition of *hegemony* itself. See Robert Gilpin, *War and Change in World Politics* (New York: Cambridge University Press, 1981), and *The Political Economy of International Relations* (Princeton: Princeton University Press, 1987); Robert O. Keohane, *After Hegemony: Cooperation and Discord in the World Political Economy* (Princeton: Princeton University Press, 1984); Stephen Krasner, "State Power and the Structure of the International Trading System," *World Politics* 28:3 (1976): 317–47; David Lake, "International Economic Structures and American Foreign Policy," *World Politics* 35:4 (1983): 517–43, and David Lake and Scott James, "The Second Face of Hegemony," *International Organization* 43:1 (1989): 1–29.

11. This indicator is equivalent to that used by David Lake in his discussion of British hegemony at the end of the nineteenth century. Lake (1983), p. 543. Alternatively, relative Gross National Product (GNP) or Gross Domestic Product (GDP) could be used as indicators of national size. For the purposes of this study, proportion of world trade was chosen over GNP or GDP in order to maintain as much consistency as possible among the data sources used to estimate hegemony, dominance, and dependence.

12. Gilpin (1981), (1987); George Modelski and William Thompson, *Sea Power and Global Politics, 1494–1983* (Seattle: University of Washington Press, 1987); Charles Doran and Wes Parsons, "War and the Cycle of Relative Power," *American Political Science Review* 74 (December 1980), pp. 946–65; Alan Ned Sabrosky, ed. *Polarity and War* (Boulder, Colo.: Westview, 1985); and A. F. K. Organski and Jack Kugler, *The War Ledger* (Chicago: University of Chicago Press, 1980). There is also a strong coincidence between trade volume and alliance membership. For a discussion of the link between trade and alliances, see Gowa (1994).

13. Using the relative number of armed forces as an indicator of the military component of hegemony provides comparable results to analyses which rely on indices of relative military expenditure. The difference in the results from using either indicator is not statistically significant.

14. There is also a strong coincidence between trade volume and alliance membership. For a discussion of the link between trade and alliances, see Gowa (1994).

15. This indicator of concentration highlights the same trends as the Hirschman-Herfindahl index and other concentration indices. It was selected rather than the others because it is easy for the reader to interpret and, more importantly, because it highlights differences in the dispersion of goods that tend to be concentrated in the hands of a few actors. Hirschman (1980), pp. xviii–xix, 87–97, 157–62. See

Ray and Singer (1973), pp. 403–37; Shambaugh (1996); and Ray and Taagepera (1977), pp. 367–84.

16. This study would be strengthened if export and import data as a percentage of domestic consumption and production figures were used. This is a promising area for future research.

17. This caveat has been noted by several scholars researching similar issues, see Kobrin (1989), p. 34.

18. This problem, combined with difficulties in assessing the outcomes of cases specified in the *Export Administration Annual Reports*, reduced the number of cases included in the data set used in this chapter. While the results are statistically significant and the data fulfill their primary role of bolstering the findings of the detailed case studies, it would be fruitful for the interested reader to expand the data set to include more of these cases or to apply the model specified in this chapter to other types of episodes involving economic statecraft.

19. Barry Buzan, *People, States and Fear: An Agenda for International Security Studies in the Post–Cold War Era* (Boulder, Colo.: Lynne Rienner, 1991).

20. Gary Hufbauer and Jeffrey Schott find that sanctions were successful in only five of twenty-seven cases involving "high politics." This project views cases involving export control policy as "high politics" because they involve issues that have a direct impact on the national economic and military security of the states involved. Furthermore, the enforcement of one state's export control policy over actors operating in another's territory undermines that host state's ability to control potentially vital resources within its territory. Hufbauer and Schott (1985), pp. 81–82.

21. Imre Lakatos, "Falsification and the Methodology of Scientific Research Programmes," in Lakatos and Alan Musgrave, eds., *Criticism and the Growth of Knowledge* (Cambridge: Cambridge University Press, 1970).

22. Auxiliary regression analyses may be performed to confirm that multicollinearity among the independent variables is not a problem in this analysis.

23. It is possible that compliance at time t-1 could effect the likelihood of compliance at time t. However, the amount of time between cases in the dataset varies substantially and many of the cases take place simultaneously. As a result, incorporating a lagged dependent variable into the equation would not provide a reliable indicator of the effect of compliance in one case on the outcome of the next. Furthermore, the cases include the use at sanctions against firms in different industrial sectors and it is assumed to be unlikely that firms operating in one sector would alter their behavior as a result of actions taken by firms operating in an unrelated industry at an unspecified time in the past.

24. While LOGIT curves are not designed to maximize the "goodness of fit," they provide reliable coefficients and tend to have higher explanatory and predictive power than OLS models when applied to dichotomous dependent variables. For a discussion of LOGIT models, see John H. Aldrich and Forest D. Nelson,

Linear Probability, LOGIT, and PROBIT Models (Beverly Hills: Sage Publications, 1984).

25. Lack of statistical significance means that the values of the coefficients in the equation are not statistically different from zero when applied to the population at large. The lack of statistical significance may be caused by the fact that LOGIT coefficients are sensitive to the number of cases and the number of cases is relatively small, or that the model may be misspecified because it does not include other factors that, while difficult to quantify accurately, may affect the likelihood of compliance. These limitations suggest that supplementing the statistical analyses with the detailed comparative case studies in the following chapters is important for the analysis and evaluation of the hypotheses. The detailed comparative case studies help to identify and analyze the causal links suggested by the statistical analyses, and they can be used to analyze variables that cannot be quantified accurately over the time period analyzed in the LOGIT analyses.

3

Maintaining Power in an Alliance Conflict:
The Trans-Siberian Pipeline Embargo, 1980–84

COMPARATIVE CASE STUDIES OF SECONDARY SANCTIONS

This chapter and the next provide detailed comparative studies of American attempts to secure extraterritorial compliance with its export control policy by firms operating in Europe and Asia in the 1980s. Comparing American successes and failures facilitates the identification of the causal connections between the independent and dependent variables by examining the process that intervenes between cause and effect.[1] If the generalizations of the statistical analyses in the previous chapter are correct in predicting when the United States will be able to compel foreign actors to conform to its export control policy, then the individual cases should document the role of U.S. trade dominance and net foreign dependence on access to American markets and American suppliers. When the United States dominates trade in a particular sector or foreign firms that possess or could produce restricted goods are more dependent on the United States than it is on them, one would expect it to be able to secure their compliance by manipulating economic incentives and sanctions. The cases are not intended to be comprehensive historical explanations of actions taken during each crisis. Rather, each case is analyzed for the purpose of assessing the relevance of particular explanatory variables on the successful enforcement of United States export control policy abroad.

This chapter and the next analyze the ability of the United States to control actors across international borders during two periods: the pipeline crisis from 1980 to 1984 and the noncrisis surrounding Operation Exodus from 1982 through the 1980s. These cases are politically and theoretically relevant. The first involves American attempts to block the construction of the trans-Siberian Pipeline, which the United States believed would make Europe dependent on Soviet energy, thus giving the Soviet Union a source of leverage over Europe, while providing it with an infusion of hard currency earnings that would bolster its economic and military potential. The second concerns American efforts to restrict Soviet access to high-technology goods and information through Operation Exodus. Both of these efforts were centerpieces of the Reagan administration's policy of economic Cold Warfare against the East Bloc, yet their outcomes varied significantly. While many scholars view efforts to block construction of the trans-Siberian Pipeline as a complete and destructive political failure, many others see Operation Exodus as a success achieved at very little political cost. The varying degree of political conflict within and between the cases sets the context for the more fundamental question of securing extraterritorial corporate compliance with U.S. policy that is at the heart of current U.S. sanctions policy against Cuba, Iran, and Libya. Compliance by foreign companies varied both during the trans-Siberian pipeline dispute where the intensity of intergovernmental conflict was high and foreign governments strenuously challenged unilateral enforcement efforts by the United States, and during Operation Exodus where the intensity of intergovernmental conflict was generally less and more issue-specific, and counteractions by foreign governments were more constrained.

These events served as catalysts that brought to light the basic conflict of interests regarding the goals and means of economic statecraft that pervaded the Cold War era and continue today. In each case, a state was trying to get foreign actors to do something they did not want to do. Despite varying perceptions among national governments regarding the threat posed by Soviet actions during the Pipeline Case and Operation Exodus, the conflict between corporate interests and U.S. government interests remained intense. At some points, when national interests converged or the U.S. government was able to entice or coerce foreign governments to enforce its policies, the extraterritorial application of sanctions by the U.S. government was supported by the foreign government as a means of enhancing local enforcement efforts against wayward firms or individuals. At other points, when national interests diverged and the U.S. government failed to entice or coerce foreign governments to enforce its policies locally, secondary sanctions were used to compel wayward foreign firms and individuals to comply despite the support of local governments against the enforcement of U.S. regulations over their activities.

The cooperation of foreign governments with U.S. enforcement efforts decreased the potential for intergovernmental conflict regarding the de jure basis of U.S. authority over foreign actors, but it did not minimize the importance of secondary sanctions in securing corporate or individual compliance in cases where the local government either lacked the means or the will to enforce compliance. On the other hand, the lack of cooperation by foreign governments dramatically increased the degree of intergovernmental conflict regarding the de jure basis of U.S. authority, as it is currently doing in the U.S.-European dispute regarding the Helms-

Burton Law and the Iran-Libya Sanctions Law. As argued in Chapter 1, however, sovereign authority is not necessarily equivalent to sovereign control. Successful control over firms in cases involving intergovernmental conflict during the trans-Siberian Pipeline crisis, Operation Exodus, and the Helms-Burton Law and Iran-Libya Sanctions Law demonstrate the power and de facto control that sanctions gave the U.S. government over dependent firms and individuals operating abroad even when it lacked legal authority to do so.

The trans-Siberian Pipeline crisis and Operation Exodus took place almost simultaneously in the same geostrategic environment. Traditional explanatory variables used to explain international enforcement, such as the international distribution of capabilities, remain relatively constant. Yet the outcome of U.S. enforcement efforts varied substantially within and between the cases. Variation in the dependent variable—the successful enforcement of U.S. policy abroad—covaries strongly with the independent variables of dependence as suggested by the proposed hypotheses. Comparing the success and failures within and between the trans-Siberian Pipeline crisis and Operation Exodus highlights the sources, extent, and limitations of the U.S. ability to use economic statecraft as a means of securing the compliance of foreign actors with its domestic interests and policy.

This chapter analyzes American and European actions during the alliance crisis surrounding the construction of the trans-Siberian Pipeline from 1980 through 1984. The period was marked by a persistent disagreement regarding the objectives, appropriateness, and application of sanctions against the Soviet Union, with the U.S. government favoring strict application and enforcement of a strategic embargo, and European governments, foreign firms, and individuals operating abroad favoring a symbolic embargo followed by constructive economic engagement. Given this divergence, instances of corporate compliance (and lack there of) with U.S. pipeline restrictions throughout the crisis can be explained in terms of American influence resulting from their dependence on American suppliers or consumer markets.

This case is often cited as an example of a complete failure of U.S. influence within the Western alliance.[2] The analysis below will concur that, in the end, the United States failed to convince, entice, or coerce the majority of its allies or the foreign companies operating in their territories to comply with its policies. To make such a judgment, however, one must analyze the events systematically in terms of the goals the United States sought to accomplish and who it sought to influence. A closer analysis of this crisis, fully considering these factors, reveals that American influence was not completely absent. U.S. pressure did affect the behavior of some important firms. Firms that were highly dependent on the supply of technology from U.S. firms or on access to American markets to export their goods altered their behavior as a direct result of U.S. actions. Similarly, foreign governments that were dependent on the United States for the supply of vital resources and, to a lesser extent, access to the American market for their exports, complied with U.S. initiatives. In short, when foreign firms were highly dependent on the United States, the U.S. was often able to get them to do things they would not otherwise have done— despite conflicting interests or divergent national beliefs about the nature of the Soviet threat and the application of sanctions. When their relative dependence on the U.S. diminished, its ability to secure compliance diminished and, as a result, the United States was not able to enforce its export control policy successfully. Even if this case as a whole represents a failure of substantive sanctions, success in certain specific instances demonstrates that sanctions work under conditions of dependence.

This chapter consists of four parts. The next section provides a synopsis of the trans-Siberian Pipeline crisis in historical context, identifies the goals and targets of the pipeline embargo, and examines the failure of American attempts to persuade or induce extraterritorial compliance. "Sources of U.S. Influence and Predictions of U.S. Success, 1980–84" analyzes American attempts to entice and coerce compliance in terms of both dominance and dependence arguments. The final section evaluates these predictions in terms of the actual decisions made and actions taken by various firms and European governments in response to U.S. initiatives during the crisis.

THE PIPELINE CRISIS IN U.S. EXPORT CONTROL POLICY

The pipeline crisis evolved through several stages. The first stage involved European and American efforts to construct a series of pipelines linking the vast natural gas supplies of the Tiumen region in northwest Siberia to Western consumers. These efforts began in 1968 and culminated in the 1981 trans-Siberian pipeline project.[3] The trans-Siberian project connected the Urengoi gas fields to the countries of Western Europe through 4,465 kilometers of existing and proposed pipes. While European efforts to tap Soviet gas supplies were evolving, U.S. and European interests and involvement in East-West trade diverged. An early American attempt to copy European successes lost political support and failed. This failure reflected the beginning of a general shift in American policy from participation and benign neglect in East-West trade during the early 1970s to economic warfare in the early 1980s.

The second stage of the pipeline crisis began on 29 December 1981 with an American-led embargo against the Soviet Union covering oil and gas equipment enacted in response to the imposition of martial law in Poland.[4] The de jure domain of U.S. export restrictions included only domestic companies, but de facto, the restrictions had a direct effect on the activities of firms operating abroad by eliminating the ability of American firms to supply them with goods and services. European governments joined the United States in condemning the imposition of martial law, but the United States was unable to secure European cooperation in limiting East-West trade, embargoing energy and related technology, or restricting credits to the East.

The inability of the United States to evoke the cooperation it desired led to the third phase of the crisis, beginning on 22 June 1982. During this phase, U.S. goals shifted from influencing Soviet behavior through a co-ordinated allied embargo, to securing the compliance of those actors who could produce or supply restricted goods to the pipeline. The United States targeted the second round of sanctions to corporate actors operating within European countries. The U.S. applied these new pipeline sanctions retroactively to foreign firms and subsidiaries of American corporations operating within and outside of U.S. territory. National and corporate reactions to U.S. threats and actions during this phase of the crisis represent a contest of power that challenged the sovereign control of European states over actors within their borders. American attempts to secure corporate compliance during this phase of the crisis are the focus of this case study.

Following a bitter confrontation within the alliance, the U.S. lifted sanctions against its allies as well as firms operating abroad in exchange for a multilateral agreement to increase monitoring and the control of high-technology items. This compromise sets the foundation for the second comparative case discussed in chapter 4. Natural gas began to flow through the pipeline on route from the Soviet Union on 1 January 1984. This date represents the termination point of this case.

Goals of American Pipeline Sanctions

The initial goal of the pipeline sanctions was to demonstrate Western anger regarding Soviet involvement in Poland in 1981. The sanctions were intended to impose heavy economic and political costs on the Soviet Union because of what President Reagan argued was its "heavy and direct responsibility for the repression of Poland."[5] To implement the sanctions, the Reagan administration broadened existing export controls on oil and gas to include goods and technology related to the transportation, exploration, and production of petroleum and natural gas.[6]

On 22 June 1982, the Reagan administration issued a second set of sanctions. Like the earlier regulations, the new policy was officially issued under Section 6 of the Export Administration Act with the stated objective "to advance reconciliation in Poland."[7] In contrast to the first round of sanctions, however, these sanctions focused specifically on halting the construction of the trans-Siberian Pipeline. The sanctions were intended to prevent the Soviet Union from obtaining, either directly or indirectly, any American equipment or technology that could assist in the building of the proposed trans-Siberian Pipeline.

While the president justified U.S. actions in the name of the Polish people, decision makers in Washington and Europe understood the actions to be in response to the lack of sufficient European cooperation with the first set of sanctions. As Alexander Haig argued, "the Polish crisis provided a convenient pretext for dealing with the pipeline issue, which had long nettled their [Defense and the NSC's] strategic sensitivities."[8] According to Antony Blinken, "the pipeline became both a target of American policy and a means to assure European compliance with Washington's restrictive East-West strategy."[9] Echoing this sentiment, the State Department defended the sanctions, arguing that they sent "an important message to our allies . . . about the seriousness of purpose."[10] Finally, the Defense Department summarized the central objective of the sanctions as a step in a "long-term alliance strategy on East-West economic relations that has the coherence and depth of our military strategy."[11]

These statements indicate that while the sanctions were designed originally as a response to a security threat, securing European compliance had become an increasingly important objective. European cooperation in June of 1982 would help the Reagan administration achieve three foreign policy goals. First, if the Soviet Union lost the hard currency earning potential from the pipeline, its economy would weaken. Second, Europe would be less threatened from a potential cut-off of Soviet energy. Finally, the Western alliance would show the Soviets a strong and unified front.

Targets

The ability of the trans-Siberian Pipeline sanctions to achieve Reagan's three stated objectives rested on the ability of the United States to secure the compliance of actors who could produce or supply restricted goods with the embargo. If the Soviet Union acquired enough advanced Western gas transport equipment and technology from non-American sources to complete the project, then the American sanctions would do little to deter pipeline construction. Moreover, Soviets access to hard currency would be maintained, their economy would be strengthened, and they would gain a potential source of power in the form of European reliance on Soviet energy supplies. The provision of restricted goods and technology by an

American ally or its firms would also undercut the symbolic value of the pipeline sanctions by challenging the American interpretation of Soviet actions and by questioning the legitimacy of the sanctions as an appropriate response to the military crackdown in Poland. For its policy to be effective, the United States had to secure the participation of both its allies and those firms that could produce or supply the embargoed goods and technology.

As the crisis evolved, securing European compliance became an increasingly prominent objective of the policy. With the imposition of the second set of sanctions in June 1982, the Western allies superseded the Soviet Union and the military leadership in Poland as the primary targets of U.S. policy. From that point on, European firms that possessed or could produce goods related to the pipeline became the targets of U.S. sanctions.

Means of Enforcement

The United States had three primary mechanisms for securing the participation of European governments and firms in its embargo. First, it attempted to persuade the others that the embargo was an appropriate and necessary response to Soviet involvement in Poland. Second, it offered inducements to entice others to participate. Third, it threatened to impose penalties against those that failed to comply with its policies.

While the U.S. motivation for securing European compliance was very high, the European motivation for enforcing U.S. export control policy locally was very low. Gaining the support of European governments in enforcing local corporate compliance was difficult because European perceptions of the potential military threat posed by the Soviet Union were often not the same as those of the United States.[12] Variation in the perception of the threat and the resulting conflicts of interest regarding the application of sanctions had important implications for the ability of the U.S. government to secure host government cooperation in enforcing its export controls. From a realist perspective, one would predict that the lower the level of threat the allies saw, even if they were deluding themselves, the more inclined they would be to resist U.S. pressure. Indeed, one reason that the allies were less likely to enforce U.S. restrictions at home during the trans-Siberian Pipeline than during Operation Exodus (discussed in the next chapter) may be that they perceived the level of threat from Soviet espionage efforts to be higher in the computer and telecommunications sectors covered by the latter as opposed to those related to pipeline construction. As a result, national governments were more likely to have supported their firms against U.S. restrictions during the Pipeline Case than during Operation Exodus. Variations in national perceptions of external threats can explain some of the variation in the behavior of national governments in the two cases, but it cannot explain variation in the successes and failures of U.S. efforts to secure corporate compliance within them. The inability of the United States to persuade or entice foreign governments to participate in the initial embargo led to an attempt by the United States government to impose negative sanctions directly on firms operating abroad as a means of securing their compliance with its policies unilaterally. The ability of the U.S. to secure compliance by firms during the Pipeline Case indicate the effectiveness of these secondary sanctions even in the face of strong opposition by foreign governments and firms exist.

The failure of diplomatic persuasion.   Numerous authors have documented the conflicts of interest between the United States and European states and firms.[13] The main focus here is on the persistent conflicts of interest between the U.S. government and the firms themselves. The fact that foreign governments actively challenged U.S. enforcement efforts during the pipeline crisis makes it a "hard case" for the use of sanctions to secure extraterritorial compliance, given that host country governments tended to bolster and support local corporate opposition to U.S. initiatives. (The same is true for the Helms-Burton case discussed in chapter 5.) This section provides a synopsis of events leading up to the second set of sanctions to demonstrate that conflicts of interest existed and that the European governments actively supported corporate opposition to U.S. enforcement efforts. The ability to secure corporate compliance under these very difficult circumstances demonstrates the high degree of extraterritorial control that sanctions provided to the U.S. government.

Great Britain, France, Italy, and West Germany were concluding initial contract negotiations with the Soviet Union when the Reagan administration formally presented the American position on the Soviet pipeline. At the Ottawa Summit in July 1981, President Reagan tried to convince the Europeans not to sign any additional gas importation agreements. These agreements, he argued, were harmful to Western security for two reasons. First, importing natural gas would strengthen the Soviet military industrial complex by furnishing hard currency earnings. Second, and more importantly, importing gas gave the Soviet Union the new strategic weapon of increased European dependence on Soviet energy supplies. By 1990, European countries were expected to be importing about 30 percent (approximately 30 bcm/year) of their natural gas from the Soviet Union.[14] Hard-liners in the U.S. government saw European acceptance of Soviet energy sources as greatly increasing European dependence on the Soviet Union which Moscow, in turn, could use as a vehicle for political and economic coercion. This view is reflected in the following statement by a U.S. Department of Defense official:

If I were a Soviet leader, I would have rubbed my hands with delight when the Europeans signed the pipeline contracts. Can you imagine getting a primary adversary in the position of depending on you knowing that the tap can be turned off at any time? That's the kind of leverage strategists usually only dream about.[15]

Furthermore, President Reagan argued that the inability of the Soviet Union to build the large compressors and sufficient quantities of large diameter pipe needed to develop and fully exploit its natural gas reserves provided the allies with a chance to exploit Soviet dependence for Western benefit. To hard-liners, the Soviet energy sector itself appeared particularly vulnerable to external economic pressure and made a good potential target for economic sanctions.

In contrast to U.S. concerns about European dependence on Soviet energy, the Europeans argued that their long-term dependence on Soviet gas would remain small. Rather than increasing their vulnerability to the Soviet Union, the pipeline served to mitigate the costs of an unwanted dependence on a limited number of energy suppliers from OPEC. Most importantly, while a Soviet cut-off of natural gas supplies would be costly for Europe, numerous alternate suppliers were available. Unlike oil, which is supplied by a small number of states concentrated in a specific geographic region, international reserves of natural gas are widely distributed.[16] If imports from one or more of the top three producers of natural gas (the Soviet Union, the United States, and the Netherlands) were terminated, additional supplies could be acquired from Algeria, Australia, Canada, Great Britain, Iran, Malaysia, Mexico, Nigeria, Norway, and Qatar.[17] If dependence is defined in terms of both the availability of alternate trading partners as well as the value of trade with the sender, then European dependence on suppliers of natural gas can be interpreted as low, whereas its dependence on suppliers of oil is potentially high. Based on the dependence arguments presented in chapter 1, U.S. fears of European dependence on Soviet energy were exaggerated. The continued abundance of natural gas, and the geographic and political dispersion of natural gas exporters, make the threat of any OPEC-like cartel unlikely. Even if the European belief was inaccurate, the belief itself naturally stiffened their resolve against the U.S. embargo. They were, therefore, less likely to help enforce the trans-Siberian pipeline restrictions over their constituents and would be more likely to challenge U.S. efforts to do so.

The United States and the Europeans also disagreed about the likelihood that the Soviet Union would attempt to exploit this dependence by cutting off the flow of gas. From the European perspective, the Soviets had been a stable and reliable supplier of energy.[18] In the event that trade with the Soviets was cut off, Europe would still possess large stockpiles of energy supplies. Moreover, the majority of its energy-producing and defense facilities have the capability to be "dual fired," using oil as well as gas.[19] In the event of a protracted conflict, the gas shortages would disproportionately affect residential and commercial sectors of the economy that depended on natural gas for heating and cooking. These sectors would only be affected in the interim before alternate sources of natural gas could be secured.

Finally, the Europeans disputed the American assessment of strategic benefits that the acquisition of pipeline technology would give to Moscow. The Soviet Union was dependent on the continued influx of Western technology and spare parts to keep its energy sector running efficiently. The United States interpreted this dependence as an indication that an increase inflow of technology and hard currency from the pipeline would upset the strategic balance by enhancing Soviet development, particularly in its military sector. In contrast, the Europeans played down the impact of energy trade on the Soviet military and instead argued that continued Soviet dependence on Western resources and technology further decreased the likelihood that it would use its energy trade as a strategic weapon.

The merits of either perspective are not of primary concern here. Rather, it is important to understand the extent to which European and American interests and perceptions of their dependence on others varied. Each step along the way, the United States tried to get the European governments to support its efforts to secure the compliance by their constituents with its policies. As Bruce Jentleson argues, divergent foreign policy objectives and divergent economic interests made securing European support for American export control policies difficult.[20]

The failure of incentives. In November of 1981, one month before the crackdown in Poland, President Reagan tried a different tactic and attempted to entice the allies by offering to provide an alternate source of energy in the form of coal or Norwegian natural gas. The package was not particularly appealing to the Europeans.[21] From a practical standpoint, it was not clear that the United States could deliver the vast amounts of coal that it promised. Furthermore, public awareness of the problems of acid rain, the high costs of antipollution devices, and pressures from European coal miners made American coal a poor alternative to natural gas. The second suggestion was also problematic. Norwegian gas was more expensive than Soviet gas and, moreover, Norwegian production of natural gas and Norwegian-European trade had declined from 1980 to 1982. Overall, the American proposal failed to offer compensation for the loss of exports, production, and employment in pipeline- and gas-related industries at a time when European economies were in the midst of a recession.

American attempts to entice the allies through promises of alternate sources of energy were ineffective. Furthermore, conflicting beliefs of the benefits of East-West trade and the appropriateness of sanctions remained largely unchanged. The failure of the United States to convince or entice its allies to accept its views, and the continuing divergence of these differences, came to a head following the imposition of martial law in Poland on 12 December 1981.

European reaction to Soviet actions in Poland. The European allies joined the United States in condemning the Soviet actions in Poland. At an emergency meeting in January 1982, NATO presented a joint statement that "Soviet actions towards Poland make it necessary to examine the course of economic and commercial relations . . . longer-term East-West economic relations, particularly energy."[22] The NATO members agreed to impose a number of economic sanctions against Poland and the Soviet Union.

The formal condemnation of the Polish crackdown was united, but the NATO sanctions were nonbinding, stating merely that "each of the allies will act in accordance with its own situation and laws."[23] French President Mitterrand declared that the "loss of liberty" in Poland "should be denounced clearly, vigorously, and consistently."[24] Similarly, German Chancellor Schmidt expressed support for Solidarity, declaring that he was "on the side of the worker in Warsaw and in Siberia and Gdansk."[25] The British government imposed political and economic sanctions against Poland, restricted the movements of Soviet officials in Great Britain, and reduced the degree of cooperative agreements between the U.K. and the Soviet Union.[26] Finally, Ministers of the European Community warned the Soviets against further intervention and eventually agreed to reduce their collective imports from the Soviet Union by 1.35 percent, or about $150 million in 1982.[27] Yet despite the common outrage reflected in all of these as related efforts, none of the sanctions agreed on at the NATO meeting were as explicitly linked to the pipeline as the U.S. had wanted. The allies questioned sacrificing the guaranteed benefits of the pipeline for the limited benefits of embargoing its construction. They argued that the overall political and economic impact of embargoing the pipeline in addition to their other protests was questionable and that even without embargoing the pipeline, their actions would send a "clear political signal to the Soviet Union."[28]

The perception of an external disturbance or potential threat to international peace created by Soviet involvement in Poland did not provide the NATO alliance or the Reagan administration with a common solution concerning how to react to it. At the national level, the limits of European cooperation with the United States' efforts to secure compliance with a trans-Siberian pipeline embargo became apparent almost immediately. Less than a month after the Polish coup, Gaz de France signed a long-term gas import contract with Soyouz Gaz Export of the Soviet Union. The transaction was supported by the French government; similarly the West German government supported several trade agreements by German firms related to pipeline construction.

French and German support for U.S. initiatives involving East-West security issues indicate that both governments cooperated with U.S. initiatives that they considered vital to their national security. The Mitterand government had taken a far stronger, pro-U.S. and anti-Soviet position on issues of arms control and military security than his predecessors. Similarly, Chancellor Kohl had supported U.S. initiatives on short-range nuclear missiles and European defense policy. The lack of French or German willingness to enforce the pipeline embargo resulted from the fact that they disagreed with the U.S. government regarding the nature of the threat and the appropriateness of the embargo, and they saw the pipeline as a source of trade to bolster the economic success of their firms. Allowing their firms to acquire pipeline contracts enabled them to diversify energy supplies after two oil shocks, and to save jobs in depressed industries.[29] Pipeline construction also provided a market for specialized exports that offered increased national revenues and promised employment in depressed regions and sectors of the British and French economies. Although East-West trade accounted for a relatively small proportion of overall trade or GNP, it was important for the economic vitality of several key industries in West Germany, France, and Great Britain.[30] This was true both in basic products, such as steel and wide-diameter pipe, and in high-technology sectors. According to the Office of Technology Assessment in Washington, 92,000 West German jobs depended on trade with the Soviet Union. While this represented only four-tenths of one percent of the West German work force, these jobs were highly concentrated in particular regions, and their loss could affect an additional 220,000 jobs that depended on related commerce with the East.[31] Similarly, Great Britain suffered from 13.5 percent unemployment, and the sanctions threatened companies that were both leading employers and exporters.[32] Twelve companies with contracts valued at $385 million were directly affected, and with elections approaching in each country, any action against the pipeline could have serious political consequences.

The importance of economic considerations, including the survival of local firms, is reflected in a declaration of French Prime Minister Mauroy in front of the National Assembly, stating, "let us not, on top of the suffering of the Polish people, add the suffering of the French people who would be deprived of heating this winter."[33] Challenging both the rationale for the embargo and the domestic economic costs, British Prime

Minister Margaret Thatcher argued that "it was too much to ask that they [Great Britain and Europe] punish their own economies and their own interests in support of policies that would inflict no noticeable wound on Moscow's interests."[34]

These issues reflect a persistent underlying controversy regarding security concerns within the Western alliance since World War II. Contrary to conventional wisdom, security concerns have not always been a unifying force and they have not provided sufficient motivation for coordination of a European response to East-West issues. Threats are often perceived differently by allies and are often evaluated on an issue-specific rather than systemic basis. The link between the pipeline and a potential security threat posed by Soviet actions in Poland was considered tenuous at best. From the European perspective, the pipeline represented a chance for economic gain and was not perceived to pose a sufficient threat to Western security to warrant the enforcement of a pipeline embargo.

In the midst of the growing controversy over the pipeline, Secretary of State Haig sent Under Secretary of State for Security Assistance James Buckley to negotiate a trade-off with the Europeans. The United States wanted the Europeans to bring existing credit agreements related to the pipeline in line with less favorable OECD credit agreements that had been renegotiated in February 1982. As reflected in a statement by Haig, Buckley invoked the threat of European dependence on American technology as a means of influencing European negotiators. Haig reported:

> I made it plain to the European foreign ministers that if we did not at least have progress on a cooperative policy to limited future . . . credits to the Soviet Union, the United States would find it difficult not to apply sanctions that would prevent the use of American technology [including licenses and patents] for the pipeline.[35]

U.S. negotiators succeeded in reclassifying the Soviet Union, thus raising the interest rates it was forced to pay for OECD credit. However, they did not gain European support for applying the reclassification retroactively. As a result, none of the pipeline contracts—all of which had been signed before the OECD policy changes—were affected.

In May, Haig again attempted to convince the Europeans to restrict credit to the East.[36] Just prior to the Versailles Summit, the Quai d'Orsay suggested that France and other European states would agree to a quid pro quo. They agreed to limit credit to the Soviet Union if the United States would agree to bolster the franc and "control imbalances in currency values," provided it agreed not to interfere in the construction of the pipeline.[37] While no formal limits were placed on credits or subsidies to the East, participants at the Versailles Summit agreed to "pursue a prudent and diversified economic approach to the USSR and Eastern Europe, consistent with our political and security interests."[38] In turn, while the pipeline was not mentioned explicitly in the formal communiqué, the agreement called for "commercial prudence" in economic relations with the East.[39] In exchange, Haig argued that all participants understood "that the United States would not apply retroactive, extraterritorial pipeline sanctions."[40]

The fragile stability of this resolution was shattered the day after it was settled by a statement by Treasury Secretary Regan claiming that the United States would not intervene in foreign exchange markets in support of the French franc. In a sharp response, President Mitterrand claimed the Summit "deal" had been compromised and that France "would not support economic warfare against the Soviet Union and was not bound by the summit declaration to cut the amount of credit extended to Moscow."[41] German Finance Minister Manfred Lahnstein echoed French sentiments arguing that West Germany, "will continue to work with Eastern European countries and the Soviet Union as usual."[42]

Lisa Martin, Michael Mastanduno, and others explain this failure by emphasizing the divisions within the Reagan administration. They argue that these divisions and other domestic constraints undermined the credibility of American threats to impose sanctions against both Europe and the Soviet Union. The perception of a common threat failed to unify the American Executive, just as it failed to unify the Western alliance. Domestic constraints and infighting within the Executive between Haig and the State Department on one side (favoring multilateral action), and Caspar Weinberger and the Defense Department on the other (favoring unilateral action), undermined American leadership, prestige, and influence in the alliance.[43]

These authors are correct in arguing that these events undermined American prestige and its ability to persuade others to participate in the embargo. It is a mistake, however, to infer that these constraints limited the ability or willingness of the American government to impose sanctions against offending firms. For instance, in addition to the often-cited grain sales to the Soviet Union, the Reagan administration was accused of hypocrisy because it granted an export license to Caterpillar Industries to sell pipelayers to the Soviet Union, after asking Prime Minister Suzuki of Japan to prevent Komatsu, a rival Japanese heavy equipment manufacturer, from exporting the same products.[44] This action is cited to indicate a lack of willingness to sacrifice domestic economic concerns for the sake of the embargo while asking others to do so. The implication is that the administration would not carry out its threats to impose economic sanctions if domestic companies were hurt by them. However, after the sanctions imposed on 29 December, Caterpillar could no longer participate in the pipeline project. As a result, a spokesperson for the company complained that, "there is no doubt that during the restrictions the Soviets came to regard us as an unreliable supplier."[45] Furthermore, when the embargo was eventually lifted, Caterpillar lost its contracts to Komatsu, whose main selling point was its guarantee to fulfill contract obligations without the fear that the Japanese government would intervene and terminate them at some point in the future. As repeatedly argued by the American business community, the sanctions were costly to American business.[46] Despite these costs, the Executive showed a willingness to impose sanctions on American firms throughout the pipeline crisis.

Given the failure of U.S. efforts to persuade its allies to enforce compliance by local firms with the trans-Siberian pipeline embargo, the United States directed its sanctions against foreign firms in order to entice or coerce their compliance itself.[47]

SOURCES OF U.S. INFLUENCE AND PREDICTIONS OF U.S. SUCCESS, 1980–84

Beginning in 1982, the Reagan administration sought to control the activities of firms involved in the construction of the trans-Siberian pipeline by enforcing its export control policy at home and abroad. Using the arguments developed in chapter 1, this section offers predictions at a corporate level of analysis. This is followed by an analysis of the use of secondary sanctions by the U.S. government to secure extraterritorial compliance with its policies in order to demonstrate the causal links between dependence and political power.

The Use of Secondary Sanctions

At the urging of National Security Advisor Clark and Defense Secretary Weinberger, President Reagan reacted strongly against the European renunciation of the Versailles Summit. On 22 June 1982, the U.S. government amended its previous foreign policy controls to prohibit exports and reexports of oil and gas equipment to the Soviet Union by U.S.-owned or controlled foreign companies, wherever organized or doing business. Restrictions were also placed on equipment containing technical data that originated in the United States. Unlike the earlier sanctions, this policy enacted retroactively. All past and existing contracts were subject to the regulations. The amended regulations made American export policy more extraterritorial in range and greatly increased its scope.

The sanctions carried penalties of indictment under U.S. law including imprisonment for executives and fines of up to $100,000 per offense. These penalties threatened companies operating within American territory more so than those operating abroad, since without the acquiescence of foreign governments, the domestic law of one state generally carries no legal force in another state's territory. The lack of a de jure means of enforcement across international boundaries is the primary limitation of enforcing domestic regulations abroad. The United States has successfully fined several individuals and firms that have violated its export control policy abroad, but this success is contingent on extradition agreements which can be politically sensitive, costly, and time consuming.

The U.S. government has at its disposal, however, a far more enforceable and fearsome penalty for noncompliance. Foreign dependence on American suppliers and markets gives the administration a potential source of de facto control over foreign firms. The backbone of American threats against noncooperative firms involved in the construction of the trans-Siberian Pipeline on the denial list maintained by the Department of Commerce.[48] Being placed on the denial list effectively terminates access to all American suppliers and markets in a particular sector by making it illegal for Americans to conduct business with the denied firm or individual (see Appendix for more information on these restrictions). As a result, the threat of placing firms on the denial list provides the American government with a potent means of exploiting foreign dependence on American suppliers or access to American markets. The next section uses the argument developed in chapter 1, to evaluate the success and failure of these threats during the trans-Siberian Pipeline crisis.

Predictions of Success, 1980-84

The pipeline embargo affected several major industries involved in the production of wide-diameter pipe, gas pumps, compressors, and related gas transport technology. The actions of four firms are analyzed: Mannesmann (a German firm), Alsthom-Atlantique and Dresser-France (French firms), and John Brown Engineering (a British firm). Mannesmann produces wide-diameter pipe, while the others, Alsthom-Atlantique, Dresser, and John Brown, produce compressors and related equipment.[49]

At the time of the pipeline crisis, the United States was the world's largest market and supplier of pumps and compressors. In 1982, it accounted for 11.3 percent of world imports and 22.8 percent of world exports in this industry.[50] It was also the world's largest market for wide-diameter pipe, accounting for 28.5 percent of world imports, though it accounted for a more modest 6.8 percent of world wide-diameter pipe exports. A sector-specific power argument would predict that the United

States should be able to use its dominance in the sale and purchasing of pumps and compressors to exert influence over companies operating in that sector, while its dominance in the wide-diameter pipe market industries should enable it to exert influence over exporting companies in that sector.

Dependence arguments emphasize that dominance alone is not sufficient to guarantee U.S. power over corporate activities. Indeed, the degree of U.S. dominance is an indicator of the availability of alternate suppliers rather than indicating the degree of influence likely in a relationship. The greater U.S. dominance, the fewer alternate non-U.S. trading partners are available. This indicator suggests that alternate markets for wide-diameter pipe were relatively limited, whereas alternate markets for pumps and compressors more likely to be available. In contrast, the availability of alternate suppliers of wide-diameter pipe was relatively high, whereas the availability of alternate suppliers for compressors is low.

In addition to the availability of alternate trading partners, dependence arguments focus on power as the relational concept and, consequently, emphasize the impact of one country's actions on others in the relationship. U.S. markets accounted for 17 percent of German exports of wide-diameter pipe, about 3 percent of French, and 7 percent of British exports of pumps and compressors.[51] Multiplying these proportions times the availability of alternate trading partners indicates that, despite the dominance of U.S. markets, the degree of corporate dependence on U.S. markets was low in every case, with a degree of dependence less than .048 on a scale from 0 to 1. Of those, French and British firms in the pump and compressor industry were even less likely than German companies to be dependent on U.S. markets in the wide-diameter pipe industry (see table 3.1).

U.S. exports accounted for only 2.7 percent of German imports in the wide-diameter pipe industry, but they account for 18.6 percent of French and 26.8 percent of British imports in pumps and compressors. Thus estimates of dependence based on these values suggest that corporate dependence on U.S. suppliers was also low in every case, and it was much lower for firms in the wide-diameter pipe industry than for those in the compressor industry.

Given the low level of the targets' dependence on the United States, dependence arguments at this level of aggregation would predict that the U.S. sanctions are not likely to compel firms in these industries to alter their behalf. At the same time, the United States was as dependent on European suppliers or markets in either sector. This suggests that while its influence would be minimal, the cost of retaliatory sanctions would be small as well. What these firms actually did and why is the subject of the next section.

Table 3.1 Dominance and Dependence during the Pipeline Crisis

	Year	Dominance of U.S. Suppliers	Dominance of U.S. Markets	Foreign Dependence on U.S. Suppliers	Foreign Dependence on U.S. Markets
Fed. Rep. Germany (F) *Mannesmann*—Wide Diameter Pipe Industry	1982	6.78%	28.54%	0.006	0.049
France (S) *Alsthom-Atlantique*—Compressor Industry	1982	22.8% (World's Largest)	11.3% (World's Largest)	0.042	0.003
France (F) *Dresser Industries*—Compressor Industry	1982	22.8% (World's Largest)	11.3% (World's Largest)	0.042	0.003
United Kingdom (F) *John Brown*—Compressor Industry	1982	22.8% (World's Largest)	11.3% (World's Largest)	0.061	0.008

Source: United Nations, *International Trade Statistics Yearbook,* vol. 2 (New York: United Nations Publishing, 1984). Using SITC 678 for the wide-diameter pipe industry and SITC 743 for the compressor industry.

(S) = Successful Sanctions
(F) = Failed Sanctions

CASE ANALYSES: U.S. INFLUENCE ATTEMPTS BY INDUSTRY

This section analyzes American efforts to control the activities of firms in industries related to the production of wide-diameter pipe, gas pumps, compressors, and related gas transport technology. These cases highlight the unique characteristics, trade patterns, and concerns of individual firms in each industry. This analysis traces the links between trade dominance, firm and state dependence, and the ability of U.S. sanctions to alter their behavior. The outcome of each case is then compared with the predictions made in the previous section.

Dominance and Dependence in the Steel Pipe and
Compressor Industries

Declining American hegemony is one of the most common explanations of the difficulties the American government faced throughout the pipeline crisis.[52] Stephen Kobrin argues, for example, that "there is little question American power has declined relative to host countries, and that decline is manifest in diminished control over outcomes. The American government no longer is able to enforce its export sanctions extraterritorially."[53] A close examination of dependent relationships among actors involved in the pipeline case reveals that overall American power measured in terms of its ability to enforce sanctions extraterritorially had not necessarily declined in all areas, but rather was contingent on the sector-specific dominance of American firms and markets and foreign dependence on them. While dominance in a particular industry was important, the relative availability of alternate suppliers determined whether threats to exploit that dominance would result in changes in corporate and national behavior.

The United States was the world's largest market for wide-diameter pipe and pumps and compressors during the trans-Siberian Pipeline crisis. In 1982, it accounted for 28.5 percent of world imports of wide-diameter pipe and 11.3 percent of world imports of pumps and compressors.[54] At the same time, it accounted for 22.8 percent of world exports of pumps and compressors (it was the world's largest supplier), and 6.7 percent of wide-diameter pipe exports.[55] Following the predictions of sector-specific dominance in these industries, these statistics suggest that the United States should be able to exert more influence over firms in the wide-diameter pipe industry by threatening to cut off access to the American market than by threatening to cut off American suppliers. At the same time, U.S. dominance in production and purchasing in the pump and compressor industry suggest that it should be able to use sanctions to secure the compliance of actors in this sector.

Supporters of dominance arguments may argue that the general failure of the United States to secure compliance in these sectors is reflected by the fact that it did not dominate each industry sufficiently. From this perspective, possessing 11.3 percent of the world markets and 22.8 percent of world exports of pumps and compressors, or 28.5 percent of world markets in wide-diameter pipe, may be sufficient to exercise control over outcomes. A larger degree of sectoral dominance would have increased leverage.[56] This criticism, however, directs attention away from the more important criticism that the availability of alternate trading partners can undercut the ability of large states to exploit their dominant trading positions.

Despite its position as the world's largest market and supplier of compressors and the world's largest supplier of steel pipes, the volume of each country's and each firm's trade to the United States in these sectors must be compared to potential business related to the trans-Siberian Pipeline. Independent German contracts related to the pipeline amounted to $840 million, independent British contracts were valued at $135 million, and independent French contracts were valued at $615 million.[57] These individual contracts are substantial when compared to the amounts of total exports to the United States from all producers in each country, $556 million, $121 million, and $184 million for West Germany, Britain, and France, respectively.[58] These independent contracts alone were larger than each country's individual exports to the United States. In addition, a consortium led by Mannesmann of West Germany and Creusot Loire of France subcontracted additional agreements valued at over one billion dollars. Thus, the availability of attractive alternate markets suggests that despite being the world's largest trader of goods in these sectors, American threats to exclude these companies from access to its markets should have little effect on tbeir behavior.

At the same time, however, France, Great Britain, and West Germany received a large proportion of their compressors and related equipment from American suppliers. General Electric (GE), for example, was the world's largest supplier of industrial turbines and compressors, and many of the companies involved in the pipeline project relied on access to General Electric parts. The dominant position of General Electric and foreign dependence on its products gave the United States government a potential leverage over firm activities, but this dependence and the resulting leverage remained contingent on the lack of viable alternate suppliers. If costs of producing non-American compressors are prohibitive (due perhaps to a lack of technological expertise, for example), then the threat to cut off access to American compressor suppliers may give the United States government a source of leverage.

In sum, American markets accounted for 17 percent of German imports in the steel pipe industry. However, the value of United States' imports was less than the value of Soviet imports related to the trans-Siberian Pipeline for France, Great Britain, and West Germany. American exports in the steel pipe industry also played a relatively small role in European trade. As a result, the threat to cut off access to the American market or American suppliers in the steel pipe industry should be expected to have little effect on the ability of the U.S. government to secure the compliance of foreign firms in this sector. In the compressor industry, foreign dependence on U.S. markets was minimal, while foreign dependence on U.S. suppliers was moderate. A corporate level analysis suggests, however, that corporate dependence on General Electric itself may give the United States the additional leverage it needed to influence several of these firms.

U.S. Influence over Firms: The First Round of Sanctions

The initial American sanctions on 29 December 1981 did not directly apply to companies operating outside of the United States. They did, however, have a strong indirect effect on these firms. At this stage, the export controls covered only "foreign origin products which incorporated U.S. technology subjected to controls when exported from the United States."[59] While Secretary of State Haig and others further argued that the sanctions were not intended to be retroactive, the Commerce Department interpreted the sanctions to be retroactive in effect. This meant that General Electric, Caterpillar, Dresser, and Cooper Industries were forced to cancel existing contracts relating to the construction of the pipeline. Consequently, the sanctions effectively cut off foreign access to American exports essential for pipeline construction, including pipe layers manufactured by Caterpillar and components for pipeline compressors from General Electric.

The technical dominance of American firms in Western markets provided the United States government with potential leverage over foreign firms and governments. General Electric produced a number of "bottle-neck" items including the rotors, nozzles, and sator blades necessary for the construction of the turbines used to pump natural gas throughout the pipeline.[60] Companies including AEG-Kanis (FRG), Alsthom-Atlantique (FR), John Brown (UK), and Nuovo Pignone (IT) all relied on equipment and parts provided by General Electric for future sales of products, valued at over $175 million.[61] By the time the initial sanctions were imposed, GE had already shipped twenty-three rotor sets to Europe, but the pipeline would be limited to about 70 percent of capacity with no backup or replacement equipment if additional supplies from GE were not forthcoming.[62] In order to build additional compressors, firms that relied on American-made materials and components had to find alternate sources of supply.

Alternate sources of supply usually take one of two forms: either alternate producers are found, or the restricted goods are produced internally. The latter option requires investment in the research and development necessary either to produce the restricted goods, or to alter its development process to use substitute components. If the costs of these options outweigh the costs of the sanctions, then the sanctions are likely to be effective.[63] Initially, Alsthom-Atlantique appeared to be an ideal alternate supplier of the equipment embargoed by General Electric. Alsthom-Atlantique was the only manufacturing associate of General Electric that possessed a license to make the rotor kits necessary for the pipeline. Further, it had already agreed to produce forty spare rotor kits for the Soviet Union by 1984.[64]

Alsthom-Atlantique. Alsthom-Atlantique could supply the equipment embargoed by General Electric. Supplying the rotors would require it to build a new production plant or retool an existing one. This alternative would require a large amount of capital, but once the initial investment was made, the firm could expect to reap greater profits as the sole producer of the rotor kits for the pipeline. A more important consideration was, however, the potential long-term costs of alienating GE. Alsthom-Atlantique depended on continued access to General Electric's equipment and technology to remain financially viable. Furthermore, the parent company of Alsthom-Atlantique, Compagnie Générale d'Electricité, was one of the largest French investors in the United States. It, too, feared retaliation if its subsidiary did not cooperate with the American restrictions. Retaliation would cut off access to the American market, which accounted for a large proportion of the current and future business of Compagnie Générale d'Electricité.[65]

Alsthom-Atlantique's dependence on General Electric gave the Reagan administration leverage over corporate actions. In addition, explicitly invoking the nationality principle of international law, the GE-Alsthom contract contained a clause allowing the U.S. government to penalize the company severely if it delivered the oil and gas equipment without recommendation from General Electric.[66] If Alsthom-Atlantique, and others under similar circumstances, chose to violate U.S. policy, they would breach their American contracts and violate American law. In addition to the standard criminal fines and imprisonment, such actions would place them on the denial lists, potentially making it illegal for any American company to conduct any business transactions with them.

Citing "the obvious political risks" and the importance of their relationship with GE, Alsthom-Atlantique declined to accept the role of alternate supplier.[67] Alsthom-Atlantique's decision not to produce additional rotor kits was based on its dependence on a stable future relationship with General Electric. Moreover, American threats against Alsthom-Atlantique served an additional purpose. By controlling Alsthom-Atlantique, the U.S. government eliminated the most cost-effective alternate supplier of compressor equipment.[68] Aside from Alsthom-Atlantique, all additional alternate suppliers would require project alterations that would complicate and delay construction, and increase the costs of the project.[69] By exploiting Alsthom-Atlantique's dependence on access to American technology and access to the American market, the U.S. government was able to eliminate the most cost-effective alternate supplier of the embargoed goods. This outcome supports predictions of both the dominance and dependence arguments based on the analysis of trade in the pumps and compressors industry. Convergent predictions are a positive occurrence, especially when they match the outcome. The next case demonstrates that the predictions are not always congruent with each other or with the outcome.

Lisa Martin and others argue that the credibility of American threats was extremely important throughout this period. She notes that "if European governments believed that the administration was bluffing, they could simply ride out the storm of rhetoric and go ahead with their contractual commitments."[70] This observation is reasonably accurate for national governments, but not for private companies. European governments could "ride out the storm" because the U.S. sanctions did not affect them directly. The imposition of sanctions would affect national governments in the medium-term rather than the short-term and would do so only when a sufficient number of companies were hurt to have a negative impact on national economic health or when those companies that were negatively affected had sufficient political clout to lobby for policy changes. Unlike their governments, however, foreign firms were directly and immediately affected by the sanctions. Linkages to other issues were unimportant. In order to avoid unacceptable financial and political costs, several European companies dependent on GE initially adopted a "wait and see" approach to the sanctions, assuming that the sanctions would be lifted before the compressor stations would be needed. Some firms, however, could not adopt such a strategy. In the middle of the embargo controversy, AEG-Kanis, as subsidiary of AEG-Telefunken, went bankrupt. It represented West Germany's largest corporate bankruptcy since World War II. The failure of such companies became both a political symbol of national governments' ability to defy U.S. actions, and an economic symbol to firms of the costs of doing so.[71]

U.S. Influence over Firms: The Second Round of Sanctions

The goal of the second round of sanctions shifted from punishing the Soviet Union to blocking the construction of the trans-Siberian Pipeline. On 22 June 1982, the U.S. imposed a second round of sanctions that placed multinational firms at the center of the pipeline crisis. These companies were caught in an awkward position between European and American governments vying for influence over their activities. They were forced to choose between the costs of U.S. sanctions and those of breaking their contracts and defying their local governments.

The costs of challenging the U.S. embargo and severing links with U.S. suppliers and the American market had to be balanced against the costs of canceling existing orders and jeopardizing business relationships with current and future clients. Unlike Alsthom-Atlantique, other firms placed a higher value on existing business relationships with the East than on either their market or supply relationships with the United States. When the embargo was first imposed, it was estimated that U.S. companies would lose $300 to $600 million in export earnings. This is a sizable loss, but it is small in comparison to the projected loss of $1.6 billion for foreign subsidiaries of American firms or foreign licensees of American goods and technologies.[72] Abiding by American export restrictions meant outright losses in sales for these firms, and it had the potential to diminish future sales by creating the unwanted stigma of being a poor and unreliable supplier. John Brown Engineering, for instance, depended far more on access to the Soviet market than on either the U.S. market or American suppliers. As predicted, when faced with the relative cost of breaking existing contracts or challenging American export controls, John Brown Engineering reacted very differently than did Alsthom-Atlantique.

John Brown Engineering. John Brown Engineering (JBE) is a British company that produces industrial turbines. Thirty of those it produced between 1975 and 1983 were exported to the Soviet Union.[73] Along with five other European firms, John Brown won contracts with the Soviet trade organization V/O Machinoimport for materials related to the trans-Siberian Pipeline. On 6 October 1981, the company signed a £61 million contract for gas turbines with the Soviet Union, each of which contained rotors produced by General Electric.[74] The agreement also included a contract for service and spare parts for the twenty-one turbines valued at £42 million. The £103 million pipeline contract alone accounted for 66 percent of corporate business in 1981.[75]

Like Alsthom-Atlantique, John Brown Engineering relied on products produced by General Electric. The first U.S. embargo in December 1981 had made it illegal for General Electric to export its rotors and related technology. General Electric had subsequently stopped its shipments, effectively cutting off John Brown Engineering's supply of the rotors needed to produce its compressors. When the embargo was implemented, John Brown had six of the twenty-one rotors it needed to complete the order. However, even if these turbines were built using the rotors it had in stock, export control regulations would block their export because they contained GE components. This prohibition also applied to turbines produced by John Brown, AEG-Kanis, and Nuovo Pignone.

John Brown had two principal choices. It could comply with U.S. restrictions or it could break the embargo, try to complete the contract, and bear the costs of U.S. sanctions. Completing the contract would result in a profit of £103 million and would allow the firm to retain the Soviet Union as a future customer.[76] To do so without General Electric, an alternate sources of rotors would be needed. John Brown could purchase the rotors from Alsthom-Atlantique, though the resulting delay would result in a 5 percent loss due to late delivery charges. Unfortunately, even if John Brown had been willing to pay the late charges, Alsthom-Atlantique's decision not to act as an alternate supplier eliminated its most likely and cost-effective alternate source of rotors. In lieu of parts from GE and Alsthom-Atlantique, the rotors could be developed internally or the compressors could be redesigned to use other technology. Pursuing either of these options would, however, require a large investment in retooling production equipment and there was no guarantee of future sales sufficient to make the conversion profitable. Failing to find or create an alternate source of rotors, John Brown could deliver the turbines it had produced and default on the remaining contract. Doing so would result in a loss of approximately £45 million, though at least part of the contract would be saved.

These options had to be balanced against the costs of breaking the American embargo. Like Alsthom-Atlantique, John Brown risked losing long-term access to General Electric products and the American market. However, it had no direct sales to the U.S. and alternate suppliers were available for the American-made components it needed. The costs of breaking the embargo were minimal in comparison to the direct cost of either £45 million for partial completion or £104 million for canceling the agreement, plus penalties and damages for failing to fulfill a contract.[77] These potential losses, not American sanctions, "threatened the very survival of JBE."[78] Because of the high costs of terminating the agreement, John Brown Engineering chose to continue producing the turbines as long as possible, and to search out other alternate suppliers without making the sizable investment of producing the rotors internally.

The costs of abiding by the embargo might have been lessened some-what by the Export Credit Guarantee Department, which traditionally insures British companies against payment defaulting foreign customers. Ideally, this insurance would cover 85 percent of the lost contract,[79] but would not cover any of the associated penalties and could not make up for the loss of future business stemming from a company that breaks a contract. This relief, however, was not guaranteed. In order to minimize the costs of abiding by regulations, John Brown chose to pursue its legal options in the United States and through the British Department of Trade and Industry.

While the second set of sanctions did not directly affect John Brown Engineering since its supply had already been cut off, it appealed to the British government for assistance. John Brown Engineering was a leading exporter in Great Britain and a leading employer in Scotland. Termination of the pipeline contract would mean financial disaster for the company, a loss of numerous jobs in a depressed sector in a depressed region of the country, and a loss of export earnings during a recession. Loss of the contract was, thus, bad for both John Brown Engineering and Great Britain. In response to the second wave of U.S. sanctions, the British government instructed British companies not to comply with U.S. export control regulations. It did not, however, declare that the companies involved were required to fulfill their contracts. On 9 September 1982, the day the British government made its announcement, John Brown Engineering shipped six of its turbines to the Soviet Union. As a result, the U.S. government placed a denial order on the company, effectively terminating its access to American suppliers and the American market.

Prior to shipping its turbines, John Brown Engineering also sought to clarify the legal and political issues surrounding the scope of U.S. policy and gain legal counsel on how best to respond to the embargo.[80] Once a denial order was issued against it, the company requested a formal hearing before the Commerce Department. It argued that the regulations could not legally affect contracts that were concluded three months before the first embargo was enacted.

The actions of John Brown Engineering support the notion that firms react based on their assessment of the costs and benefits of particular relationships. John Brown Engineering's actions match predictions made based on its dependence on American producers and markets, but they are not consistent with those based on the dominance of American industry and markets in that sector. John Brown Engineering relied on rotors and rotor technology from General Electric. However, the costs of finding or developing alternate sources of supply of these rotors and technology were far less than the value of the contract in question. The threat of closing off U.S. technology, therefore, was not sufficient to gain the firm's cooperation. Similarly, access to the American market was not highly valued in comparison to the Soviet market. North and South America accounted for 27.4 percent of sales in 1982 for the John Brown Group of Companies, PLC.[81] While John Brown Engineering itself had no sales in the United States, 66 percent of its sales were to the Soviet Union.[82] In sum, the company chose the most profitable and only financially viable option.

Dresser-France. In response to the sanctions, Dresser-France, a wholly owned subsidiary of Dresser Industries of the United States, stopped production of its compressors. The company, however, continued to deliver several compressors it had already manufactured. Doing so enabled it to fulfill an agreement with a second French company and a Soviet trading company. The compressors in question were built with American technology that had been obtained prior to the first wave of U.S. sanctions against the Soviet Union. The U.S. Department of Commerce threatened to penalize Dresser if the deliveries were completed. In response, the French government threatened to penalize Dresser severely, potentially requisitioning Dresser-France's facilities, if the contract was not fulfilled.[83]

Faced with this dilemma, Dresser Industries and Dresser-France filed suit against the regulations for declaratory and disjunctive relief.[84] Dresser petitioned the Commerce Department to abandon the denial order and remove Dresser and its subsidiaries from the Black List. Dresser challenged the U.S. actions on the grounds that the denial of export privileges without trial violated due process and were unlawful because of their extraterritorial and retroactive effects.[85]

A detailed discussion of the litigation by the companies that challenged the pipeline sanctions at the administrative level and in the U.S. District Court in Washington is not necessary at this point.[86] It is important, however, to appreciate the high costs of such litigation and the small likelihood of success. The companies involved had to risk the possibility of civil, criminal, and administrative sanctions in order to get a judicial hearing on the merits of their cases. For instance, Dresser argued that the U.S. government's actions were inconsistent with international law and went beyond the legal limits of its authority as specified by the Export Administration Act. This claim would have challenged the president's legal authority to take action under the Export Administration Act. Dresser Industries never succeeded in getting a hearing on these issues in court.

Like John Brown Engineering, Dresser-France was dependent on access to American suppliers but was not dependent on access to the American market. As predicted, Dresser-France's policy was mixed. While it did stop production of compressors, it did not stop delivery of compressors it had already completed. Furthermore, rather than bow to American threats like Alsthom-Atlantique, it attempted to clarify its position and change American policy.

Retaliation and Rebuttal by European and American
Governments

As noted above, the European governments disagreed with U.S. policy
regarding the trans-Siberian pipeline embargo. Given this disagreement,
the failure of the U.S. government to secure European cooperation in
enforcing its export control policy over firms operating within their territories indicates that the threat and imposition of sanctions did not change
national behavior. This failure is consistent with the perceived lack of
national dependence on U.S. markets and suppliers. As argued above,
U.S. incentives failed because the United States did not offer a suitable
alternative supply of energy, nor did it provide an alternate market for the
embargoed goods.[87] Similarly, U.S. sanctions were ineffective because limited access to American rotors was not considered to be of vital importance to the European governments.

It is interesting to note that European governments and the European Community cited the violation of sovereignty, rather than economic
hardship or international security concerns, as the primary justification
behind strong condemnation of American enforcement efforts. European
leaders were unified in their indictment of American policy as a violation
of their sovereign authority. The German, French, British, and Italian
governments, as well as the European Community, all claimed that this
extension of U.S. jurisdiction was contrary to international law.[88] A leading
commentator in the West German weekly *Der Spiegel* noted that "the
Americans were treating us as if we were not sovereign states. We could
not sit still and let them run our lives for us."[89] The European Community
called the U.S. actions an "unacceptable interference" in its sovereign
affairs.[90] Even the Mitterrand government, which had proven to be squarely
Atlanticist and a staunch and reliable ally in dealings with the East, con-
demned U.S. enforcement efforts. French Foreign Minister Claude
Cheysson claimed that the sanctions represented a "progressive divorce"
between the U.S. and France.[91] A spokesman for the ministry argued that
"[a] major mistake has been to underestimate national pride in France, to
think that we would be so easily willing to abide by what the Americans
impose on us."[92]

The breakdown in American-European relations was compounded
when, just one month after the second wave of sanctions took effect,
President Ronald Reagan announced that the United States and the Soviet Union had signed a new deal for twenty-three million metric tons of
grain. From the European perspective, it was the height of hypocrisy that
the U.S. should ask the Europeans to forego the economic advantages of
the pipeline while making grain deals and claiming that the "Soviet mar-

ket is the biggest in the world, and we want to recapture it. . . . Our national economy needs it."[93]

Again, rather than focusing public attention on strategic or domestic economic issues, Thatcher extolled the sovereign integrity of Great Britain while condemning the extraterritorial and retroactive nature of Washington's demands, declaring that "[i]t is wrong for one very powerful nation. . . [to try to prevent the fulfillment of] existing contracts that do not, in any event, fall under its jurisdiction."[94] Britain's Trade Secretary, Lord Cockfield, invoked the Protection of Trading Interest Act, ordering four of the largest British companies with pipeline contracts to disregard the U.S. embargo.[95] In an even stronger measure, the French Minister of Industry, Jean-Pierre Chevenement, signed an administrative decree ordering Dresser-France to deliver its compressor equipment. For reasons of national security, the French Government reinstated a wartime ordinance to direct French companies to fulfill their contracts.[96] Similarly, the West German and Italian governments both stated their intentions to defy the U.S. sanctions. However, neither government forbade its firms from abiding by U.S. policy or ordered them to fulfill their agreements.

The significance of the severity of these reactions becomes apparent when they fail to reappear in response to American efforts to control the movements of computers and other high-technology goods. As the next chapter will demonstrate, the extent of extraterritorial sovereign control by the U.S. government were far more severe during Operation Exodus than during the Pipeline Case, yet the foreign governments did not protest to the same degree. The difference was not the credibility of the sanctions and countersanctions. In both cases, despite domestic opposition, the United States imposed sanctions that were costly to its firms. If the credibility of the threat were the deciding factor, in terms of an unwillingness to accept the cost of countersanctions against domestic actors, then the results would be the same.

The primary differences between the Pipeline Case and Operation Exodus are variation in the convergence national interests and the level of dependence between these countries and the United States. The convergence of threat perception and the convergence of national interests varied, but were generally higher during Operation Exodus than the Pipeline Case. When threat perceptions and/or common interests converged, foreign governments tended to increase their support for the application of U.S. sanctions against wayward firms or individuals operating in their territories. Yet, while this convergence tended to minimize the likelihood of intergovernmental conflict regarding the de jure basis of U.S. sanctions, it did not end the difficulty associated with securing compliance by foreign companies. Regardless of the activities of thier last governments,

U.S. sanctions generally succeeded in securing the compliance of foreign companies when they were dependent on U.S. markets or suppliers, but did not when they were not.

Dependence and trade dominance are issue specific and vary within each case. However, the general level of U.S. trade dominance and foreign dependence on the United States was higher in Operation Exodus than during the trans-Siberian Pipeline crisis. In the trans-Siberian Pipeline crisis, the European governments and firms (with the exception of Alsthom-Atlantique) did not perceive themselves to be dependent on American goods or technology. While replacing the restricted items was costly, it could be done. In contrast, throughout Operation Exodus, European governments and firms believed that they were dependent on the continued supply of American computer and other high-technology goods for their national economic and military security—a supply that could not be easily replaced. Comparison of the two cases demonstrates that government as well as firm action can be explained in terms of the dominance of American trade and foreign dependence on American goods markets.

The first shipments of pipeline equipment left European ports on 26 August 1982.[97] In direct violation of U.S. regulations, three fifty-seven-ton compressors left France at Le Havre en route to the Soviet Union.[98] The compressors had been built by Creusot-Loire and Dresser France. Four days later, a second shipment was sent from Glasgow, Scotland, carrying six turbines built by John Brown Engineering with General Electric parts.[99] Two turbines manufactured in Italy using GE rotors were shipped by Nuovo Pignone, a state-owned Italian company, on 4 September 1982.[100] And, on 1 October 1982, AEG-Kanis shipped two gas turbines built with American-originating parts and technology to the Soviet Union.[101]

In response, the United States carried out its threat. Under Secretary of Commerce Lionel Olmer invoked Section 11 of the Export Administration Act and Section 388.19 of the Export Administration regulations, placing these companies on a temporary denial list, forbidding access to all American goods, services, and technology, and subjecting them to a fine of $100,000. The U.S. imposed sanctions on Dresser-France on 27 August, Nuovo Pignone on 4 September, John Brown Engineering on 9 September, and AEG-Kanis on 5 October. By the end of October, Mannesmann had joined twelve European companies as a blacklisted violator of the embargo.[102] Of these companies, only Dresser-France was a wholly owned subsidiary of a U.S. corporation. The others were allegedly subject to sanctions because they were licensees of technology from U.S. corporations. The United States sanctioned Mannesmann because of the Department of Commerce's belief that it had entered into contracts for the delivery of gas turbine engines to the Soviet Union even though no such engines had actually been exported.

The temporary denial orders did the following:[103]

1. revoked all outstanding validated export licenses concerning U.S.-origin commodities or technical data for or relating to oil and gas exploration, production, transmission, or refinement in which the respondent or any related party agrees or participates;
2. prohibited the respondent as well as its successors, officers, etc., from participating directly or indirectly in any way in any transaction involving U.S. origin commodities or technical data for, or relating to, oil and gas exploration, etc.;
3. extended the denial of export privileges, not only to the respondent, but also to its agents and employees and to any successor company; and
4. prohibited any person or company without prior departmental authorization from participating in any export, reexport, transshipment, diversion, etc., or any gas-related commodity or technical data exported from the U.S. on behalf of or in association with any of the respondent companies.

At the request of Secretary of State George Shultz and Commerce Secretary Malcolm Baldrige, the secondary sanctions were narrower in range than initially intended, and were restricted to equipment, services, and technology directly related to oil and gas.[104] These minor adjustments did not moderate European anger or protest. Rather, as argued in a *New York Times* editorial on 1 September 1982, "incompetent American diplomacy. . . turned the disagreement into a battle over sovereignty that mocks the unity of the Atlantic alliance."[105]

End of the Pipeline Crisis

After five months of litigation, much public debate, and resistance by the allies, President Reagan rescinded that the December 1981 and June 1982 controls as of 13 November 1982.[106] The U.S. Government stated officially that the decision resulted from the fact that the U.S. and Western Europe had reached "substantial agreement" on a policy regarding East-West trade. The White House initially presented the agreement as a trade-off in which it agreed to lift the sanctions in exchange for European acceptance of a more restrictive trade policy towards the Soviet Union, especially with respect to credits. On 15 November, however, President Mitterrand challenged the U.S. interpretation of the agreement, stating that "France is not a party to what is *perhaps* not even an agreement."[107] Subsequently, the White House and State Department admitted that the pipeline sanctions were not mentioned during the recent trade negotiations, and that the lifting of the sanctions was a unilateral act by the president. This amounted to an awkward withdrawal from a misconceived and divisive policy. The British, French, and German governments remained defenders of the pipeline throughout the crisis. Despite U.S. enforcement actions, some firms, including Dresser France, continued to ship equipment and technology related to the pipeline to the Soviet Union.[108]

The volume of East-West trade did decline in the 1980s, but while the decline in U.S.-Soviet trade was politically motivated, the decline in European-Soviet trade was primarily the result of economic factors. A recession in the West led to an overall decrease in world trade by 2 percent in 1982, and the growing East-European debt to Western banks—combined with the failure of the Soviet Union to guarantee East European loans—made European investors wary.[109]

Despite all its efforts, the United States was unable to solicit sufficient European cooperation to terminate the construction of the trans-Siberian Pipeline. With only minor delays, and amidst great Soviet fanfare, natural gas began to flow through the trans-Siberian Pipeline on New Year's Day, 1984.

CONCLUSION

The United States largely failed to persuade, entice, or coerce foreign actors to comply with its trans-Siberian Pipeline embargo. Prominent scholars have argued that the inability of the United States to offer sufficient incentives to secure extraterritorial compliance with its policies was an indication of declining American leverage and prestige within the Western alliance.[110] U.S. influence was, however, not completely absent. Foreign dependence on access to American markets and the products and technology produced by its firms enabled the U.S. government to secure the compliance of certain actors across international borders. This case demonstrates that firms that were dependent on access to the American market or the supply of American components or technology during the trans-Siberian Pipeline crisis chose to abide by U.S. regulations, whereas those that were not dependent on the United States or were more dependent on others chose not to accept U.S. initiatives.

This case also supports the proposition that firms value access to markets more highly than supply of resources. Firms are often able to find or develop alternate sources of supply when access to needed items is restricted, but they often cannot find or create alternate markets for their goods. In the pipeline case, most of the restricted components could be reproduced outside of the United States. Conversely, the Soviet Union offered a market for goods that the United States did not provide. Consequently, restricting access to American suppliers and the American consumer market had a minimal effect on these particular firms.

Host government intervention is an intervening variable, mediating the effect of dependence on firm actions. If foreign governments support U.S. initiatives, they can greatly facilitate the application of sanctions and the general enforcement of U.S. restrictions over their constituents. If, however, foreign governments disagree with U.S. policy and the U.S. government is unable to entice or coerce them into enforcing its policies at home, then they may intervene on behalf of their local constituents against U.S. initiatives. In the event of intergovernmental conflicts of interest, host government reactions to U.S. policy can also be explained in terms of dependent relationships. In the Pipeline Case, the allies believed that they were dependent on energy imports and were particularly vulnerable to external oil suppliers. Diversification of energy sources to include Soviet natural gas was a means of minimizing this dependence. Pipeline construction guaranteed access to the Soviet gas fields. Furthermore, the pipeline stimulated depressed sectors of the economy by providing employment and export earnings. The United States did not offer a comparable energy alternative and could not compensate the countries involved for the loss of economic activity from the embargo. Furthermore, counter to American interpretations of the Soviet threat, European governments argued that the pipeline increased rather than decreased their security. Given this conflict of interest and a lack of viable leverage due to minimal European dependence on the U.S. in this issue area, the United States was not able to get its allies to do something they did not want to do.

Corporations must act within the legal limits prescribed by the countries in which they operate. As a result, initial corporate decisions to acquiesce to American pressure may be challenged by national legislation in host countries. At the same time, however, the compliance of Alsthom-Atlantique and other firms during the pipeline crisis despite de jure protection by their host governments demonstrate the de facto effect of sanctions and the corresponding ability of the U.S. government to control actors and resources across national boundaries.

Notes

1. For other examples of research that combines comparative case studies with statistical analysis, see Paul K. Huth, *Extended Deterrence and the Prevention of War* (New Haven, Conn.: Yale University Press, 1988), and Martin (1992).

2. See for example Abbott (1987); Jentleson (1986); and Kobrin (1989).

3. For a summary of the pipeline project, see Ed A. Hewett, "The Pipeline Connection: Issues for the Alliance," *The Brookings Review* (fall 1981): 15–20.

4. Other items covered by the embargo included high-technology exports, the suspension of negotiations on a long-term grain agreement, the suspension of negotiations on a new U.S.-Soviet Maritime Agreement, the suspension of Aeroflot flights to the United States, and the closing of the Soviet Purchasing commission. Martin (1992), p. 211.

5. Soviet Involvement in Poland, Statement on U.S. Measures Taken against the Soviet Union, December 29, 1981, 17 *Weekly Compilation of Presidential Documents 1429* (4 January 1982). See also Homer Moyer and Linda Mabry, *Export Controls as Instruments of Foreign Policy: The History, Legal Issues, and Policy Lessons of Three Recent Cases* (Washington, D.C.: University of America Press, 1983), p. 67.

6. 47 Federal Regulation 141 (1982). The preexisting regulations required a validated export license for exports relating to oil and gas exploration and production equipment and technology. See also Moyer and Mabry (1983), p. 67.

7. 47 Federal Regulation 27, 250.

8. Antony Blinken, *Ally Versus Ally: America, Europe, and the Siberian Pipeline Crisis* (New York: Praeger, 1987), p. 103.

9. Blinken (1987), p. 104.

10. "East-West Economic Issues: Questions and Answers," State Department Background Paper for Williamsburg Summit, (26 May 1983), Section IV, Question 1. See also Jentleson (1986), p. 194.

11. Jentleson (1986), p. 194.

12. Ibid.

13. See for example Abbott (1981), (1987); Bertsch (1983); Blinken (1987); Kenneth W. Abbott, "Linking Trade and Political Goals: Foreign Policy Export Controls in the 1970s and 1980s," *Minnesota Law Review* 65 (1981); Abbott (1987); Bertsch (1983); Blinken (1987); Lawrence Freedman, ed. *The Troubled Alliance: Atlantic Relations in the 1980s* (London: Heinemann, 1983); A. H. Herman, *Conflict of National Laws with International Business Activity: Issues of Extraterritoriality* (London: British-North American Committee, 1982); Bruce W. Jentleson, "From Consensus to Conflict: the Domestic Political Economy of East-West Energy Trade Policy," *International Organization* 38:4 (1984); Jentleson (1986); Kobrin (1989); Stephanie Lenway and Beverly Crawford, "When Business Becomes Politics: Risk and Uncertainty in East-West Trade," *Research in Corporate Social Performance and Policy: A Research Annual* 8 (1986); Martin (1992); Mastanduno (1985), (1992); Moyer and Mabry (1983); Neale and Stephens (1988); Olmstead (1984); Stanley Woods, *Atlantic Paper No. 63, Western Europe: Technology and the Future* (Paris: Croom Helm, 1987); and Stephen Woolcock, *Western Policies on East-West Trade,* Chatham House Papers, #15 (London: Royal Institute of International Affairs, 1982).

14. Martin (1992), p. 207; Jonathan Stern, *East European Energy and East-West Trade in Energy,* British Institutes' Joint Energy Policy Programme, Energy Paper Number 1 (London: Policy Studies Institute, 1982), p. 52; and Jentleson (1986), p. 186.

15. Blinken (1987), p. 49.

16. Of the European states, Great Britain, the Netherlands, and Norway produce enough gas domestically for their own consumption. In contrast, West Germany, France, Italy, and Austria import between 55 percent and 70 percent of their natural gas, about half of which is imported from non-OECD states. See Blinken (1987), p. 20.

17. Blinken (1987), p. 21.

18. The Soviets had decreased their export of natural gas to Europe during the winters of 1976–77 and 1978–79, but the reductions were justified by Soviet and East European demand for gas during particularly severe winters, and the reductions were within limits agreed to by the West. The Soviets did cut off oil to Yugoslavia in 1948, Israel in 1956, Albania in 1961, and China in 1962, but only in response to actions taken by these states. Moscow never instigated a conflict by cutting off energy supplies. See Blinken (1987), p. 53.

19. Blinken (1987), p. 54.

20. Jentleson (1986), pp. 37–40.

21. For a review of these offers, see Jentleson (1986), pp. 185–91.

22. Bernard Gwertzman, "NATO Allies Assail Soviets on Poland and Hint Reprisal," *New York Times* (12 January 1982), p. A2. See also Jentleson (1986), p. 192.

23. Jentleson (1986), p. 192.

24. *Newsweek* (28 December 1981), p. 19.

25. "Exerpts on Schmidt Interview on Key Issues," *New York Times* (3 January 1982), p. A14, and William Borders, "Common Market Cautions Moscow," *New York Times* (16 December 1981), p. A16. See also Moyer and Mabry (1983), p. 79.

26. Moyer and Mabry (1983), p. 80.

27. The regulations went into effect on 15 March 1982. The reductions were much smaller than the $425 million reduction proposed in February. *U.S. Export Weekly* (2 March 1982), p. 597; Martin (1992), p. 213; Moyer and Mabry (1983), p. 80.

28. "European Community Members Agree to Cut Imports from the Soviet Union," *U.S. Export Weekly* (BNA) No. 397 (2 May 1982), p. 597. See also Moyer and Mabry (1983), p. 80.

29. Denis Lacorne, "Giscard's and Mitterrand's East-West Policies," in Baldwin and Milner (1990), p. 129.

30. Soviet trade at this point accounted for only 1.14 percent of American trade, and only 4.14 percent of overall EEC trade. West Germany and France had the largest West European trade with the Soviet Union, yet it only accounted for 6.20 percent and 4.20 of their trade, and 2.90 and 1.58 percent of their GNP, respectively. Woolcock (1982); Bertsch (1983), p. 26; and Blinken (1987), pp. 91–92.

31. Office of Technology Assessment, *Technology and East-West Trade* (Washington D.C.: U.S. Government Printing Office, 1979), p. 63. See also Blinken (1987), p. 92.

32. Rita Dallas, "Britain Orders Firms to Defy Pipeline Ban," *Washington Post*, (3 August 1982), p. A11.

33. Pierre Hassner, "The View from Paris," in Lincoln Gordon, ed., *Eroding Empire* (Washington, D.C.: Brookings Institution, 1987), pp. 228–29.

34. Alexander Haig, *Caveat: Reagan, Realism, and Foreign Policy* (New York: Macmillan, 1984), p. 256; Martin (1992), pp. 213–14.

35. Haig (1984), p. 305; cited in Blinken (1987), p. 101.

36. Blinken (1987), p. 105.

37. Blinken (1987), p. 102. It is interesting to note that the Europeans and notably the French are asking the United States to perform a function often attributed to a "hegemon." In essence, it is asking the United States not to give up its hegemonic role.

38. Jonathan Carr, "Trade Sanctions Widen Gulf in Trans Atlantic Strategy," *Financial Times* (25 June 1982), Section I, p. 2, cited in Jentleson (1986), pp. 193–94.

39. *New York Times* (7 June 1982), p. D7.

40. Blinken (1987), p. 102.

41. Carr (25 June 1982), Section I, p. 2. See also Blinken (1987), p. 102.

42. Carr (25 June 1982), Section I, p. 2. See also Blinken (1987), p. 102.

43. Martin (1992), p. 209; Mastanduno (1985), (1992).

44. Martin (1992), p. 208.

45. *Mini-Micro Systems* (July 1984), p. 84.

46. Lenway and Crawford (1986). Numerous articles in the popular press cite the costs of U.S. export control policy for American firms. See, for example, Christian Tyler and Nancy Dunne, "The High-Tech Row That Split Washington," *Financial Times* (23 March 1984), Section I, p. 18.

47. Thomas Schelling emphasizes a link between credibility and bearing self-imposed costs. Thomas Schelling, *The Strategy of Conflict* (Cambridge: Harvard University Press, 1980), pp. 123–24. See also Martin (1992), p. 37.

48. De Mestra and Gruchalla-Wesierski (1990), p. 78; Lowenfeld (1983), p. 22.

49. World trade data are gathered from both the United Nations and the Organization for Economic Cooperation and Development broken down by Standard International Trade Classifications (SITC). SITC 678 (iron and steel tubes, pipes, etc.) is an aggregate indicator of wide-diameter pipe trade, and SITC 743 (pumps, turbines) is an aggregate indicator of compressors, turbines, and related equipment trade.

50. United Nations, *International Statistics Yearbook*, vol. 2 (New York: United Nations Publishing, 1983–86).

51. All data in this section are estimated using United Nations estimates of trade flow in a particular sector. United Nations, *International Statistics Yearbook*, vol. 2 (1983–86).

52. See for example Kobrin (1989) and Jentleson (1986).

53. Kobrin (1989), p. 47. This appropriate quote was also cited by Martin (1992), p. 225.

54. United Nations, *International Statistics Yearbook*, vol. 2 (1983–86).

55. Ibid.

56. March's basic force model does not place a low bound on relative distribution of resources and power in a particular relationship.

57. Jentleson (1986), pp. 184–85.

58. United Nations, *International Statistics Yearbook*, vol. 2 (1983–86).

59. Lacorne, in Baldwin and Milner (1990), p. 130; and Haig (1984), p. 305.

60. Mastanduno (1992), p. 45. Goods and technology for which demand is highly inelastic, and the costs of production is prohibitively high, at least in the short run, are considered "bottle-neck" items. Mastanduno (1992), p. 45; Wiles (1968), p. 462.

61. Lenway and Crawford (1986), p. 44.

62. Ibid.

63. As Michael Mastanduno has argued, the costs of designing alternatives to American components can be considerable, and numerous firms have found it impractical to do so. See Mastanduno, "CoCom and American Export Control Policy: The Experience of the Reagan Administration," in Baldwin and Milner (1990), pp. 208–209.

64. Blinken (1987), p. 97.

65. Ibid.

66. *Wall Street Journal* (23 July 1982), p. 16; Blinken (1987), p. 113.

67. Blinken (1987), p. 97.

68. Axel Krause, "Europeans Seek to Circumvent Pipeline Ban: Replacing Rotors Embargoed by Reagan Is Key Element," *International Herald Tribune* (26 July 1982), p. 1.

69. A second potential alternate supplier was available, but as is true with many alternate sources of supply, its products were inferior to the original. If a product superior to the original existed, it would most likely have been selected in the first place. Rolls Royce of Great Britain, for instance, produced rotors that could be used in the pipeline compression stations. Its rotors were, however, not well matched to the pipeline compressors. As a result, the transition to Rolls Royce rotors would have required that the turbines be redesigned and several current contractors would have to be replaced.

70. Martin (1992), p. 219.

71. Steven Rattner, "Brown Engineering: Pipeline Stakes Big for British Concern," *New York Times* (20 August 1982), p. D4, and "Compressors Leave LeHavre for Soviet," *New York Times* (27 August 1982), p. D1.

72. Joseph E. Pattison, "Extraterritorial Enforcement of the Export Administration Act," in Michael R. Czinkota, ed., *Export Controls: Building Reasonable Commercial Ties with Political Adversaries* (New York: Praeger, 1984), p. 90.

73. Stanley D. Nollen, "The Case of John Brown Engineering and the Soviet Gas Pipeline," in Czinkota (1984), p. 113.

74. John Brown Engineering Ltd., "Press Release," (13 October 1981), cited in Nollen, in Czinkota (1984), p. 117.

75. Ibid.

76. Nollen, in Czinkota (1984), pp. 111–140.

77. Unlike standard international business contracts, those related to the pipeline did not contain a *force majeure* clause. This clause absolves the supplier from delivery in the event of unforeseen or unavoidable circumstances. The removal of this clause from the contracts obligated the firms that abided by the American embargo to pay a substantial penalty for failing to deliver the goods.

78. Nollen, in Czinkota (1984), p. 127.

79. Ibid., p. 127–28.

80. Ibid., pp. 128–31.

81. Ibid., p. 114.

82. John Brown Engineering Ltd., "Press Release," (13 October 1981), cited in Nollen, in Czinkota (1984), p. 117.

83. Martin (1992), p. 222.

84. Moyer and Mabry (1983), pp. 72–73.

85. Motion for Temporary Restraining Order, *Dresser Industries v. Baldridge*, No. 82-2385, at 20–24 (D.D.C., filed 23 August 1982).

86. For further discussion of the legal proceedings see Arthur Appleton, "Dresser Industries: The Failure of Foreign Policy Trade Controls under the Export Administration Act," *Maryland Journal of International Law* 8, 1 (1984), pp. 122–43.

87. The Reagan administration offered American coal and Norwegian natural gas as an alternative to Soviet natural gas. Both options contained political complications, and neither provided an efficient alternative to Soviet natural gas. See Jentleson (1986), pp. 185–90.

88. "European Protests Reagan Sanctions on Pipeline Sales," *New York Times* (13 August 1982), p. A1. Test of the European message is reprinted in the same article. See also *International Legal Materials* 21 (1982), p. 891. For a comparison to European reactions to American efforts to embargo pipeline equipment in 1962, see "U.S. Efforts to Block Soviet Gas Pipeline Recalls Failed Embargo of 20 Years Ago," *Wall Street Journal* (14 July 1982).

89. Blinken (1987), p. 105.

90. John Tagliabne, "Europe Protests Reagan Sanctions on Pipeline Sales," *International Herald Tribune* (13 August 1982), p. A21.

91. Jentleson (1986), p. 194.

92. Felix Kessler, "France Disavows Allied Accord on Trade Cited by Reagan in Lifting Pipeline Ban," *Wall Street Journal* (15 November 1982), p. 14.

93. Ernest Halsendolph, "U.S. May Narrow Focus on Sanctions," *New York Times* (31 July 1982) Section I, p. 35.

94. "Rees Steps up Pressure for U.S. Policy Changes," *Financial Times* (30 June 1982), Section I, p. 7, cited in Blinken (1986), p. 105. *The Economist* (26 June

1982), pp. 52–53; *Newsweek* (2 August 1982), p. 27; *New York Times* (2 July 1982), pp. A1, A4.

95. These companies included John Brown Engineering, Ltd., Smith International Ltd., Baker Oil Tools Ltd., and AAF Ltd.

96. The French Government could not rely on its 1980 blocking statute because it was only applicable as a "discovery blocking statute." Olmstead (1984), p. 64.

97. "Compressors Leave LeHavre for Soviet Union" *New York Times* (27 August 1982), p. D1, col. 3.

98. Ibid.

99. Michael Blumstein, "Stable Dresser's Rocky Year." *New York Times* (1 September 1982), p. D1.

100. *The Washington Post* (5 September 1982), p. A1, (8 September 1982), p. A4.

101. Paul Lewis, "Sanctions Hurting France: Dresser Order Shifted to GE," *New York Times* (2 October 1982), Section I, p. 40.

102. Office of Technology Assessment (1983), p. 31; *New York Times* (13 August 1982), p. 37. See also Blinken (1987), p. 107; and Jentleson (1986), pp. 195–96.

103. Olmstead (1984), p. 51.

104. Jentleson (1986), p. 196.

105. "Pipeline Machismo," *New York Times* (1 September 1982), p. A22, cited in Jentleson (1986), p. 196.

106. Twin bills were introduced in the House and Senate on 22 July and 13 August, respectively, to repeal the 30 December 1981 and 22 June 1982 regulations against the Soviet Union. The House bill was narrowly defeated—206 to 203—on 29 September, and the Senate had not yet acted on its bill before the president rescinded the regulations on 13 November 1982. *Weekly Compilation of Presidential Documents* (13 November 1982), pp. 1475–76. 47 Fed. Reg. 51,858 (1982).

107. Olmstead (1984), p. 52. See also Kessler, (15 November 1982), p. 14.

108. See Moyer and Mabry (1983), p. 72.

109. The Soviet debt to the West was about $10.2 billion in 1982, while the East Bloc owed over four times as much—approximately $48 billion.

110. Jentleson (1986), pp. 228–33, see also Kobrin (1989).

4

Tethering Technology:
Operation Exodus, the IBM Letter, and Beyond

INTRODUCTION

Beginning in 1981, just prior to the eruption of the trans-Siberian Pipeline crisis, the Reagan administration tried to reinvigorate existing export controls on high-technology goods and information. To accomplish this objective, the Reagan administration increased its unilateral monitoring and enforcement of export restrictions through a program called Operation Exodus, while simultaneously spearheading a drive in CoCom to increase multilateral monitoring and enforcement of high-technology export controls. The Reagan administration used persuasion, diplomacy, and economic statecraft to convince foreign governments and firms to conform to its policies. When foreign governments supported the desired export restrictions, the U.S. government used secondary sanctions to supplement their local enforcement efforts against noncompliant firms. As in the trans-Siberian Pipeline Case, when intergovernmental interests diverged, the U.S. tried to persuade, entice, or coerce CoCom or non-CoCom governments to enforce export controls locally. When this failed, it used secondary sanctions to compel foreign firms and individuals to comply with its policies despite the lack of support by local governments.

A general consensus of CoCom member governments on the need to restrict the sale of a limited number of high technology strategic goods reduced the intensity of intergovernmental conflict regarding the de jure basis of U.S. authority over foreign actors relative to the trans-Siberian Pipeline crisis. This limited consensus did not, however, extend to corporate and individual actors who produced and sold restricted goods, and it did not minimize the importance of extraterritorial sanctions in securing their compliance in cases where the local government either lacked the means or the will to enforce multilateral export controls domestically. Furthermore, the U.S. government maintained and promoted controls on a much broader range of goods and technology than other CoCom members and the companies operating within their borders were willing to accept.[1] As was the case during the trans-Siberian Pipeline crisis, when sufficient compliance was not forthcoming, the U.S. government used economic incentives and sanctions to secure extraterritorial compliance with its policies. Indeed, the scope and domain of the de facto control that sanctions gave the U.S. government over dependent firms and individuals operating abroad was much broader during Operation Exodus than it had been during the trans-Siberian Pipeline crisis.

This chapter covers the period from the start of Operation Exodus in 1981 through January 1988, at which point the United States agreed to reduce multilateral export control restrictions within CoCom and to relax its efforts to restrict the movement of goods and technologies to and from other Western countries.[2] (Current high-technology controls are discussed in chapter 5.) In contrast to the pipeline embargo, the extraterritorial enforcement of high-technology controls during the 1980s may be cited as an example of successful American influence within the Western alliance. As in the previous chapter, however, before making such a judgment, it is necessary to analyze the events systematically in terms of the goals the United States sought to accomplish, who it sought to influence, and what actions it wanted the targeted actors to take. Even though the secondary sanctions were largely successful, there was more success (and failure) with some actors than others. Despite persistent protests, foreign firms that were highly dependent on access to American markets or the supply of technology from its firms often altered their behavior as a direct result of U.S. actions. Those that did not bore the brunt of American sanctions and, in some cases, were driven out of business as a result. In several instances, national governments that concurred with U.S. policy relied on the threat of U.S. sanctions to enforce the policy locally. At the same time, national governments that either disagreed with U.S. policy or were not members of CoCom (and therefore not obligated to comply with it) tended to change their behavior in response to sanctions when they were dependent on the American suppliers or markets. American influence was, however, not absolute. When firms or states disagreed with U.S. policy and were either not dependent on its suppliers or markets or it was dependent on them, the United States was not able to use sanctions to secure compliance with its export control policies.

This chapter contains four parts. The next section provides a synopsis of Operation Exodus and other technology controls in historical context. It identifies the goals of U.S. policy, its primary targets, and its primary mechanisms for securing compliance, and offers predictions of the American government's ability to secure extraterritorial compliance based on the hypotheses presented below. The next section evaluates these predictions based on decisions made and actions taken by various firms and CoCom member governments in the computer and telecommunications industries during the 1980s. This is followed by an analysis of U.S. efforts to secure the compliance of non-CoCom members, or "Third Countries," with export restrictions. These cases demonstrate that sanctions can be used to secure the compliance of states and firms regardless of membership in CoCom.

OPERATION EXODUS AND U.S. EXPORT CONTROL POLICY

The resurgence of U.S. and multilateral efforts to secure compliance with export controls on strategic goods and technology evolved through several stages.[3] The seeds of the 1980s debate regarding the need to reestablish a more restrictive and better enforced export control policy were planted domestically by a 1976 report from the Defense Science Board.[4] The so-called Bucy Report argued for tighter national security controls particularly on "design and manufacturing know-how," with a focus on "active" technology transfer mechanisms like the building of factories overseas, licensing agreements accompanied by extensive teaching or instruction, and joint ventures.[5] One of the most significant aspects of the Bucy Report was its recommendation to expand export controls on high technology trade between the United States and other Western nations. The Bucy Report argued that CoCom members often maintained lax controls, and that such practices undermined the American lead in a variety of crucial technologies. Furthermore, the Bucy Report recommended that the United States government protect its strategic technology by restricting access to it by any CoCom member that had allowed restricted items to be passed on to targeted countries.[6]

The issues raised in this report bolstered the Reagan administration's arguments that export controls were a vital element of its defensive military build-up against the Soviet Union from 1981 to 1988. The development and military application of advanced American technology were key components of this defensive military buildup. It followed that tightening control over the movements of strategically "sensitive" products at home and abroad was necessary to guarantee continued American superiority in advanced technologies.

The U.S. government implemented this policy through domestic legislation, multilateral negotiations, and unilateral policing and enforcement on a global scale. With the support of the Defense Department, "Operation Exodus" was established under the Customs Service of the Treasury Department in 1981. The new program provided increased financial and human resources for the export control division of the Customs Service. It began with a budget of $30 million and a complement of four hundred new customs agents assigned to foreign offices in trading centers including London, Paris, Bonn, Rome, Tokyo, Hong Kong, and Singapore.[7]

Goals of American High-Technology Controls

The primary objective of U.S. export control policy is to prevent strategically sensitive technology and products from being diverted to potentially threatening countries. The declared goal of Operation Exodus was to interdict the flow of technology to the Soviet Union and other targeted countries by cracking down on illegal shipments of technology. Operation Exodus concentrated its efforts on exports of microelectronic systems and computers, telecommunications equipment, lasers, weapons guidance equipment, and the products and knowledge that made the production of these goods possible. As one observer noted, "[t]he program was designed to make Customs agents as vigilant at stopping high-tech smuggling as they traditionally have been at halting drug imports."[8]

Targets

The targets of Operation Exodus included any actor who could provide the goods or technology restricted by U.S. export control regulations. The broad domain of these targets was highlighted in the early 1980s by intelligence reports of an expansive and growing Soviet effort to obtain strategic Western technology from a long list of specific Western countries, companies, and individuals.[9]

This chapter analyzes U.S. efforts to persuade, entice, and coerce CoCom and non-CoCom members to increase their local monitoring and enforcement of American and multilateral export controls. With or without intergovernmental cooperation, however, the primary focus of U.S. sanctions was on securing the compliance of firms operating abroad that possessed or could produce the restricted goods. Consequently, this chapter focuses on U.S. efforts to secure the compliance of seven computer and telecommunications firms that were involved in public disputes regarding U.S. export control policy. These firms include International Computers Limited (ICL), Plasma, and Systime PLC of the UK; the Thomson Group of France; Datasaab and LM Ericsson of Sweden; and Toshiba of Japan. The actions of each firm are analyzed based on trade patterns reflecting U.S. trade dominance and its dependence on U.S. markets and suppliers in each industry.[10] Where possible, the interests and actions of particular firms are analyzed.[11]

When evaluating sector-level data, it is important to recognize that each of these industries is strongly integrated with the others. Changes in technology and national regulatory policy have dramatically diffused what had previously been considered distinct industries. For instance, while the "telecommunications industry" is still used pervasively as a convenient label, telecommunications equipment is composed of a myriad of sophisticated computer and electronic components.[12] This means that attention must be given to trade and potential dependence among actors across different industrial sectors. The use of advanced computer technology in the telecommunications industry has increased the potential dependence of actors in this industry on those in the computer industry. Similarly, as discussed below, dependence on American and Japanese semiconductors and computer chips has made the European computer industry vulnerable to the threat of foreign sanctions in these industries, despite massive long-term government efforts to build competitive European "champions" in the computer industry.

Means of Enforcement

Throughout the 1980s, the American government tried to persuade CoCom and non-CoCom governments to enforce export control restrictions locally against noncompliant firms. After extended negotiations, CoCom members reached a general consensus on the need to increase the effectiveness of restrictions on certain "high priority items" containing "critical" technology.[13] These included strategic materials, optics, sensors, floating docks, spacecraft, space launch vehicles, and some computers and telecommunications equipment.[14] The consensus on export restrictions was not, however, absolute. As Beverly Crawford argues, despite agreement on the need to increase local enforcement of these controls, European firms and their host country governments continued to challenge U.S. restrictions on a variety of "critical" technologies, particularly computer and telecommunications equipment that had commercial as well as potential military uses.[15] More importantly, as argued above, while intergovernmental cooperation diminished the likelihood of confrontations regarding conflicts of jurisdiction and facilitated U.S. enforcement efforts, it was neither always necessary nor sufficient to guarantee corporate compliance.

The United States has three primary means of securing the participation of foreign governments and firms in its policies. First, it can persuade others that its high-technology controls are an appropriate and necessary response to a current enemy's military build-up and espionage efforts. Second, it can try to prevent violations through early detection efforts and by closely reviewing license applications. Finally, if these efforts fail, it can use economic sanctions and incentives to enforce its policies abroad.

Persuasion and a limited multilateral consensus. The United States has continuously tried to secure multilateral cooperation in restricting the export of high-technology goods. In 1979, the U.S. Department of Defense urged CoCom members to adopt its newly established "military-critical technologies list." The list included technologies that could improve existing military or weapons systems, contribute to their development, or transform existing nonthreatening systems into military or weapons systems.[16] Disagreements over the nature of the threat and the scope of the embargo lists led to a formal list review beginning in 1982. The most contentious issues involved the control of computers, telecommunications equipment, and related technology for which the United States argued for more comprehensive controls than its CoCom partners were willing to accept.[17] On 15 July 1984, after over two years of heated negotiations, the United States and CoCom reached a compromise: they agreed to place new export controls on the sale of small computers, computer software, sophisticated telephone equipment, industrial robots, printed circuits, electronic-grade silicon, spacecraft equipment, and other high-technology items considered useful to the Soviet defense effort.[18]

Part of the American success in negotiating a new and more stringent set of multilateral controls can be attributed to the common perception of a threat resulting from Soviet espionage efforts resulting from the French release of information regarding the "Farewell Affair." At the Ottawa summit in July 1981, Mitterand provided the Reagan administration with numerous documents obtained by French intelligence services from a high-ranking KGB agent. The disclosure of the "Farewell Affair" led to a detailed reconsideration of Soviet military needs and espionage efforts, as well as the arrest and expulsion of numerous Soviet agents and business executives accused of industrial spying. The Farewell documents, obtained by French counterintelligence between 1972 and 1982, consist of a set of secret internal reports on the whole range of Soviet technical espionage in the West.[19] The Farewell documents provided a window into the organization and depth of Soviet technological espionage between 1978 and 1980, which proved to be more extensive than had ever been available. The documents included charts showing the fulfillment of tasks in the area of rocket and space technology, a detailed list of collection tasks for 1981 through 1985, and a list of the Western companies that produced the desired items.

The documents also specified several aims of the KGB-Directorate T (the technology division), including "[t]imely identification of military/technical plans of the U.S., the other NATO countries, Japan, and China with respect to preparing a possible nuclear attack on the Soviet Union and the countries of the socialist community," and "identification of any breakthroughs in U.S., capitalist countries and China in the military field."[20] Another goal of Directorate T was to promote the "[a]cceleration of Soviet scientific and technical progress by acquiring information and samples of equipment" from the West.[21]

The Farewell Affair provided dramatic evidence of a common threat to the West resulting from Soviet espionage, and served as a catalyst for CoCom efforts to revise high-technology restrictions. However, this "threat" was not sufficient to secure the cooperation of CoCom members states with all of the American export control initiatives. Variation in French and British reactions to these initiatives vividly demonstrate that policy makers viewed external threats in different ways, often on a case-by-case basis. Scholars who emphasize the role of U.S. leadership in CoCom negotiations and the importance of consensus in promoting the CoCom list review are correct and can explain the success behind the 1984 CoCom negotiations, but these arguments cannot explain variations in the resulting enforcement actions within and across various issue areas and between CoCom member countries.[22]

Implementation of the new CoCom agreement on high-technology controls required domestic action on the part of each member country. In France, disclosure of the Farewell documents led to the immediate expulsion of forty-seven Soviet diplomats and renewed interest in the French export control policy. On the domestic front, in October 1981, the prime minister signed a classified directive enhancing the export licensing process and establishing a permanent dialogue between customs, SGDN, and the ministries of finance, industry, foreign affairs, and defense regarding export controls.[23] In 1987, the French government implemented a final set of improvements placing the SGDN in charge of coordinating the export control procedures of "hard-core" technologies, arms sales, and the export of nuclear products and technology.[24] Internationally, France became a key European supporter of the controversial U.S.-inspired creation of a military arm in CoCom, the Security and Technology Experts Meetings group (STEM), designed to give a military assessment of high-technology sales to the East. French officials also attempted to convince other CoCom members to adopt more stringent controls over hard-core technologies.

At the same time, however, despite both international and domestic pressures, French policy towards the Soviet Union varied dramatically across different issues. For example, French President Mitterand's uncompromising, pro-American position on certain high-technology computer controls (and the INF deployment), contrasted significantly with his refusal to impose sanctions on the Soviet Union after the imposition of martial law in Poland, his promoting of an unprecedented gas import agreement with the Soviet Union in 1982, and his defense of the export of high-technology telecommunications equipment to the East despite the fact that the export of all large telecommunications switches and technology used in the development of switching technology was banned by CoCom.[25] (This case is discussed in the telecommunications section below.)

Similarly, the United Kingdom was the first CoCom member country to publish a revised list of what technology its companies could and could not export to the East Bloc and other restricted countries. By 1984, the British list reflected the new CoCom agreement to expand controls on high-speed computers, software, and telecommunications equipment. British actions taken in the ICL, Systime, and Brian Butcher cases (discussed below) demonstrated its willingness to comply with the export restrictions. However, it is important to note that British compliance in the computer sector took place at the same time that it adamantly rejected American demands regarding the trans-Siberian pipeline embargo. The "threat" from the Soviet Union in the computers and telecommunications industries did not alter British behavior in other high-technology or strategic sectors, such as the production, transportation, and use of Soviet natural gas.

Tensions between the United States and its European allies became apparent almost immediately following the July 1984 agreement to control certain high-technology goods. The Europeans were particularly sensitive to American efforts to impose independent restrictions that were more stringent than those agreed to in CoCom. They expressed concern about the effect of the more stringent controls on small local firms that were dependent on access to the Eastern market. In particular, they objected very publicly to the "IBM letter" (discussed below) and what they considered unilateral American attempts to manipulate and control U.S. technology after it had left the United States.[26]

As in the trans-Siberian Pipeline Case, when sufficient cooperation from CoCom or non-CoCom governments was not forthcoming, or when cooperative foreign governments lacked the will or the means to enforce export controls locally, the U.S. government targeted its sanctions against negligent foreign firms. If local governments wanted to comply with U.S. or multilateral export controls but were unwilling or unable to enforce them, the threat of U.S. sanctions could be used to bolster local enforcement efforts. At the same time, if local governments opposed the extraterritorial application of U.S. regulations, the sanctions provided a means of threatening or rewarding foreign firms without the support of the local government. As discussed earlier, the backbone of American threats against firms operating abroad involves the possibility of placing these noncooperative firms on denial lists such as the Economic Defense List (also known as the Gray List) and "Atlas" (also known as the Black List). Being placed on the denial lists could effectively terminate access to all American suppliers and the American market by making it illegal for an American company to conduct business with any blacklisted firm. These lists provide an effective means of exploiting the U.S. trade dominance and foreign dependence on American suppliers or access to American markets in high-technology industries. The remainder of this chapter examines the use and effectiveness of these sanctions.

Aggregate Predictions of U.S. Influence

The dominance and dependence arguments specified in chapter 1 can be used to make predictions about the likely success of American sanctions. Table 4.1 lists the trade dominance of U.S. suppliers and U.S. markets in the computer, telecommunications, and electronics industries during Operation Exodus. It also lists sector level estimates of foreign dependence on U.S. suppliers and U.S. markets as a function of the proportion of the Target's trade accounted for by the United States and the availability of alternate trading partners. Based on the degree of U.S. dominance in each industry, one would expect that threats to cut off access to American suppliers would be more likely to succeed in the computer and electronics sectors and less likely in the telecommunications sector, while the threats to cut off access to American markets would succeed in all three.

Based on the degree of foreign dependence in each sector, one would predict that threats to cut off access to American suppliers would be more effective than threats to cut off access to American markets, and that threats involving access to American suppliers would be most likely to succeed in the computer and electronics industry, and least likely to succeed in the telecommunications industry.

CASE ANALYSES: U.S. INFLUENCE IN THE COMPUTER INDUSTRY

This section analyzes American efforts to control the activities of actors operating abroad in the computer industry. It focuses, in particular, on corporate actions in 1984 at the height of Operation Exodus, following both the CoCom agreement and increased unilateral action by the United States through the "IBM letter." These cases highlight the unique characteristics, trade patterns, and concerns of individual corporations that form the link between dominance, dependence and the ability of the U.S. government to secure corporate compliance using economic sanctions.

Dominance and Dependence in the Computer Industry

The United States dominated the computer industry in the mid-1980s to an even greater degree than it does today. In 1984, at the peak

Table 4.1 Dominance and Dependence in the Computer, Telecommunications, and Electronics Industries

CASE	YEAR	DOMINANCE OF U.S. SUPPLIERS	DOMINANCE OF U.S. MARKETS	FOREIGN DEPENDENCE ON U.S. SUPPLIERS	FOREIGN DEPENDENCE ON U.S. MARKETS
United Kingdom (S) *ICL, Systime*—Computer Industry	1982	36.4% (World's Largest)	6.46%	0.176	0.002
Sweden (S) *Datasaab*—Computer Industry	1984	29.9% (World's Largest)	14.6% (World's Largest)	0.125	0.069
United Kingdom (S) *Plasma*—Computer Industry	1985	28.4% (World's Largest)	15.0% (World's Largest)	0.097	0.013
Japan (F) *Toshiba*—Computer Industry	1987	22.8% (World's Largest)	16.4% (World's Largest)	0.185	0.063
Norway (F) *Konigsberg*—Compressor Industry	1987	22.8% (World's Largest)	16.4% (World's Largest)	0.067	0.002
France (F) *Thomson*—Telecom Industry	1983	16.6% (World's Largest)	27.5% (World's Largest)	0.024	0.009
Sweden (S) *IM Ericsson*—Telecom Industry	1984	15.8% (World's Largest)	33.3% (World's Largest)	0.007	0.036
Sweden (S) *ASEA*—Electronics Industry	1985	22.6% (World's Largest)	25.6% (World's Largest)	0.094	NA

Source: United Nations, *International Trade Statistics Yearbook*, vol. 2 (New York: United Nations Publishing, 1984–89). Using SITC 752 for the computer industry, SITC 764 for the telecommunications industry, and SITC 776 for the electronics industry.

(S) = Successful Sanctions
(F) = Failed Sanctions

of Operation Exodus, it was both the world's largest supplier and market of computer equipment, accounting for 29.9 percent of world exports and 14.6 percent of world imports in computers and related products.[27] At that time, all of the top ten world importers of computer products (excluding the United States itself) relied on the United States for 30 percent or more of their supplies, and four of the top ten non-American exporters of computer components (including Japan, Canada, and Singapore) relied on the American consumer market for 20 percent or more of their sales.[28] Furthermore, of the ten largest exporters of computer products, only the United States and Japan maintained positive trade balances and were net exporters of computer goods from 1981 through 1985.[29] The trade dominance argument suggests that the dominant position of American suppliers and markets in this sector should have enabled the United States government to secure the compliance of foreign actors in the computer industry.

The trade dependence argument largely supports these predictions. While U.S. markets accounted for only 3.23 percent of British computer exports in 1982 during the International Computer Limited case and 38.4 percent of Japanese computer exports in 1987 during the Toshiba case, U.S. suppliers accounted for 48.4 percent of British and 81.3 percent of Japanese imports, respectively.[30] At the same time, given U.S. dominance in this sector, fewer alternate suppliers are available than alternate markets. The implications of these data become clear when they are combined into the dependence indicators. While foreign dependence on U.S. markets is minimal (largely due to the local dominance of U.S. suppliers), foreign dependence on U.S. suppliers is higher. The dependence indicators presented in table 4.1 thus also suggest that threatening to cut off access to American suppliers would have a greater impact on firms that threaten to cut off access to American markets.

Dependence in the European computer and semiconductor industries. The structure of the British and French computer and semiconductor industry made them particularly vulnerable to American threats and promises. Beginning in the 1960s, both governments promoted the development of domestic computer industries by supporting national champions that were intended to compete against American leaders in the industry.[31] For example, French support of national champions was a direct response to U.S. efforts to exploit French dependence on U.S. computers in order to control the French development of its nuclear *force de frappe* (see chapter 5). The United States tried to compel France to alter its nuclear policy by forbidding IBM and Control Data to export high performance computers to the French *Commissariat a L'energie Atomique.*[32] In addition to other political and economic repercussions, this sanction infuriated the French

government and created a strong incentive to minimize French dependence on American technology. As argued at the time, creating national champions was important "not merely in France, but throughout
Western Europe. . . . [it is] unwise to become over-dependent on [a
limited number of suppliers] for the supply of any advanced technological equipment."[33]

Significantly, however, European efforts to bolster the domestic computer industry were not extended into the semiconductor industry. As a
result, Europe became the world's largest importer of computer components, with the United Kingdom alone accounting for 22 percent of world
imports of digital central processors at the peak of Operation Exodus in
1984.[34] The most important component for the computer and telecommunications industries is the integrated circuit, yet less than one third of
integrated circuits used by European industry and consumers were produced by European suppliers. In 1984, for example, European firms obtained 62 percent of their supplies from American producers and 8 percent
from the Japanese.[35] In this case, few alternate suppliers were available,
with the top five accounting for 66 percent of world markets and 81
percent of world suppliers in 1984.[36]

The British computer industry was dominated by foreign suppliers as
well.[37] American suppliers alone maintained a British market share of 50
to 53 percent throughout Operation Exodus.[38] Furthermore, American
manufacturers supplied an additional 25 percent of the market from British
and European subsidiaries. The leading British computer company at the
time, International Computers Limited, had domestic sales amounting to
$2.3 million in 1983, most of which contained components from Ameri-
can suppliers. During the same year, imports from American companies
amounted to $1,170 million worth of sales in the UK.[39] IBM, DEC,
Burroughs, and Honeywell account for 51 percent of all computers in-
stalled.[40] The British computer industry was also becoming increasingly
dependent on Japanese suppliers, one of whom recently purchased ICL.[41]

In addition to its dependence on American and Japanese suppliers,
the British computer industry was also dependent on access to foreign
markets. Over 60 percent of Great Britain's domestic computer production
was intended for export.[42] Its largest domestic firm at the time, ICL, tried
to increase its presence in European and American markets throughout the
1980s by selling peripheral parts and computer subassemblies.[43] Again,
however, most of these products, however, contained components made by
American firms and were therefore subject to American export controls.

British dependence on American components has important implications for arguments that relying on one's "own" local companies as
suppliers can protect a country from foreign competition and foreign
control. Despite the political appeal of such arguments, as Theodore Moran

has argued, "having one's own companies provides no protection against foreign manipulation when monopoly or oligopoly concentration in the upstream industry allows foreign governments to dictate how the firms must operate."[44] The dominance of the U.S. semiconductor industry combined with the high concentration of suppliers in the United States and Japan, meant that European computer producers were dependent on upstream U.S. (and Japanese) suppliers in those industries. This meant that sanctions involving access to these suppliers could provide the U.S. or Japanese governments with a source of leverage over European computer firms.

It is interesting that in 1984 the United Kingdom was the world's second largest exporter of digital central processors. At first glance, this may appear to indicate that the United Kingdom was not necessarily dependent on the United States and that it might be able to take advantage of its dominant position in that part of the computer industry. In actuality, however, a large proportion of these exports were goods that were purchased elsewhere, especially from the United States and Japan, and re-exported to third parties. Thus the fact that the United Kingdom provided 18 percent of the world's exports of digital central processors may have increased rather than decreased its vulnerability to American sanctions.[45]

It is also interesting to note that as of 1984, largely due to the dominance of American firms, the United States accounted for only 14.6 percent of world imports of computer products (SITC 752), and was not among the top ten importers of digital central processing units.[46] This indicates that while promising access to American consumer markets may serve as a carrot to foreign firms, the threat to cut off access would have little effect. American reliance on foreign suppliers of computer products has increased steadily during the early 1980s. By 1987, during the Toshiba affair, the United States was the world's fourth largest importer of CPUs.

The U.S. government responded to the increasing dominance of Japanese firms in the memory chip market through two strategies. First, it created a new domestic consortium, like Sematech, to replicate Japanese patterns of industrial collaboration. Second, it negotiated the 1986 U.S.-Japanese semiconductor agreement to control Japanese dumping and secure a promise that twenty percent of the Japanese market would be open to foreigners.[47] The Europeans responded to the U.S.-Japanese agreement by challenging some aspects of the 1986 agreement in the GATT, by negotiating an E.C.-Japan antidumping pact, and by increasing funding for E.C.-sponsored programs like Esprit and RACE to support the expansion of European semiconductor firms.

While these governmental programs and intergovernmental agreements were intended to bolster domestic industries relative to foreign competition, their success has been limited. For example, despite continued financial assistance, Groupe Bull of France was one of the few European computer companies that sold widely outside of its home country, and even required financial assistance from the French government (Ffr 2.5 billion in 1995) to stay afloat against outside competition.[48] Furthermore, these domestic assistance programs may actually have helped foreign competitors who gained access to them through transnational corporate alliances, like the production alliance between the dominant European firm Siemens, IBM, and Toshiba. The rise of collaborative alliances has had several critical implications for the European computer and semiconductor industries. First, interfirm alliances between European, Japanese, and American companies have given U.S. and Japanese firms access to the pan-European research programs and funds. This undercut the advantage such funding would give to European firms and it helped U.S. and Japanese firms maintain their dominant positions in the industry. Second, increased collaboration between Japanese and American firms increased their combined ability to exploit continued European dependence on their products and technology by eliminating themselves as potential alternate suppliers for each other.

In sum, imports from American suppliers accounted for a large proportion of computer trade throughout Europe and Japan during the peak of Operation Exodus.[49] The rise of Japanese suppliers in the semiconductor and memory chip markets in the late 1980s led to a flurry of intergovernmental efforts to bolster domestic industries and a dramatic rise in inter-firm alliances. The rise of these alliances enabled U.S. and

Table 4.2 Top Ten World Consumers and Producers of Automatic Data Processing Peripheral Units in 1984, SITC 7525

CONSUMERS	TOTAL, $M	%	PRODUCERS	TOTAL, $M	%
World Economy	10,424,749	100	World Economy	12,111,063	100
Europe	6,490,316	62	Europe	4,424,739	37
United Kingdom	1,820,738	17	Japan	3,686,171	30
Canada	1,495,995	14	United States	3,319,640	27
Fed. Rep. Germany	1,345,583	13	Fed. Rep. Germany	1,143,970	9
France	1,084,072	10	United Kingdom	897,821	7
Italy	768,965	7	Italy	778,963	6
Netherlands	604,923	6	Netherlands	508,613	4
Australia	400,802	4	France	441,823	4
Japan	398,043	4	Singapore	278,009	2
Belgium-Lux.	354,481	3	Hong Kong	216,047	2
Spain	270,245	3	Belgium-Lux.	109,717	1

Source: United Nations, *International Trade Statistics Yearbook,* vol. 2 (New York: United Nations Publishing, 1986).

Table 4.3   Top Ten World Consumers and Producers of Digital Central Processors in 1984, SITC 7523

CONSUMERS	TOTAL, $M	%	PRODUCERS	TOTAL, $M	%
World Economy	4,366,032	100	World Economy	4,364,267	100
Europe	3,016,003	69	Europe	2,085,497	48
United Kingdom	961,960	22	United States	1,739,839	40
Fed. Rep. Germany	710,781	16	United Kingdom	799,961	18
Japan	435,898	10	France	358,645	8
France	431,313	10	Fed. Rep. Germany	325,435	7
Italy	329,191	8	Japan	284,375	7
Netherlands	193,787	4	Spain	250,114	6
Spain	137,512	3	Ireland	127,443	3
Belgium-Lux.	136,839	3	Belgium-Lux.	106,886	2
Australia	108,831	2	Hong Kong	101,921	2
S. African Rep.	93,118	2	Brazil	78,689	2

Source: United Nations, *International Trade Statistics Yearbook,* vol. 2 (New York: United Nations Publishing, 1986).

Table 4.4   Leading World Computer Equipment Producers during Operation Exodus

(CURRENT $ BILLION)

1981		1985	
FIRM	REVENUE	FIRM	REVENUE
IBM (U.S.)	$24.48	IBM (U.S.)	$50.06
DEC (U.S.)	3.59	DEC (U.S.)	7.03
NCR (U.S.)	3.07	Sperry (U.S.)	4.76
CDC (U.S.)	2.89	Burroughs (U.S.)	4.69
Sperry (U.S.)	2.78	Fujitsu (Japan)	4.31
Burroughs (U.S.)	2.67	NCR Corp. (U.S.)	3.89
Fujitsu (Japan)	2.03	NEC (Japan)	3.76
Honeywell (U.S.)	1.77	Control Data (U.S.)	3.68
Hewlett-Packard (U.S.)	1.73	Hewlett-Packard (U.S.)	3.68
NEC (Japan)	1.51	Siemens (FRG)	3.27
ICL (U.K.)	1.44		
CII-HB (France)	1.34		
Hitachi (Japan)	1.31	STC ICL (U.K.)*	1.33
Olivetti (Italy)	1.09	British Telecom (U.K.)	0.46
Xerox (U.S.)	0.97	Racal (U.K.)	0.38
Siemens (FRG)	0.84	Feranti (U.K.)	0.28

Sources: U.S. Department of Commerce, *High-Technology Industries: Profiles and Outlooks— The Computer Industry* (Washington, D.C.: U.S. GPO, April 1983), pp. 19–20; *Datamation* (June 1986); and Tim Kelly, *The British Computer Industry* (London: Croom Helm, 1987), p. 222.

*The last four companies listed in 1985 are included to indicate the relative size of the British computer industry and are not among the top ten computer producers.

Table 4.5   Ten Leading Computer Manufacturers in the United Kingdom, 1984

COMPANY	TURNOVER (£ MILLION)	EMPLOYMENT
IBM U.K. (U.S.)	2,349.0	17,506
STC ICL (U.K.)	942.6	21,056
Racal Electronics (U.K.)	309.0	n/a
DEC (U.S.)	302.9	2,967
Hewlett-Packard (U.S.)	293.1	2,783
Burroughs Machines (U.S.)	232.3	3,880
Control Data (U.S.) (incl. Systime, acq. 1985)	227.3	2,972
Commodore (U.S.)	158.4	338
Ferranti Computer Systems (U.K.)	152.2	4,800
NCR Ltd. (U.S.)	141.8	3,313

Sources: Company Annual Reports, Tim Kelly, *The British Computer Industry* (London: Croom Helm, 1987), p. 214.

Japanese companies to take advantage of European support funding and programs. This has, in turn, enabled U.S. and Japanese companies to maintain their mutual dominance over European industries. Furthermore, the global supply of computer products remains highly concentrated. As a result, many countries and firms remain dependent on access to American (and Japanese) suppliers of computer products and technology. The cases discussed in the next section demonstrate the degree of control gained as a result of foreign dependence on American suppliers and markets during the 1980s at the peak of Operation Exodus.

U.S. Influence over Firms in the Computer Industry

The extraterritorial reach of this U.S. enforcement effort in the computer industry greatly exceeded earlier American attempts to regulate foreign corporations during the trans-Siberian Pipeline crisis. Yet unlike the trans-Siberian Pipeline Case, and despite parliamentary protests and corporate requests for national assistance, host country governments largely supported and even relied upon the application of U.S. sanctions to enforce export controls within their borders. The varying success of U.S. sanctions in both sets of cases can be explained in terms of American trade dominance and foreign dependence on American suppliers markets in this sector.

In December 1983, IBM (U.K.) sent a "letter" to thirty leasing companies reminding them that they must obtain permission from the United States Commerce Department before selling or reselling any of their products and technology. The letter was intended to clarify the scope and range of American regulations:[50]

> As you are aware, transactions *within* the United Kingdom involving "Advanced Systems" are also subject to the obtaining of U.S. export license approval. Such transactions include not only the initial installation of a new machine with a user, but also any subsequent dealing or transfers in such machines. [emphasis in the original]

This regulation required getting an appropriate American license whenever and wherever the products were moved, even within the same country. Furthermore, it required that the final destination, customer, and use of the products be reported to the Commerce Department.

Texas Instruments and Control Data Limited announced similar restrictions for their British and European clients. In May 1984, Texas Instruments informed its British customers:[51]

> We seek an assurance from you, our customer of T.I. programmable controller devices and systems, that your company will not, without prior authorization, export technical data to any destination or country which is prohibited under the laws of the USA.

Later, in August 1986, Control Data Limited informed its European customers that they had to complete a similar letter of assurance under threat of future orders being rejected.[52]

Corporate reactions to these letters reflected the ability of the United States to control technology transfers through dependence, and can be seen in the following internal memoranda from two European high-technology firms:

> Non-compliance with the regulations on U.S. re-export control . . . would . . . prove disastrous to the company! . . . Unless we are willing to risk being denied access to all U.S. equipment in the future and heavy fines begin imposed on our U.S. representation, we have no alternative than to comply, as onerous a task as it is! . . . The most important point to stress is that these regulations are unfortunately unavoidable and MUST BE COMPLIED WITH IN ALL CIRCUMSTANCES BY ALL PERSONNEL! [emphasis in the original][53]

> The company has been obliged to protect is imports/exports from the USA. by complying with U.S. Export License regulations. A procedure has been written into the Contractual Commitment Form which is mandatory for ALL orders. Failure in applying the procedures can result in the Company losing all American technology, £b losses in sales and criminal prosecutions. [emphasis in the original][54]

These corporate memoranda indicate both a perception of dependence on American suppliers and a belief that the threats were both credible and potentially extremely costly. The next sections analyze corporate and national reactions to the threat of sanctions by examining the actions of International Computers Ltd., Systime PLC, Brian Butcher, and others like them. These cases demonstrate the ability of the U.S. government to impose costly penalties on foreign actors who do not comply with U.S. or multilateral policies.

International Computers, Ltd. In May 1982, the United States Commerce Department fined International Computers Limited (ICL, later STC ICL) of Great Britain $15,000 for selling a large computer to South Africa. The original transaction took place in 1978 with appropriate export licenses from the United Kingdom.[55] The Commerce Department claimed, however, that because the computer contained two memory discs built by the American company CDC Corporation, the sale should not have been completed prior to obtaining U.S. export control licenses as well. In addition, the Commerce Department required a full release of all of ICL's major exports from the United Kingdom including the destination, recipient, and likely use of ICL's major exports containing American-made components.

To secure compliance with its regulations, the Commerce Department threatened to sanction ICL by placing it on the U.S. export Denial Lists, thus effectively terminating all American business contacts, and seizing all corporate assets in the United States.[56] ICL requested assistance from the British government and asked that the Department of Trade and Industry (DTI) intervene on its behalf. The case of ICL was brought to the attention of Sir Michael Havers, Attorney General of the U.K., in a letter from MP Paddy Ashdown. The letter summarizes the threat of sanctions used to enforce compliance by British companies:

> In the event of breach of the regulations by the non U.S. national in their own country the U.S. Department of Commerce has imposed heavy fines and additional conditions.
>
> As the enclosed extract of the 1982 Report of the Export Administration shows clearly, fines have been levied on non U.S. companies, including a fine of $15,000 on the UK company ICL. Currently, a Leeds based Company called Systime Limited faces fines of $400,000, despite its compliance with UK export control regulations. Attached to the fines are conditions, which, in ICL's case, include a requirement to obtain the consent of the Office of Export Administration for import sales transactions involving the relevant computer system.
>
> If the fine is not paid and the conditions not met, orders are made, and names are entered on the U.S. Export Denials list.[57]

Through DTI, the British government responded by providing guarantees to banks for a bail-out package for ICL, but did not challenge the extra-territorial extension of U.S. regulations on ICL's behalf.

The British government justified its failure to challenge U.S. actions by arguing that both the company and the country itself were dependent on American suppliers in the computer industry. The actions against ICL took place at a time when the company was in a financial crisis.[58] After achieving at a 23.6 percent growth rate from 1973 through 1980, ICL suffered a £49.8 million loss in 1981.[59] In order to save Great Britain's only major indigenous computer producer, the DTI was willing to arrange a financing package and accept corporate restructuring that led to a loss of over 10,000 British jobs in the industry. However, it would not challenge the application of U.S. regulations within its borders. DTI believed that ICL was dependent on the supply of American technology and components and would not survive if that supply was terminated.[60] If provoked, the United States Department of Commerce would likely blacklist ICL, cutting off its access to American companies and goods. This outcome would violate DTI's primary objective of saving the company and was therefore rejected.

A second motivation for British cooperation with U.S. enforcement efforts was a perception of national dependence on IBM and DEC for the supply of computer components as a base of British economic and military security. IBM (U.K.) is the largest manufacturer of computer products in the U.K., with an output more than two and one half times as large as STC ICL. The dominance of American firms like IBM and DEC has given the United States a means of controlling the activities of firms operating within Great Britain (see table 4.6). The British Minister of Information Technology Ken Baker summarized the government's fear of losing access to American computer technology if the American initiatives were challenged. He expressed this concern by arguing that "[i]f we are dependent on the Americans or the Japanese, they [the computers] may not be here tomorrow."[61]

Finally, the British government concurred in part that a limited number of high-technology goods should be controlled. Given this partial consensus, the threat of American sanctions was sufficient to spur the British government into dramatically increasing its local enforcement efforts. In 1983, for example, it created "Project Arrow" to monitor and enforce export controls in Great Britain.[62] This was followed by increased diligence in monitoring license applications at the Department of Trade and Industry, and an increasingly active role by Customs and Excise agencies reflected in an increasing number and frequency of searches. As the case of Systime Ltd. will demonstrate, these agencies often conducted searches on behalf of American enforcement agencies.[63] As Richard Perle noted at the time, "the British have taken some positive steps in the areas of enforcement and intelligence. Some of the best cooperation we have had has been British."[64] While part of this behavior shift can be explained in terms of the "Farewell Affair" and a base level of agreement on the need to control the proliferation of certain goods and technology, various Members of Parliament argued correctly that British behavior in the computer sector was inconsistent with its behavior during the pipeline crisis. The basic assertion of extraterritorial jurisdiction by the United States and the infringement of British sovereignty remained unchanged; the difference was that the British government was dependent upon the United States in this sector and, as a result, took strong efforts not to endanger its relationship.

In this case, both ICL STC and the British government were dependent on access to American products, but neither was dependent on access to the American market. ICL's willingness to fulfill its original contracts despite U.S. restrictions, and the British government's reluctance to challenge the United States on its behalf, support the hypothesis that firms are less likely than national governments to be swayed by dependence on supply.

While also dependent on access to American suppliers, other firms, such as Systime PLC and Brian Butcher, did not anticipate the full cost circumventing U.S. export control policy. Their cases demonstrate the ability of the United States to use the threat of sanctions to assist local governments in enforcing multilateral export restrictions.[65] The costs imposed on these two firms served as an example for others contemplating circumventing the American regulations.

Systime PLC. A large proportion of Systime PLC's business involved the resale of DEC computers obtained from American vendors. Systime was blacklisted by the Department of Commerce and fined $600,000 as a penalty for allegedly shipping up to four hundred DEC computer systems to the Eastern Bloc via Switzerland without an American export license.[66] In 1983, it had a turnover of over £40 million and employed twelve hundred people. By 1985, in the aftermath of U.S. sanctions, the company was virtually destroyed. Corporate investors withdrew their financial support and all but two hundred people had been laid off. The remaining corporate assets were acquired by Control Data Corporation of the United States.[67]

In order to sell American-made products, Systime was obligated to obtain an export license from the U.S. Commerce Department in addition to a standard export license from the British Department of Trade and Industry. In 1982, Systime made a voluntary disclosure to the U.S. Department of Commerce regarding sales to Eastern Europe without an appropriate American export license and agreed to pay a fine for doing so. At that time, however, attorneys from DEC UK accused Systime of shipping up to an additional four hundred DEC computers to the Eastern Bloc via Switzerland.[68] The allegations led to a grand jury investigation in the United States.

Systime appealed to both the British Department of Trade and Industry and to Parliament, but to no avail. Rather than challenging the American actions within British territory, the British government tried to demonstrate that it was fully committed to preventing high-technology exports that might be detrimental to American interests. In essence, it used the threat of American sanctions to enhance its own enforcement capabilities. With information provided by U.S. Customs, British Customs raided Systime in July 1984. The information provided by British Customs, combined with DEC investigators and the initial voluntary disclosure by Systime, provided the Department of Commerce with the justification needed to indict the company. The U.S. cited Systime with forty-six violations of the Export Administration Act, imposed fines on the firm, and placed it on the Black List.[69] By 1985, prior to being taken over by the American company CDC, Systime was effectively cut off from its American suppliers and driven out of business.

Brian Butcher. The case of Brian Butcher demonstrates the effectiveness of American sanctions against a foreign individual or firm even when the targeted actor itself is not directly dependent on American suppliers or markets. As in the ICL case, officials from the Department of Trade and Industry agreed that the American Embassy had broken British law by interfering in the business transactions of a British company. Citing a fear of upsetting Anglo-U.S. relations, however, they chose not to interfere with U.S. enforcement efforts or the actions taken against the British firm. As in the Systime PLC case, U.S. sanctions supplemented British enforcement efforts. The costs imposed against Brian Butcher as a result of U.S. sanctions were far more severe than those inflicted by the British court.

Brian Butcher, a computer software broker for a British electronics equipment company in Basingstoke, was indicted by the Department of Commerce for selling an integrated circuit tester to a Polish television station in 1979. The television station had been part of a $72 million American development project supported by the World Bank.[70] The project, however, lost American support when Martial Law was declared in Poland. Subsequently, Butcher was arrested in the United States for violating an American export embargo against the Polish regime, but he jumped bail and returned to Great Britain. The U.S. government attempted and failed to extradite him. Although a British court fined him £2,500 for exporting restricted equipment to Poland, the U.S. Department of Commerce imposed the additional penalty of placing Butcher and his company on its denial list.

As a result of being placed on the Black List, Butcher lost his client base at CEMI, Ltd. During a judicial review of his case in London, Butcher complained: "Within a few weeks of details of the list being published in 1984, I had lost 75 percent of my customer base for buying and selling because I could not deal with U.S. companies in Europe."[71] During the judicial review of the Butcher trial in London, companies including Ferranti, GEC, and Hewlett Packard (U.K.), claimed that they needed continued access to American markets and future contracts with American companies, including participation in the Strategic Defense Initiative (SDI). As a result, they did not want to offend U.S. authorities and would not do business with blacklisted firms. Similarly, after being notified by the U.S. Department of Commerce that Butcher had been placed on the denial list, Bell Telephone of Belgium withdrew a £400,000 contract with his company.[72] Japanese firms including Toshiba, Fujitsu, and Canon also terminated their contracts, arguing that they wanted to avoid any possible allegations of not cooperating with American efforts to restrict technology to the East Bloc.[73]

As in the ICL case, the Department of Trade and Industry agreed that U.S. interference in this case represented an unwarranted encroachment on British sovereignty. However, the DTI claimed that its purpose was not to intervene in individual cases. Despite continued statements made in Parliament that the American blacklisting of British companies was illegal, DTI refused to get involved. Spokesmen from the DTI supported the argument that taking up the case would be futile and, because Butcher was on the denial lists, intervention could potentially damage British interests by antagonizing the United States.[74]

In sum, the U.S. government was able to use corporate dependence on American suppliers and markets in the computer industry to enforce its policies abroad. The U.S. acted both independently and with the support of the British government. In both situations, the U.S. government demonstrated a willingness to impose sanctions that inflicted heavy, and often fatal, costs on offending firms. Its willingness to do so bolstered British enforcement efforts by penalizing negligent British firms. The willingness of the British government to promote the application of American sanctions against their firms can be explained in terms of both a consensus among CoCom members that certain high-technology controls were needed, and a combination of U.S. dominance in the computer industry and a large degree of national (as well as corporate) dependence on American suppliers and markets.

U.S. Influence over National Governments in the
Computer Industry

While a general consensus existed among CoCom members regarding the need for certain high-technology export controls, the European governments expressed outrage at the broad scope and domain of U.S. control asserted by the IBM letter. Given the general consensus and the de facto control the threat of sanctions gave to the U.S. government, the public outcry over U.S. infringements on European sovereignty was not followed by the intense legal retaliation that characterized their response to the trans-Siberian Pipeline crisis just two years earlier.

In response to the IBM letter, West German Economics Minister Martin Bengemann warned Washington in August of 1994 that Bonn would "not tolerate" American attempts to impose additional controls on its companies. He argued that if challenged, West Germany would impose a law to prohibit domestic companies from complying with extraterritorial trade restrictions imposed by a foreign power, as they had done during the pipeline crisis.[75] French officials supported the West German position, arguing that, "the United States is waging economic war with all the means at its disposal," and that American efforts to curb trade with the East would weaken West European technology in favor of its American competitors.[76] Even the British government, which openly cooperated with CoCom and had assisted U.S. enforcement efforts, argued that it did not condone American efforts to control equipment and technology that were not on the lists.[77] British Trade Minister Norman Tebbit argued, for example, that "we can't impose our law within the U.S. and frankly they can't impose their law in Britain . . . we can't allow other governments to exert their law in our country."[78] National presses published articles about the implications of the IBM letter for national sovereignty, and government officials promised to resolve the issue immediately.[79] Some members of Parliament argued that the government could apply the Protection of Trading Interests Act of 1980 as it had during the Pipeline Case.

In response, the U.S. government issued a warning that all companies that refused to cooperate would be held accountable and sanctioned under U.S. law.[80] And, later that year, after the delivery of several VAX computers to the Soviet Union by Digital U.K., Assistant Secretary of Defense Richard Perle threatened that unless dramatic changes in European policies take place, "[w]e are seriously considering ending licensing of really sensitive technology altogether to the alliance in Europe."[81] Director of Central Intelligence William Casey charged three hundred foreign companies with diverting technology to the Soviet Union. Moreover, in an address to British computer executives in London, another U.S. government official threatened: "We have got enough on you all to clap most of you in irons."[82]

When Paddy Ashdown and other legislators raised this issue in Parliament, British Attorney General Sir Michael Havers argued that the regulations were "an unwarranted encroachment on U.K. jurisdiction and are contrary to international law," though the government did nothing more about the issue at the time. When pressed on the issue in Parliament, Geoffrey Pattie, Minister for Information Technology and spokesman for the prime minister, argued that: "We reject out of hand claims by the U.S. government to have jurisdiction of U.S. goods based on U.S. technology while they are in the UK. . . . If we could compel the U.S. to withdraw this claim, the problem would be eliminated easily, but we cannot."[83] This statement reflects the tension between autonomous de jure sovereign authority of one government over actors within its territory and the de facto control of those actors by another government.

Lack of government action resulted from both the recognition that some export controls were necessary and the combination of American dominance and British dependence on continued access to American suppliers at the national and corporate levels in this sector. In particular it reflected a national response to the U.S. Defense Department's threat that it would "facilitate" sharing technology only with those firms that "cooperate effectively" in safeguarding technology from potential adversaries.[84] Moreover, a spokesman for the British government argued that the government was not willing to challenge U.S. actions because "the U.S. threatened to blacklist companies which failed to meet their demands. In this way British industry was denied access to U.S. technology not available elsewhere."[85]

As the trade statistics discussed above indicate, more than 70 percent of the British computer industry was controlled directly or indirectly by American corporations, and therefore, at least according to American sources, fell under American jurisdiction.[86] American firms also provided the largest source of foreign investment in Great Britain, accounting for $32.1 billion (over 50 percent) by the end of 1984.[87] In the 1980s, the majority of the investment had been by American high-technology firms including IBM, its subsidiary Rolm telecommunications, DEC, Hewlett Packard, and Dupont. European firms and governments have perceived the lack of access to these resources as a threat to national economic and military security, as well as to corporate survival.[88]

CASE ANALYSES: U.S. INFLUENCE IN THE
TELECOMMUNICATIONS INDUSTRY

Throughout the 1980s, the U.S. government also sought to maintain far more stringent controls on telecommunications equipment and technology than its CoCom partners. The U.S. government argued that improved command, control, and communication systems made possible by advanced telecommunications equipment and technology rendered strict CoCom controls vital to international security. European governments, in contrast, tended to emphasize the beneficial political impact of telecommunications trade with Eastern Europe and Asia, as well as the large economic benefits of participating in a new Eastern market. After intense negotiations, CoCom members agreed on stricter controls in high technology in 1984, but disputes over the telecommunication equipment and technology remained prevalent.[89]

Recent changes in this industry including a dramatic liberalization of the international telecommunications market and a corresponding increase in trade, combined with the convergence of telecommunications, computer, and electronics technology have given the U.S. government a source of leverage of foreign actors in this industry.[90] These changes began in the mid-1980s near the peak of Operation Exodus and continue today. The cases discussed below involve Thomson Group of France and LM Ericsson of Sweden. While they took place at virtually the same time, LM Ericsson and the Swedish telecommunications industry better reflected coming changes in the industry towards liberalization and internationalization than Thomson Group and the French telecommunications industry. As discussed below, this distinction bodes well for the use of U.S. sanctions against European firms in the future as the European Union gradually liberalizes its telecommunications industries and the convergence of the computer and telecommunications industries grows.

Dominance and Dependence in the
Telecommunications Industry

Telecommunications industries in most countries have traditionally focused on supplying a domestic market with a high degree of protection against foreign competition. In the early 1980s, for example, the domestic telecommunications industries in seventeen out of twenty-four Organization for Economic Cooperation and Development (OECD) countries were organized government-controlled postal, telephone, and telegraph organizations (PTTs). PTTs generally excluded foreign competition through specific legislation or through the stringent application of national standards, testing, and certification practices. These practices have secured legal monopolies for domestic public or private telecommunications firms.[91] PTT monopolies generally include the procurement, licencing, distribution, and maintenance of telecommunications equipment as well as the operation and service of domestic telecommunications networks.[92]

Preferential procurement and secured local markets would seem to minimize the usefulness of sanctions in the telecommunications industry.[93] On the supply side, in 1984—at the peak of Operation Exodus and the IBM letter fall out—U.S. suppliers accounted for less than 16 percent of world telecommunication equipment exports. Japanese suppliers dominated world exports, accounting for roughly twice as much as U.S. firms.[94] From 1984 through 1996, Europe's major telecommunications equipment manufacturers, including Alcatel, Siemens, LM Ericsson, and Philips have relied primarily on European suppliers.[95] The majority of European countries continue to keep government telecommunications equipment procurement restricted to domestic or European venders, thereby limiting the access of American telecommunications suppliers.[96]

Despite this initially dire assessment, recent changes in the global telecommunications industry have greatly increased the U.S. government's ability to manipulate foreign dependence on supply and market access to its advantage. Two of the most consequential changes have been the convergence of the telecommunications and computer industries, and the dramatic liberalization, deregulation, and privatization of the international telecommunications industry. The first change increased the role of American computer and telecommunications equipment suppliers in the international telecommunications trade. Foreign dependence on American computer and telecommunication equipment and services offered a potential carrot and stick to use against wayward, dependent foreigners consumers. The second change, symbolized by the breakup of AT&T, increased this leverage by enabling the United States to use access to its market (currently the world's largest) to entice foreign producers.

The lack of U.S. dominance in this industry did not mean that the use of sanctions in this industry would be ineffective. On the contrary, foreign dependence on access to American (and Japanese) computer technology offered and continues to offer a spill-over effect resulting from foreign telecommunication producers' dependence on American suppliers in the computer and other related industries.[97] Computer technology plays an increasingly large role in telecommunication services and operations including advanced data transmission and information services, new generations of international cellular and satellite communications networks, and digital switching and fiber-optic communication networks. U.S. and Japanese firms are the dominant suppliers of these components and services. Controlling foreign access to these suppliers provides the U.S. and Japanese governments with a source of political leverage.

On the demand side, international telecommunications markets liberalized substantially in the 1980s and 1990s, with the United States, Great Britain, and Japan opening their domestic markets to competition in the provision of both telecommunication and data transmission services. Others, like Sweden, Australia, Canada, New Zealand, and South Korea are also liberalizing, particularly, in the area of mobile communications, satellite communications, and global data networks.[98] On January 1, 1998, the European Union opened their networks to increased competition.[99] However, while Great Britain and Sweden have substantially liberalized and privatized their telecommunications industries, other European countries—notably France, Belgium, Portugal, and Spain—have largely maintained monopolies on infrastructure and services.[100]

The trend towards organizational reform, deregulation, liberalization, and privatization was accelerated by the breakup of AT&T. The divestiture of AT&T was significant because it began to force open the U.S. and global telecommunications markets to competition in the supply of infrastructure and technology, the provision of services, and the running of public telecommunications and data networks. Foreign access to American markets and American imports of telecommunications technology increased dramatically in the 1980s. In the early 1980s, AT&T was the largest American consumer of telecommunications equipment; it alone accounted for 58 percent of total U.S. spending on telecommunications equipment and, through its Bell system, maintained 80 percent of the American telephone network.[101] Deregulation of the American telecommunications industry and the divestiture of AT&T in 1983 and 1984 opened the United States market to foreign competition. Between 1983 and 1984, U.S. imports of telecommunication equipment rose 38 percent to $7.6 billion.[102] Japan was the primary beneficiary of this new market, but exports to American consumers as a proportion of overall telecommunications exports rose in Sweden, France, Great Britain, and West Germany as well.

Promising increased access to its market (or alternatively limiting access to it), gives the United States a carrot to dangle and a stick to wave in front of monopolistic telecommunications firms. In order to promote continued European liberalization while protecting U.S. telecommunications firms, President Clinton refused to let European companies enter the U.S. market until telecommunication regulations in their home countries were judged to be as liberal as those of the United States. This effectively cut off all European companies, except those from Sweden and the United Kingdom where telecommunication markets had been liberalized, from the U.S. market until full liberalization in the E.U. is completed.[103]

In order to bypass this restriction, American and European firms formed a series of interfirm alliances. Examples include a British Telecom merger with MCI; a joint venture by France Telecom and Deutsche Telecom to purchase a $4.2 billion share of Sprint's international network service; the AT&T World Partners alliance comprised of Kokusai Denshin Denwa Company of Japan, Singapore Telecom, and Unisource (including Dutch, Swedish, and Swiss telecommunications companies); and Bell Atlantic of Philadelphia's alliance with Olivetti to create Telecom Italia in Rome. Finally, in January of 1995 the first French license was granted to a foreign company enabling a joint venture of MFS Communications Company of the U.S. and France Telecom to construct a fiber-optic network in France.[104]

European manufacturing companies have also set up joint ventures with
American companies in order to gain access to American markets and
technology. For example, Alcatel Alsthom acquired ITT Corporation in
1986 and Rockwell International Corporation's Networks Transmission
Division and Sprint in 1995.[105]

Equally important, the Computer and Business Equipment Association in the United States negotiated an agreement with the European
Telecommunications Standards Institute (ETSI) to ensure common standards and secure an agreed means for European access to American pat-
ents. This is significant because 10 percent of ETSI's membership of
European operators and equipment manufactures are American owned.[106]
The compatible standard will further open European markets to U.S.
suppliers and visa versa. European countries enjoyed a trade surplus in
telecommunications equipment in the 1980s. This surplus indicates a
reliance on external markets, since domestic producers supply more equipment than can be consumed by the domestic market. This makes access
to foreign markets in the U.S., and potential markets in East Europe,
Russia, and China appealing.

An analysis of the European telecommunications industries on a
country-by-country basis reveals a distinctly different picture than the
European computer industry. In the early 1980s, the European telecommunications industry was robust, with 80 percent of equipment exports
outside the European Community going to OPEC countries. By the mid-
1980s, however, the European Community began to run a telecommuni-

Table 4.6   Trade Balance of Major Telecommunications Producers, SITC #764.1
(\$ THOUSANDS)

	1982	1983	1984	1985
West Germany	+510,097	+409,413	+379,500	+375,285
Sweden	+458,470	+422,809	+457,757	+474,535
France	+122,484	+226,744	+147,348	+176,695
Netherlands	+117,520	+61,200	+100,907	+22,663
Belgium/Luxembourg	+41,202	+20,955	+10,312	-23,646
Italy	+46,141	+16,857	+6,738	-8,194
United Kingdom	+27,024	-11,983	-43,035	-46,909
United States	+209,658	-427,099	-1,059,537	-1,193,320
Canada	+319,754	+368,660	+524,621	+486,384
Japan	+764,148	+904,891	+1,078,447	+1,321,527

Source: United Nations, *1985 International Statistics Yearbook*, vol. 2 (New York: United
Nations Publishing, 1987).

cations deficit with the United States and Japan, amounting to 657 million ECU and 582 million ECU by 1985.[107]

Between 1983 and 1984, when the Thomson and LM Ericsson cases took place, the United States had the world's largest market in the telecommunications sector, accounting for 27.5 percent of telecommunications imports in 1983 and 33.3 percent in 1984. During the same period, the dominance of U.S. suppliers declined somewhat from 16.6 percent to 15.8 percent of world exporters in telecommunications equipment.[108] As a result of deregulation, foreign competitors gained access to the world's largest telecommunications consumer market. While dominance arguments suggest that U.S. sanctions might be effective, dependence arguments are less optimistic. Foreign dependence U.S. markets and suppliers in the telecommunications sector remained low in 1983 and 1984, suggesting that U.S. sanctions were not likely to be effective—at least not unless they were extended to cover computers and related technology where European dependence on American suppliers was greater.

U.S. Influence over Firms in the Telecommunication Industry

The majority of the world's telecommunications exports come in a small number of states and firms. As the telecommunications industry becomes more reliant on sophisticated digital switching and transmission equipment, and as international telecommunications trade is further liberalized, these countries and firms may continue to dominate trade in this industry. Two of these firms were targets of American actions under Operation Exodus. The differing reactions of Thomson of France and Ericsson of Sweden to U.S. efforts to control their activities illustrate the extent and limitations of U.S. influence resulting in U.S. dominance and foreign dependence on access to American suppliers and markets in a particular industry.

Thomson Group. Since 1979, Thomson had established several contracts with the Soviet Union that were a source of contention with both the French and the United States governments. Three sets of contracts were particularly troublesome. The first was a $110 million deal in 1979 involving digital communication exchange technology, the second involved $350 million in computerized monitoring equipment that was to be used on the trans-Siberian Pipeline in 1981.[109] In each of these cases, the French government intervened before allowing the sales to go through. In order to minimize the risk of technology transfer, the French government required Thomson to downgrade its technology in the first case. In the second case, it allowed Thomson to export the components for the monitoring equipment, but it forbade Thomson from exporting related production technology.[110] These

Table 4.7 Leading Telecommunications Equipment Producers
(CURRENT $ BILLION)

BY FIRM	1981
Western Electric (U.S.)	$11.53
ITT (U.S.)	5.50
Siemens (FRG)	4.40
Ericsson (SW)	2.48
GTE (U.S.)	2.23
NEC (JA)	2.05
Northern Telecom (CA)	1.88
Motorola (U.S.)	1.60
Thomson (FR)	1.45
GEC (U.K.)	1.45
Phillips (NETH)	1.30
CGE (FR)	1.00
Plessey (U.K.)	0.81

Sources: U.S. Department of Commerce, *High-Technologies Industries: Profiles and Outlooks, The Telecommunications Industry* (Washington, D.C.: U.S. GPO, April 1983), p. 18.

modifications indicated an awareness on the part of the French government of the need to control the proliferation of certain technologies. The United States, however, did not consider the modifications to be sufficient.

In December 1983 the Thomson Group announced that it would continue deliveries of a sophisticated telephone exchange system to Leningrad. The French government supported Thomson's decision to continue its deliveries despite intense protests from the U.S. government during CoCom meetings and in other fora throughout the year. Thomson had signed the original agreement in 1979, shipments of the sophisticated MT20 digital telephone exchange equipment began in 1980, and they were scheduled to continue through 1984. Thomson did not stop its sale. Rather, as in the earlier cases, it chose to avoid using American parts by modifying certain "sensitive" components of its system. By altering the equipment, Thomson sidestepped the American request, but the underlying problem remained unsettled.

The disagreement between the French and American governments over the Thomson case mirrored the continuing conflict within CoCom over what items should be considered "sensitive" and, therefore, placed on restrictive embargo lists maintained by the organization. In the end, the sale was completed with the support of the French government, despite the threat of American sanctions. As a French CoCom negotiator stated, "[w]e agree to disagree."[111]

In light of earlier French policy and its general unwillingness to abide by more stringent U.S. export restrictions, the success of getting

Thomson to modify its equipment has been interpreted by some analysts to indicate an increase in U.S. influence. Mastanduno argues, for example, that the new French policy "contributed to a stronger CoCom by restricting access to French technology."[112] Increased French compliance may be due to the "Farewell Documents" as well as other factors that affected a general shift in French policy. Such a shift, however, does not diminish the fact that the United States failed to secure the degree of compliance it desired from either the French government or Thomson. As a result, despite a minimal convergence in behavior, U.S. influence in this case was minimal.

LM Ericsson. In contrast to the failure of U.S. efforts to control Thomson, the United States was able to inhibit the activities of the Swedish telecommunications firm LM Ericsson. LM Ericsson suspended its efforts to sell an advanced telephone exchange system to Bulgaria in August 1984 as a result of the threat of U.S. sanctions.[113] This action was extremely important because rival firms within CoCom countries, including Plessy and GEC from Great Britain, were not willing to sacrifice the expected £50–100 million in sales to Bulgaria unless their non-CoCom competitors did the same.[114] Furthermore, should rivals intervene once Plessy, GEC, and others had withdrawn, the British and French governments agreed to allow their firms to reopen their negotiations.[115] As Mastanduno notes, this made securing the compliance of firms like LM Ericsson in non-CoCom countries a vital part of U.S. leadership within the organization.[116] The ability of the U.S. to secure compliance and promote this leadership was a function of Sweden and LM Ericsson's dependence on the United States.

Sweden was not a CoCom member and was not under agreement to abide by its decisions. However, in practice, the CoCom decision had a direct effect on the Swedish company's actions. CoCom influence was the result of LM Ericsson's dependence on the supply of American parts for its most sophisticated systems. LM Ericsson reported 25 billion crowns ($3 billion) of sales in 1983, the majority of which involved its principal and most sophisticated product, the AXE digital exchange system, which, in turn, used American-made components.[117] As Magnus Lemmel, Vice President for Corporate Marketing for LM Ericsson, stated, without continued access to U.S. components and the permits to use them, "we will not be able to deliver our latest technology to Eastern Europe."[118]

Dependence and the Success of U.S. Influence

The divergent actions of the French and Swedish governments and their firms, Thomson and LM Ericsson, can be explained in terms of variation in their dependence on American suppliers and the American market. The telecommunications industries in France and Sweden place different emphases on production and trade. The French telecommunications market is essentially closed, and it sales are primary to its domestic market. In contrast, the Swedish telecommunications market is small and relatively open. Its industries produce primarily for an export market. These different emphases have led to different degrees of national and corporate dependence on trade which, in turn, explain the reactions of each player.

The French government had gone to great lengths to maintain a viable domestic base in the telecommunications, electronics, and computer industries. Under the *Plans Composants* in 1977, the French government provided FFr 3 billion to upgrade the nation's high-technology industries. This project selected the Thomson Group as a national champion to receive preferential treatment in order to sustain substantial defense electronics, computer, and communications production facilities in France. Government intervention in support of these industries peaked in 1981, when it formally nationalized C.G.E., Matra, Saint Gobain, Point à Mouson, and Thomson Brant. In 1983, Thomson Group expanded, acquiring the defense and consumer electronics divisions of the firm C.G.E. A subsidiary of Thomson, Thomson-CSF, produced defense electronics, avionics, radar, and integrated circuits, while Thomson Brant focused on telecommunications and computers.

French government support of Thomson against the United States was part of its ongoing campaign to maintain a strong domestic high-technology industry. The French government was not dependent on the United States in this sector. French telecommunications trade with the United States was low and alternate suppliers, both domestic and international, were readily available. As a result, the French government was free to challenge U.S. efforts to control Thomson, it did so, and the contract was completed. As a compromise, the French government modified some of the equipment in the Leningrad telephone system and increased its export control procedures.[119] The government, however, continued to fight American efforts within and outside of CoCom to expand controls over high-technology goods. Similarly, Thomson itself was not dependent on access to the American market. In 1988, Thomson expanded into the American defense market by acquiring Wilcox Electronics, a former subsidiary of Northrop. Prior to that time, however, Thomson's primary market was European and predominately French. Its dependence on American suppliers, as well as on the American market remained low. As predicted, American influence over its actions was limited.

In contrast to Thomson and the French government, LM Ericsson and the Swedish government were dependent on American suppliers and access to the American market. LM Ericsson was vulnerable to U.S. threats because of its reliance on U.S. components for its telecommunications products. Its primary products, including the AXE digital exchange system it was to sell to Bulgaria, relied heavily on American-produced computer and electronic parts. Magnus Lemmel argued that the AXE system was extremely popular and had been sold to fifty-four countries, including China and Yugoslavia. He argued that defying the United States in order to gain access to Eastern Europe, which accounted for less than 1 percent of the world telecommunications market, was not worth losing the ability to service its current customers.[120]

In addition to relying on American suppliers, confrontation with the United States occurred just as the American consumer market opened to foreign competition. Unlike the French, the Swedish telecommunications market was small and relatively open. Its industries produced primarily for an export market, as approximately 80 percent of sales from Ericsson and the Dutch firm Phillips came from abroad.[121] In 1981, Sweden accounted for 16 percent of world exports in telecommunications equipment and, following Japan, had the second largest trade surplus in telecommunications equipment: $711 million.

Of the other European countries, Germany is similar to France, and the Netherlands are similar to Sweden, with the United Kingdom falling in between. Several countries, including Austria and Ireland, have little or no domestic sources of telecommunications equipment and rely heavily on foreign suppliers. The potential for future access to the American market provided a strong incentive for corporate officials not to antagonize the U.S. government. As a result, potential access to the American consumer market, combined with dependence on American components, gave the U.S. government leverage over LM Ericsson.

Summary of U.S. Influence in the
Telecommunications Industry

The success of U.S. influence over LM Ericsson and the Swedish government, and the U.S. government's inability to influence Thomson and the French government, confirm the hypotheses that foreign dependence is a critical component of economic statecraft. The contrast is particularly significant because unlike Sweden, France was a member of CoCom. While general agreement on the need for export controls among members were CoCom does not guarantee cooperation, non-CoCom member are even less likely to voluntarily restrict their exports to conform to multilateral export restrictions.

Despite general liberalization of CoCom controls since June of 1990, strict controls on telecommunications equipment remain, as do severe disagreements over the appropriateness of the restrictions.[122] Recent changes in the global telecommunications industry may increase the U.S.

Table 4.8 U.S. Dominance in the Telecommunications Industry in the 1990s

YEAR	1990		1991		1992		1993		1994	
PERCENT	SUPPLIER	MARKET	SUPPLIER	MARKET	SUPPLIER	MARKET	SUPPLIER	MARKET	SUPPLIER	MARKET
Digital Computers SITC 752	7.79	22.6	8.38	20.2	8.78	22.6	7.9	25.9	6.9	27.0
Telecommunications Equipment SITC 764	15.0	21.5	14.8	19.9	15.1	18.9	15.9	18.7	15.4	18.1

Source: United Nations *International Trade Statistics Yearbook*, vol. 2 (New York: United Nations Publishing, 1994, 1995).

government's ability to manipulate foreign dependence on supply and market access to its advantage. With the diffusion of technology, this trend is likely to continue.

DEPENDENCE, SANCTIONS, AND THE THIRD COUNTRY PROBLEM

The success of U.S. export control policy requires the cooperation of all actors that possess or can produce the controlled goods and technology. Even if the United States can secure the compliance of all members of multilateral export control fora like CoCom, its successor the New Forum, the Nuclear Suppliers Group, or the Missile Technology Control Regime and their firms, the impact of the export restrictions on the primary target may be undermined if non-member countries or firms provide alternate sources of the sanctioned goods. Furthermore, regardless of the effect on the primary target, the availability of restricted goods from non-member sources will likely undermine the degree of cooperation within these multilateral fora by decreasing the incentive for individual member countries to continue restricting their economic activities. Consequently, it is crucial that the United States secure the compliance of potential non-member or "third country" suppliers and markets even though they have not formally agreed to abide by the regulations stipulated by a multilateral export control regime. For these reasons, controlling the activities of third countries became a vital component of U.S. leadership responsibilities within CoCom.[123] In April 1983, CoCom members agreed to target third countries that were particularly susceptible to diversion.[124]

American efforts to address the third country problem were made public in 1984 in Vienna where U.S. Deputy Trade Under Secretary Olin Wethington argued for the need to expand multilateral cooperation on export controls and to include non-CoCom states such as Austria, Switzerland, Sweden, and India. He argued: "There is simply too much diffusion of technology. Semi-conductors, to take one example, are now made in some 40 countries throughout the world.... The world is simply too dangerous ... to avoid ensuring broad authority under U.S. law for the President in both foreign policy and the national security control area."[125] The success of American efforts to gain the cooperation of non-CoCom member countries and their firms is largely the result of manipulating economic rewards and penalties. On the whole, the United States has been able to secure the compliance of third countries and their firms. This success has, however, not been absolute. As in the cases analyzed below, when the targeted firms or states were not dependent on access to American suppliers or markets, the threat of American sanctions was often not effective.

Goals, Targets, and Means of Enforcement

The U.S. government focused its enforcement efforts on firms operating in Western states like Austria and Sweden, and non-Western states including countries in South and South East Asia (notably Hong Kong, India, Indonesia, Singapore, Malaysia, the Philippines, and South Korea). By the peak of Operation Exodus in the mid-1980s, Australia and Singapore were the largest producers of computer technology in Asia, outside of Japan.[126] Failure to gain the compliance of firms operating in these countries could potentially quickly have undermined other U.S. and CoCom export controls.

Equally important, the United States needed to secure the cooperation of third countries in order to maintain compliance on the part of its fellow CoCom members and their firms. This was true for two reasons. First, it was necessary for the United States to provide a guarantee that noncooperative countries would not get an unfair advantage of trading benefits while those participating in the embargo were excluded. As Mastanduno argues, by securing the cooperation of the Pacific Rim countries, the United States would fulfill a classic hegemonic leadership function by absorbing the costs of potential free riders (or stopping them entirely) and maintaining the benefits of collective action for all.[127] The Reagan administration's efforts to strengthen existing controls within Southeast Asia, particularly in those countries with the fastest-growing technological capabilities, reflected its concern that these countries could otherwise take advantage of the embargo to gain preferential access to restricted countries. Secondly, the United States relied on the threat of economic sanctions to secure compliance of CoCom members and their firms with its export control policies. These export controls would only be effective as long as few alternate non-American suppliers or markets were available. If companies in the Pacific Rim were able to produce products and components of comparable quality to those in the United States, then those companies could act as alternate suppliers for CoCom members and their firms, thereby undercutting the effectiveness of U.S. sanctions.

To gain the cooperation of third countries in the 1980s, the United States threatened to deny access to its technology or markets to all firms or countries that flout or undermine the controls, regardless of CoCom membership. The cases of Singapore and Austria demonstrate that when national and corporate dependence on the United States is high, U.S. success is likely. Sweden's support of its firms, Datasaab and ASEA, and its refusal to cooperate in the extradition of Richard Mueller suggests, however, that when states and firms are not dependent on the United States, U.S. influence will be minimal.

Dependence and the Success of U.S. Influence

Austria and Singapore. In December 1984, the Austrian Parliament unanimously approved amendments to its trade laws aimed at stopping illegal shipments of U.S. technology to the Soviet bloc. The amendment, which called for jail terms of up to two years and steep fines for offending companies and individuals, was a direct outgrowth of U.S. threats to terminate Austrian access to American suppliers and technology. The Commerce Department had delayed its approval of several high-technology joint ventures with American companies and argued that under export regulations that would take effect on 16 January 1985, the U.S. government would refuse to grant licenses to neutral countries like Austria unless tighter measures were taken to prevent technology transfers.[128] Foreign Minister Leopold Gratz indicated that his government's ruling was intended to assure Austrian industry unhindered access to American technology.[129] The move was supported by Austrian business as a means of avoiding U.S. penalties or threatening their access to U.S. technology and investment. According to one report, the amendment "reflects Austria's concern that it might lose access to U.S. technology if it fails to convince the Reagan administration that it intended to prosecute violations of U.S. export law."[130]

In April 1985, Singapore Minister of Finance Dr. Tony Tan announced that his country would follow the Austrian example and was prepared to cooperate "not only with the U.S. but also with the other members of CoCom."[131] This announcement was made as an attempt to maintain a stable trading relationship between firms in Singapore and the United States. The majority of Singapore's exports of electronic merchandise was produced by local subsidiaries or affiliates of American, European, and Japanese multinationals. These exports rose from $83 billion in 1970 to $3.9 billion in 1985.[132] In April 1986, Secretary George Shultz met with Foreign Minister Suppiah Dhanabalan of Singapore to urge Singapore to apply stricter controls on exports of advanced technologies. Early that year, the United States blocked the sale of powerful IBM mini computers worth approximately $248,000 by the Singapore Soviet Shipping Company, SinSov. As required under American law, IBM-Singapore applied for a license from the Commerce Department, and was subsequently informed that the license would be denied. Rather than challenging the United States on behalf of its firms, the Singapore government promised to tighten its export licensing system of controlled goods and technologies.[133]

The United States successfully brought similar pressure to bear on Spain by threatening to prohibit the construction of a microchip plant by AT&T in Spain unless it expanded its export control measures.[134] Similarly, under pressure from the United States, India agreed to abide by CoCom regulations in 1985, and Australia followed suit in 1987.

Sweden. Unlike the clear reaction from the Austrian government, American efforts to extend its control into Sweden were mixed. The Swedish cases involving Datasaab Contracting AB, ASEA, and Richard Mueller demonstrate the extent and limitations of U.S. efforts to secure compliance with its policy in non-CoCom member countries. If the hypotheses linking dependence and political power are correct, then the United States should have been as likely to secure compliance with its export control policy within CoCom as within non-CoCom countries under similar circumstances.

In 1985, Sweden was the only remaining Western country that did not have laws regulating the export and re-export of Western or American technology. Officially, Sweden maintains a neutral stance and does not take part in embargoes, and, as a result of several highly publicized cases, Sweden was placed on the Pentagon's list of "risky countries."

Datasaab and ASEA. In 1977 the Carter administration refused to grant re-export licenses for electronic equipment needed by Datasaab Contracting AB to complete its shipment of an air traffic control system to the Soviet Union. Datasaab circumvented the restriction by smuggling various key components to the Soviet Union during corporate visits. When the violation was uncovered in 1980, the United States attempted to punish Datasaab and discipline the Swedish government by terminating the sale of American Sidewinder missiles to the Swedish air force.

In 1982, to regain access to the American military suppliers and the missiles in particular, the Swedish Defense Department agreed to establish a covert operation to maintain surveillance over local companies using sophisticated computers. Datasaab, in turn, agreed to pay $1 million to the United States government.[135] As predicted, the threat to cut off the supply of items considered necessary for national economic or military security gave the United States a potent source of influence over the Swedish government. The *Guardian* summed up the Swedish response:

> Swedish industry is heavily dependent on advanced U.S. electronic components and if these were stopped, the local export market, which accounts for 27 percent of GNP, would collapse within a few months. Thus the U.S. is able to make its own terms and Swedish industry is being forced, despite official policies of neutrality, to join the blockade and even to submit to "voluntary" control and inspection by Americans. With little fanfare, the [Swedish] Government has put key Swedish companies under military surveillance to satisfy U.S. demands.[136]

U.S. influence in Sweden, however, was not absolute. Despite this concession, U.S.-Swedish relations were strained in October 1983 when

Swedish authorities refused to open and release containers of equipment associated with the Mueller case. In 1985, Sweden's largest electronics firm, ASEA, was brought under investigation by the U.S. Department of Trade for the smuggling of six computers to Moscow to be used to coordinate steel production. ASEA faced fines of up to £10 million and was denied access to U.S. technology.[137]

Richard Mueller. Richard Mueller, a German businessman, led a sophisticated smuggling organization that shipped American goods and technology to the Soviet Union throughout the 1970s and 1980s. According to Richard Perle, Assistant U.S. Secretary of Defense, technology leaks like those generated by Mueller greatly facilitated the development of modern industry and weapons systems in the Soviet Union by saving it billions of dollars on research and development.[138]

In November 1984, West German and Swedish officials intercepted a shipment of high-technology goods that Mueller's organization was smuggling to the Soviet Union. The shipment included fifty tons of electronics equipment, making it the largest diversion of restricted American technology yet uncovered. The shipment contained two VAX 11/782 computers produced by Digital Equipment Corporation valued at $4.5 million. These computers were widely used in the U.S. military for tasks ranging from missile guidance to satellite transmission intercepts and are considered very sensitive.[139] The computers had been shipped to Canada (where export licenses were not required), then to Europe, South Africa, Sweden, and, finally, to the Soviet Union. The Mueller case was publicized by the Pentagon to demonstrate the scope of high-technology crime. As one Pentagon spokesman stated: "This helps make our allies aware of the threat and it dramatizes our security concerns right when Congress is debating the new export legislation."[140]

Even when an "illegal" shipment of goods is discovered, however, the cooperation of allied governments and firms is not guaranteed. In 1968, as a result of pressure from local businesses who protested restrictions on trade and politicians who wanted to maintain Sweden's neutrality, Sweden had withdrawn from CoCom. As a consequence, although Swedish authorities were willing to impound the containers containing Mueller's electronic equipment, they claimed there was no legal basis that enabled or required them to confiscate the contents.[141]

In order to coerce the Swedish government into confiscating the restricted equipment and then releasing it to American officials, the U.S. threatened to terminate the shipment of American-made armaments to the Swedish military for its next generation of fighter aircraft. The Swedish government was already under pressure from the United States to change its policies following the recent discovery that the Swedish

government-owned company Datasaab Contracting AB had supplied the
Moscow airport with a sophisticated computerized air traffic control system. As a result of the Swedish government's perception of dependence
on the continued supply of American products it considered vital to its
national security, Prime Minister Olof Palme decreed retroactively that it
was illegal to ship "war material" to or from South Africa. The computers
and electronic equipment in question were labeled "war material" and
impounded. DEC, in turn, bought the products. Then, while they were in
transit back to the United States, U.S. Customs officials confiscated them
as evidence against Mueller.

Summary of U.S. Influence over Third Countries

The U.S. government has been successful in securing the cooperation of states that were not members of multilateral export control regimes. Its influence over these third countries and their firms was not
absolute. Rather, as in the other cases, it was a function of foreign dependence on American suppliers and access to the American market.

CONCLUSION

The combination of U.S. trade dominance and foreign dependence on
access to American suppliers in several high technology sectors gave the
United States government a source of leverage over foreign firms and
their host governments during Operation Exodus. This leverage enabled
the United States to use economic penalties and rewards to compel and
entice firms operating in both CoCom and non-CoCom member countries to comply with its export control policy. The contrasting outcome of
U.S. efforts during Operation Exodus and the Pipeline Case, as well as
variations within each set of cases, demonstrate the extent and the limitations of this form of economic statecraft. When U.S. trade dominates a
particular sector and others are dependent on access to American markets
or American suppliers, then the threat to terminate access to them can be
a potent tool. Nevertheless, U.S. influence in the computer and telecommunications industry was not absolute. As predicted, when firms and states
were not dependent on the United States, the threat to terminate access
did not increase the probability of success.

From 1981 through 1988, sanctions strengthened the enforcement of
U.S. and CoCom export controls. In addition to penalizing non-compliant
firms, the use of sanctions also increased the international awareness of the
proliferation of "strategic" goods and technology. This led, in turn, to increased monitoring, enforcement, and compliance with export restrictions

on the part of national governments and other foreign actors.[142] At the same time, however, the sanctions were controversial. Their success was not paralleled by an increased willingness on the part of other CoCom members to expand the role of CoCom beyond restricting goods of strategic significance. Moreover, the continued American use of sanctions to compel corporate compliance in other areas was often interpreted as an abuse of American power and leadership.[143] With the end of the cold war, the U.S. government has increased its use of sanctions dramatically. This has led to renewed criticism about the abuse of American power and leadership resulting from the power of sanctions—especially those targeted against private companies. The next chapter concludes this book by evaluating the potential costs and benefits of using sanctions to influence corporate activities in the post-cold war world.

Notes

1. Paul Lewis, "Computer Pact 2½ Years," *International Herald Tribune* (18 July 1984), p. 1. Agreement in CoCom was reached to double the number of restricted items on the denial lists, but the European delegates successfully dropped the U.S. proposal to require exit visas for programmers in order to control the movements of technological knowledge and software.

2. Mastanduno (1992), pp. 298–99.

3. Mastanduno (1992) provides an excellent detailed history of the domestic and multilateral evolution of export controls.

4. U.S. Department of Defense, *An Analysis of Export Control of U.S. Technology—A DoD Perspective* (Washington, D.C.: Office of Defense Research and Engineering, 1976); and Fred Bucy, "Technology Transfer and East-East Trade: A Reappraisal," *International Security* 5, 3 (winter 1980–81): 132–51.

5. Mastanduno (1992) pp. 187–88.

6. The report recommended even more stringent restrictions on non-CoCom member countries, arguing that "the U.S. should release to neutral countries only the technology we would be willing to transfer directly to Communist countries." Defense Science Board Task Force, *An Analysis of Export Control of Advanced Technology*, p. 40; cited in Mastanduno (1992): 195–96.

7. The distribution of responsibility for enforcing export control legislation has been a source of interagency rivalry, particularly between the Commerce Department, the Department of the Treasury, and the Department of Defense.

8. Joseph Fitchett, "Even Friends Will Be Watched Closely as U.S. Guards Its High-Tech," *International Herald Tribune* (23 May 1984).

9. "The Spies Who Steal Computers," *Financial Times* (17 May 1986), pp. I, XIII; Joseph Fitchett, "Silicon Embargo against East Bloc Revealed by U.S.," *International Herald Tribune* (25 May 1984), p. 1; Joseph Fitchett, "Technology Bandit

Led Ring for Russia," *International Herald Tribune* (5 February 1985), p. 1; David Buchan and Peter Montagnon, "Backing Reluctantly into the Limelight," *Financial Times* (8 December 1987), Section 1, p. 22; Philip Hanson, *Soviet Industrial Espionage: Some New Information* (London: Royal Institute for International Affairs, 1987). For a review of U.S. export control policy as it relates to the fear of Soviet aggression, see Robyn S. Metcalfe, *The New Wizard War: How the Soviets Steal U.S. High-Technology—And How We Give It Away* (Redmond, Wash.: Tempus Books, 1988).

10. World trade data are gathered from both the United Nations and the Organization for Economic Cooperation and Development broken down by Standard International Trade Classifications. SITC 752 (automatic data processing equipment) is an aggregate indicator of the computer industry, and SITC 764 (telecommunications equipment, parts, and accessories) is an aggregate indicator of the telecommunications industry.

11. Milner's argument that sectoral-level analyses are limited by their failure to address the actions of particular firms is well taken. Despite this limitation, I argue that generalizations at the sectoral level provides reasonably accurate predictions of firm behavior. Individual corporate actions are evaluated below as a means of testing the reliability of sectoral level predictions. Milner (1988), pp. 20–21.

12. For example, the telecommunications equipment includes communication switching equipment (now primarily electronic equipment and computers), terminals (including telephones, facsimile machines, and a myriad of electronics equipment and computers), and transmission equipment (including wire, fiber-optic cable, and electronics and computer equipment used for microwave and satellite transmission). Similarly, the computer industry consists of completed computers, peripherals (printing machines, monitors, etc.), and subassemblies (including electronic components such as printed circuit boards and computer memory and data processing chips). Within the computer industry, 35 to 50 percent of all trade involves subassemblies rather than fully functional computers. This is due to both the structure of international tariff barriers and because economies of scale make it more efficient to import basic components from specialized producers rather than develop common components internally. As a result, the distinctions between the telecommunications, computer, and electronics industries have become blurred.

13. National Academy of Sciences, Panel on the Future Design and Implementation of U.S. National Security Export Controls, Committee on Science, Engineering and Public Policy, *Finding Common Ground: U.S. Export Controls in a Changed Global Environment* (Washington, D.C.: National Academy Press, 1991); see also Bertsch (1983); Mastanduno (1985), (1992); and Adler-Karlsson (1968).

14. Crawford (1993), p. 135. For a complete list, see U.S. Department of Defense, *The Technology Transfer Control Program: A Report to the 98th Congress* (Washington, D.C.: U.S. Department of Defense, 1984), pp. 11–14.

15. Crawford (1993), pp. 132–37; Lewis, (18 July 1984), p. 1. CoCom members agreed to double the number of restricted items on the denial lists, but the European delegates successfully dropped the U.S. proposal to require exit visas for

programmers in order to control the movements of technological knowledge and software.

16. Crawford (1993), p. 134. For a complete list, see *The Military Critical Technology List* (Washington, D.C.: Department of Defense, Office of the Undersecretary of Defense, Defense Research and Engineering, October 1984).

17. *The Economist* (21 April 1984), p. 13.

18. Lewis, (18 July 1984), p. 1. Agreement in CoCom was reached to double the number of restricted items on the denial lists, but the European delegates successfully dropped the U.S. proposal to require exit visas for programmers in order to control the movements of technological knowledge and software.

19. David Buchan, "The Spies Who Steal Computers," *Financial Times* (17 May 1986), pp. I, and XIII.

20. Ibid.

21. Ibid.

22. Mastanduno (1992), pp. 318–19.

23. Christian Lamoureux, "Sanctions and Export Controls in France," in Claude Lachaux, Denis Lacorne, and Christian Lamoureux, eds., *De L'Arme Economique* (Paris: Foundation pour les Etudes de Défense Nationale, 1987), pp. 159–60.

24. The SGDN now directs a permanent "High Commission on Controls," which includes the Ministry of Foreign Affairs, the Ministry of Defense, the Chief of State, and the Ministry of Industry and Finance. Lamoureux, in Lachaux et al. (1987), p. 160.

25. It remained restricted until September 1988. Lacorne, in Lachaux et al., (1987), pp. 127–28; Mastanduno (1992), p. 270.

26. Warren Getler, "Bonn Says It Will Ignore U.S. Technology Curbs," *International Herald Tribune* (9 August 1984), p. 1.

27. Using SITC 752, United Nations, *International Trade Statistics Yearbook*, vol. 2 (1986).

28. Using SITC 752. United Nations, *International Trade Statistics Yearbook*, vol. 2 (1984–87).

29. United Nations, *International Trade Statistics Yearbook*, vol. 2 (1985–1987).

30. OECD (1984), (1989).

31. Including CII-Honeywell-Bull in France and International Computers Limited (ICL) in Great Britain. Wayne Sandholtz, *High-Tech Europe: The Politics of International Cooperation* (Berkeley: University of California Press, 1992), p. 78.

32. "America Says No," *The Economist* (16 June 1966), p. 1229; "Computers Denied to France by U.S.," *New York Times* (21 May 1986), p. 38; Theodore Moran, "The Globalization of America's Defense Industries: Managing the Threat of Foreign Dependence," *International Security* 15, 1 (summer 1990), pp. 60–61.

33. "Turning a Blind Eye," *The Economist* (29 October 1966), p. 489. Cited in Moran (1990), p. 61.

34. United Nations, *International Trade Statistics Yearbook*, vol. 2 (1986).

35. Organization of Economic Cooperation and Development (1985), p. 118.

36. United Nations, *International Trade Statistics Yearbook*, vol. 2 (1986).

37. The United States and Japanese suppliers accounted for 79 percent of sales in 1988. U.S. Department of Commerce, International Trade Administration, *Country Market Survey: Computers and Peripheral Equipment, United Kingdom* (Washington, D.C.: GPO, May 1984), p. 2.

38. U.S. Department of Commerce (1984), p. 3.

39. Ibid.

40. In 1982. U.S. Department of Commerce (1984), p. 9.

41. Following an agreement to sell Fujitsu Atlas ten computers until 1984, ICL developed its advanced Series 39 computer, which contains forty-three chips developed by Fujitsu. Sandholtz (1992), p. 116; and Tim Kelly, *The British Computer Industry* (London: Croom Helm, 1987), p. 47.

42. It is interesting that in 1984 the United Kingdom was the world's second largest supplier of digital central processors, accounting for 18 percent of world exports. At first glance, this may appear to indicate that the United Kingdom is not necessarily dependent on the United States. This is misleading, however, because a large proportion of these exports are actually goods that have been purchased elsewhere, especially from the United States, and re-exported to third parties. Kelly (1987), pp. 80–85.

43. Kelly (1987), p. 81; U.S. Department of Commerce (1983), p. 10.

44. Moran (1990), p. 62.

45. Tim Kelly provides further evidence to support this point. See Kelly (1987), pp. 80–85.

46. United Nations, *International Trade Statistics Yearbook*, vol. 2 (1986).

47. The U.S.-Japanese agreement was renewed in 1991. Peter Cowhey and Jonathan Aronson, "A New Trade Order," *Foreign Affairs* 72, 1 (1993): 187–89; Tyson (1992), chapters 2, 4, 6.

48. "Europe's Dash for the Future," *The Economist* (13 August 1994), pp. 13–14.

49. At least until 1985, largely due to the dominant market share of IBM, foreign exports to the United States market remained relatively unimportant when compared to the value of American exports.

50. Emphasis in the original. The letter is reprinted in its entirety in Macdonald (1990), pp. 130–31. See also Cahill (1986); Patrick Bloom, "U.S. Warns on High-Tech Sales," *Financial Times* (4 April 1984), Section I, p. 8; "Trade Department to Question IBM Computer Warning," *Financial Times* (10 January 1984), p. 15; Joseph Fitchett, "Silicon Embargo against East Bloc Revealed by U.S.," *International Herald Tribune* (25 May 1984), p. 1.

51. This letter is reprinted in its entirety in Macdonald (1990), p. 132.

52. This letter is reprinted in its entirety in ibid., p. 139.

53. *Re-export Controls for Goods of U.S. Origin*, internal compliance manual of large European electronics company. Cited in Macdonald (1990), p. 142.

54. *Export License Compliance*, internal compliance manual of large European computer firm. Cited in Macdonald (1990), p. 142.

55. Kevin Cahill, "Sh . . . The Following May Be a U.S. Secret," *The Times* (17 April 1984), p. 23; Mary Fagan, "British Exports Hit by U.S. Rules," *The Independent* (25 April 1988), p. 2; and Cahill (1986), pp. 82–85.

56. Cahill (1986), p. 85.

57. Ibid.

58. Kelly (1987), pp. 216–17; and Cahill (1986), pp. 82–85.

59. Kelly (1987), pp. 216–17.

60. Cahill (1986), pp. 82–85.

61. Ibid., pp. 74–75.

62. Mastanduno (1992), p. 271.

63. Ibid., p. 272.

64. *Financial Times* (1 November 1993), p. 12; cited in ibid., p. 271.

65. Other cases of blacklisting include the Spanish electronics firm Piher Semiconductor SA, which was denied access to U.S. suppliers between 1982 and 1986 for re-exporting U.S. manufacturing equipment to Cuba and the Soviet Union. *New York Times* (6 September 1985), p. D1. Also cited in Mastanduno (1992), p. 289.

66. Nancy Dunne, "Systime in $600,000 Settlement of Re-export Charges," *Financial Times* (15 May 1986). See also Cahill (1986), p. 85.

67. For more details on this case, see Cahill (1986), p. 177; and Kelly (1987), p. 81.

68. Cahill (1986), p. 178.

69. Cahill (1986), pp. 177–78; and Kelly (1987), p. 81.

70. Paul Brown, "CIA Victim on Blacklist Fights on Alone," *The Guardian* (21 December 1987), p. 2.

71. Mary Fagan, "Victim of U.S. Embargo Sues the Government," *The Independent* (28 March 1988), p. 22.

72. Brown, (21 December 1987), p. 2; and Fagan (28 March 1988), p. 22.

73. Butcher sums up the effect: "Within the last six months, companies such as Toshiba, Fujitsu, and Canon, with whom I still did business, have pulled the plug. As far as I am concerned the U.S. has won. I'm a businessman. They've got me kicked to death now. There is nothing left in the kitty." Fagan (28 March 1988), p. 22.

74. In May of 1988, Brian Butcher was arrested in Italy by Italian police and U.S. Customs agents on charges of fraud and illegal export of technology with both civilian and military uses. After a series of delicate negotiations between Members of the European Parliament, Italian lawyers, and their American counterparts, Butcher agreed to go to the United States and face trial voluntarily. While the British government continues to argue that it opposed American efforts to impose and enforce its export regulations abroad, and especially in the U.K., the Foreign Office claimed that there was nothing it could do since the original offenses took place when Butcher was in the United States. A spokesman for the

Foreign Office summed up their position, stating: "What we can do is to watch carefully to ensure that he has an absolutely fair trial." See Mary Fagan, "High-Tech Exporter Agrees to Stand Trial in the U.S.," *The Independent* (6 August 1982); Michael Sheridan, "Plea Bargain Offer to Briton Held in Rome," *The Independent* (22 June 1988).

75. Warren Getler, "Bonn Says It Will Ignore U.S. Technology Curbs," *International Herald Tribune* (9 August 1984), p. 1.

76. John Tagliabue, "U.S., Europeans Split on Sale of High Technology," *International Herald Tribune* (13 August 1984), p. A21. A spokesman for the French government argued that the new legislation challenged their sovereign integrity, and argued that, "This could be a case of our businessmen being asked for their professional secrets by a foreign government." See Paul Lewis, "Europeans Angry over the Call for New Technology Export Controls," *International Herald Tribune* (24 January 1984).

77. David Buchan, "U.K. Revises Rules for Sales of Technology Sales to Communist Countries," *Financial Times* (14 June 1985), Section I, p. 3.

78. John Lloyd, "IBM Warned on Trying to Enforce Controls," *Financial Times* (21 January 1984), Section I, p. 3. In similar fashion, the Confederation of British Industry issued a statement saying that while it agreed with the goals sought by the strategic embargo, "we object to broad announcements extending United States' jurisdiction outside United States territory." Paul Lewis, "Europeans Angry over the Call for New Technology Export Controls," *International Herald Tribune* (24 January 1984), p. 15.

79. Patrick Bloom, "Trade Department to Question IBM on Computer Warning," *Financial Times* (10 January 1984), p. 15.

80. Geoff Andrews and Kevin Cahill, "How the Pentagon Ties up Europe's Computer Industry," *The Guardian* (2 November 1984), p. 15. See also "IBM's Role in Europe," *Financial Times* (19 January 1984), Section I, p. 8.

81. Geoff Andrews and Kevin Cahill, "How the Pentagon Ties up Europe's Computer Industry," *The Guardian* (2 November 1984), p. 15.

82. Ivor Owen, "MP Protests at 'Unfair' U.S. Curbs," *Financial Times* (14 April 1984), Section I. p. 4.

83. Brown, "Thatcher Pressed to Stop CIA Surveillance of Nuclear Industry," *The Guardian* (28 July 1986), p. 6.

84. Crawford (1993), p. 136. The original document is Department of Defense Directive 2040.2, "International Transfers of Technology, Goods, Services, and Munitions" (17 January 1984), Section D.

85. Brown (28 July 1986), p. 6.

86. Paddy Ashdown, "No Go for British Know-How," *The Times* (15 May 1986), p. 18.

87. Derek Harris, "High-Tech Boom Helps Maintain U.S. Lead in Foreign Investment," *The Times* (12 February 1986), p. 20.

88. Paul Brown, "Thatcher Pressed to Stop CIA Surveillance of Nuclear Industry," *The Guardian* (28 July 1986), p. 6; John Hooper, "Havers Attacks U.S. Technology Controls," *The Guardian* (17 July 1985), p. 30.

89. *Export Control News* 2 (3 February 1988), pp. 2–5. Mastanduno (1992), pp. 3–4.

90. The telecommunications industry is composed of three primary components: switching equipment, which connects terminals and coordinates telecommunications networks; terminals, like telephones and facsimile machines, which transmit information across the networks; and transmission equipment, which provide the means of transmitting telecommunication signals. U.S. Department of Commerce, International Trade Administration, *High-Technology Industries: Profiles and Outlooks, the Telecommunications Industry* (Washington, D.C.: U.S. Government Printing Office, April 1983), p. 14. Telecommunications equipment, parts, and accessories (SITC 764 and 764.1) are aggregate indicators of the telecommunications industry.

91. Edgar Grande, "The New Role of the State in Telecommunications: An International Comparison," *West European Politics* 17, 3 (July 1994): 139–40.

92. For a discussion of the role of the state in telecommunications industries in Europe see Grande (1994), pp. 139–40.

93. Robert Crandall, *After the Breakup: U.S. Telecommunications in a More Competitive Era* (Washington, D.C.: Brookings Institution, 1991); Jill Hills, *Deregulating Telecoms: Competition and Control in the United States, Japan, and Britain* (London: Pinter Publishing, 1986).

94. United Nations, *International Trade Statistics Yearbook*, vol. 2 (1988).

95. Alan Pearce, "Competition Breaks the Ties That Bind European Vendors," *America's Network* 99, 24 (15 December 1995): 44.

96. Deborah Eby, "Rating GATT: Trade Pact's Breakthroughs and Barriers," *America's Network* 99, 1 (1 January 1995): 18–21.

97. Grande (1994), p. 146; Robin Mansell, "Rethinking the Telecommunications Infrastructure: The New 'Black Box,' " *Policy Research*, 19 (1990): 504.

98. Cowhey and Aronson (1993), pp. 189–91.

99. It is also important to note that "liberalization" and "privatization" of the telecommunications industry does not mean that governments stop intervening and extensively regulating these industries. Grande (1994), p. 149.

100. Jack Gee, "A New Era in Global Telecom," *IW Electronics and Technology* (17 July 1992): 43.

101. U.S. Department of Commerce (1983), p. 16.

102. Using SITC 764. United Nations, *International Trade Statistics Yearbook*, vol. 2 (1983, 1984).

103. Gee (1995), p. 43.

104. Gail Edmondson, John Rossant, and Julia Flynn, "AT&T Is No Smooth Operator in Europe," *Business Week* (11 April 1994), p. 48; Gee (1995), pp. 43–44.

105. Gee (1995), p. 45.

106. Ibid., p. 47.

107. Sandholtz (1992), p. 120; and Commission of the European Communities, *Towards a Dynamic European Economy: Green Paper on the Development of the Common Market for Telecommunications Services and Equipment.* COM (87) 290 final. Brussels (June 1987), p. 158.

108. Using SITC 764. United Nations, *International Trade Statistics Yearbook* (1985).

109. See Mastanduno (1992), pp. 166, 272.

110. Ibid.

111. David Marsh, "French Go Ahead with Soviet Sale," *Financial Times* (17 December 1983), Section I, p. 2.

112. Mastanduno (1992), p. 273.

113. "Swedish Firm Yields to Ban on Exports to Eastern Bloc," *International Herald Tribune* (4–5 August 1984).

114. Mastanduno (1992), p. 270.

115. Guy de Jonquieres and David Buchan, "Ministers Split over Bulgaria Phone Deal," *Financial Times* (24 March 1984), p. 1; David Buchan, "Export Curbs Apply to UK Telecom Gear," *Financial Times* (17 July 1984), p. 1; and David Brown, "Ericsson Drops Plan for East Bloc Sales," *Financial Times* (4 August 1984), p. 2.

116. Mastanduno (1992), pp. 270, 290–95.

117. "Swedes Agree to a Fine for Radar Sales to Soviets," *International Herald Tribune* (4–5 August 1984), p. 3.

118. Ibid., p. 3.

119. David Marsh, "French Go Ahead with Soviet Sale," *Financial Times* (17 December 1983), Section I, p. 2.

120. Ibid.

121. U.S. Department of Commerce, International Trade Administration, *High-Technology Industries: Profiles and Outlooks—The Telecommunications Industry* (Washington, D.C.: U.S. Government Printing Office, April 1983), p. 29.

122. Bill Root, "The Core List: Expectations vs. Reality," *Export Control News* 5 (29 July 1991), pp. 2–5. Cited in Mastanduno (1992), p. 4.

123. Mastanduno (1992), pp. 290–95.

124. U.S. Department of Defense (1984), p. 24.

125. *Financial Times* (4 April 1984).

126. Michael Schrage, "U.S. Wants Asian Technology," *International Herald Tribune* (16 August 1984).

127. Mastanduno (1985).

128. One example involves a joint venture between Voest of Austria and Microsystems of the United States to produce integrated circuits. Mastanduno (1992), pp. 291–92.

129. John Tagliabue, "Austrians Tighten Curb on High-Tech," *International Herald Tribune* (3 January 1985), p. 9.

130. Ibid.

131. Chris Sherwell, "Singapore in CoCom Hi-Tech Offer," *Financial Times* (25 April 1985), Section I, p. 7.

132. Michael Richardson, "U.S. Fears High-Tech Leakage," *International Herald Tribune* (28 May 1986).

133. Michael Richardson, "Pacific Heeds U.S. on East Bloc Exports," *International Herald Tribune* (31 October–1 November 1987).

134. Spain joined CoCom in 1984. *The Economist* (23 February 1985), p. 70, and Mastanduno (1992), p. 293.

135. "Swedes Agree to a Fine for Radar Sale to Soviets," *International Herald Tribune* (8 April 1984), p. 3.

136. Richard Stainbridge, "Sweden Awaits American Wrath," *The Guardian* (19 October 1985), p. 6.

137. Ibid.

138. Chris Farnsworth, "White House Plans to Fight Congress on Bills," *International Herald Tribune* (21 March 1984), p. 3.

139. Ibid.

140. Ibid.

141. Ibid.; *International Herald Tribune* (21 November 1983) and (21 December 1983).

142. For an assessment of the U.S. role in CoCom throughout the 1980s, see Mastanduno (1992), pp. 276–78.

143. Mastanduno (1992), pp. 276–87.

5

Conclusion: Threatening Friends and Enticing Enemies in the Post–Cold War World

POWER RELATIONS AMONG STATES AND FIRMS

As of 1 August 1996, foreign firms conducting business in Cuba may be sanctioned in accordance with restrictions specified in the Cuban Liberty and Democratic Solidarity Law. While President Clinton delayed implementation of the most contentious aspects of the legislation in July of 1996 (and has done so every six months since then), he affirmed the right of U.S. citizens to sue foreign companies who "traffic in" property in Cuba that was expropriated from them following the 1959 Cuban revolution. This affirmation established a precedent that may be used to justify another set of secondary sanctions imposed against foreign firms under the Iran and Libya Sanctions Act.[1] The goal of these secondary sanctions, like those analyzed throughout this volume, is to entice or coerce foreign actors to adopt practices consistent with U.S. policy.

The cases analyzed in the preceding chapters suggest that critics of the Helms-Burton Act and the Iran and Libya Sanctions Act are correct to warn that the use of secondary sanctions may create intergovernmental conflict. The conflict created by U.S. efforts to stop construction of the trans-Siberian Pipeline is a prime example of the potentially negative consequences of such policies (see chapter 3). In fact, many of the reactions of U.S. allies and trading partners to the United States' use of secondary sanctions today—ranging from protests regarding the violation of national sovereignty and international law, to the imposition of blocking legislation to protect local firms, to the threat of countersanctions—are similar to those during the pipeline crisis.

What critics misunderstand is that secondary sanctions tend to cause intergovernmental conflict precisely because they can provide an effective means for states to influence the activities of foreign firms and individuals operating abroad. Lessons learned from the trade dominance and trade dependence arguments analyzed in this volume help us understand how and when economic statecraft can work. In this chapter, these arguments will be used to explain the success and failure of sanctions in U.S.-Chinese relations in the 1990s, and to provide an assessment of the likely success and failure of secondary sanctions under the Cuban Liberty and Democratic Solidarity Act and the Iran and Libya Sanctions Act of 1996.

At the same time, it is important to recognize that even under ideal conditions, the use of economic statecraft may have economic, political, and social ramifications beyond their intended effect on a particular target.[2] These economic ramifications result from a variety of factors including the reciprocal nature of dependence; the potentially negative repercussions of sanctions on the reliability and competitiveness of domestic firms; and the incentives that sanctions create for the indigenous foreign development of restricted resources. These additional costs can explain in part why the U.S. has refrained from seeking to control actions of foreign subsidiaries of American firms in several relatively recent embargos including the Moscow Olympics, Afghanistan, and Uganda.[3] They also elucidate reasons for caution in current U.S. efforts to influence foreign companies doing business with the People's Republic of China, Cuba, Iran, and Libya using economic threats and incentives.

This chapter is divided into four sections. Following the introduction, the second section reviews the book's primary objectives and evaluates the theoretical and practical significance of its findings. The section entitled "Costs and Limitations of Sanctions" examines several economic ramifications of using economic sanctions as a source of political power. The next section uses the models to evaluate the likely effectiveness of the Helms-Burton Act and the Iran-Libya Sanctions Act. The chapter concludes by evaluating the impact of increasing levels of technological diffusion and interdependence on the utility and analysis of sanctions in the 1990s and beyond.

SECURING EXTRATERRITORIAL COMPLIANCE

The primary empirical objective of this volume is to explain when the U.S. is likely to succeed in securing extraterritorial corporate compliance with its policies using secondary sanctions. The results of the statistical analyses and comparative case studies in the previous chapters suggest that economic statecraft can provide the United States (or other countries) with an effective means of extending political control over firms and individuals operating across international borders. Consistent with the arguments and evidence in the preceding chapters, the successes and failures to date of current attempts by the U.S. government to use secondary sanctions to compel foreign companies to conform to its trade restrictions against Cuba, Iran, and Libya illustrate that the dynamics of dominance, dependence, and political power remain as valid and critical today as they have been in the past.

The Findings and the Implications

The findings of the statistical analysis and comparative case studies support the proposition that sanctions can be effective when used under appropriate conditions that are defined by the trade dominance of the sender, the target's net dependence on the sender, and the opportunity costs associated with sending and responding to the sanctions. In particular, the statistical analyses suggest that the target's net dependence on U.S. markets—defined as the target's dependence on U.S. markets minus U.S. dependence on the target's exports in the same sector—will have significant positive impact on the likelihood that the secondary sanctions will be successful. The estimated likelihood of corporate compliance based on the sender's trade dominance and the target's net dependence on the sender is statistically significant, as are the coefficients for the target's net dependence on U.S. markets, the proportion of the target's imports accounted for by U.S. suppliers, and host government intervention. Furthermore, the equation accurately predicts both the success and failure of U.S. sanctions 75.8 percent of the time.

Unexpectedly, the statistical analyses suggest that the target's net dependence on U.S. suppliers is not significant; however, the proportion of the target's imports accounted for by the United States is. This implies that while that target's dependence on foreign suppliers may not affect its compliance with secondary sanctions, increasing the proportion of imports in a particular sector accounted for by the sender may increase the likelihood that it will comply. Finally, counter to initial expectations, neither the sector-specific dominance of U.S. suppliers nor the sector-specific dominance of U.S. markets had a significant impact on corporate compliance. This implies that sector-specific trade dominance by the sender may not affect the likelihood that secondary sanctions will be successful. Despite data limitations and mixed outcomes, the statistical results suggest that additional analysis of corporate compliance is warranted. The detailed comparative case studies conducted in chapters 3 and 4 supplement the statistical analyses by clarifying the causal links between dominance, dependence, and political power.

The comparative case studies added further support for the hypothesized relationship between the target's net dependence on the sender and the likely success of sanctions in achieving corporate compliance. Like the statistical analysis, however, the comparative case studies also generally failed to support the predicted link between sector-specific trade dominance by the sender and the success of economic incentives or sanctions. For example, between 1982 and 1984, the U.S. government largely failed to secure the compliance of European firms with its export restrictions related to the construction of the trans-Siberian Pipeline. The majority of firms, including Mannesmann, Dresser-France, and John Brown Engineering were not dependent on either American suppliers or access to American consumer markets. Consequently, as predicted, the imposition of U.S. sanctions was insufficient to alter their behavior. American influence was not, however, completely absent. The U.S. government was, for example, able to exploit Alsthom-Atlantique's dependence on supplies from General Electric and the access of its parent company to U.S. markets as a means of altering its behavior. This success was important because Alsthom-Atlantique was the most cost-effective alternate supplier for European firms of the rotors and related technology that they could no longer purchase from General Electric.

The United States government was generally more successful in securing extraterritorial corporate compliance with its export restrictions during Operation Exodus than during the trans-Siberian Pipeline crisis. This success can be attributed to the general willingness of host country governments to allow the application of U.S. sanctions against their constituents, combined with a comparatively high degree of net corporate dependence on access to American suppliers in the computer industry. As predicted, however, U.S. influence was not absolute. When corporate dependence on American suppliers or the American market was low, as in the Thomson Group case, the U.S. government was unable to secure compliance using economic sanctions. The inability of the U.S. government to restrict the sales made by the Thomson Group is unfortunate given that a Thomson-built Crotale missile shot down the one plane lost in the U.S. bombing raid on Tripoli in 1986, and that Thomson radar systems played a critical role in Iraq's early warning systems used during the Persian Gulf War of 1991.[4]

The findings suggest that host government cooperation with U.S. enforcement efforts increases the effectiveness of its secondary sanctions against foreign firms. At the same time, the case studies suggest that governments and firms tend to respond to U.S. sanctions independently from one another. For example, based on a variety of national concerns ranging from dependence on American suppliers to the perception of a joint security threat, the British government assisted U.S. agents in enforcing its export control restrictions against the wishes of ICL and other British firms. Host government cooperation is, however, neither always necessary nor always sufficient to guarantee extraterritorial compliance by firms or individuals. In the case of Alsthom-Atlantique, for example, the company chose to abide by U.S. restrictions despite the de jure support of the French government against U.S. enforcement efforts.

Furthermore, while the statistical results suggest that dependence on access to foreign suppliers generally has a more significant impact on both corporate compliance and host government cooperation than dependence on foreign markets, the comparative case studies generally support the proposition that firms were also vulnerable to sanctions and incentives involving market access.

COSTS AND LIMITATIONS OF SANCTIONS

Under appropriate conditions, all states can use economic statecraft to exert political influence. It is important to recognize, however, that even under ideal conditions, the use of economic statecraft (and sanctions in particular) may have economic and political ramifications beyond its intended effect on a particular target. In economic terms alone, the president's Export Council report on unilateral economic sanctions in June of 1997 estimates that the direct impact of sanctions on U.S. firms resulting from foregone sales and business relationships with the targeted country amounted to lost exports in 1995 of $15 billion to $19 billion, affecting 200,000 to 250,000 export-related jobs.[5] These and other economic costs result from a variety of factors including the reciprocal nature of dependence and the threat of retaliation; the negative repercussions of sanctions on the reliability and competitiveness of domestic firms; and the incentives that sanctions create for the indigenous foreign development of restricted resources. These costs must be balanced against the benefits derived from economic statecraft before using it as a tool of foreign policy.

The Reciprocal Nature of Dependence

Just as the U.S. government can use a variety of means to control the activities of foreign countries operating abroad, so too can foreign governments affect the activities of U.S. companies operating around the globe. One of the most direct means of extending control abroad is to act through a parent company with foreign subsidiaries. Although the foreign affiliates are incorporated under the laws of their host governments, the home government can influence their activities indirectly by legally constraining their locally based headquarters. The local headquarters in turn exerts control over its subsidiaries, potentially against the interests of the subsidiary's host country's government. While the U.S. government has used this technique to control foreign subsidiaries of American companies, other governments can use the same strategy to control American subsidiaries of their companies. For example, antinuclear members of the Japanese Diet succeeded in forcing the American firm Dexcel to withhold ceramic technology from the U.S. Tomahawk missile program.[6] They did so by pressuring the Japanese Ministry of International Trade and Industry to stop the Japanese firm Kyocera from exporting related technology. Kyocera, in turn, instructed its subsidiary, Dexcel, to withhold the sale.

Similarly, just as the U.S. government can exploit foreign dependence on it suppliers and markets to its advantage, foreign governments can exploit U.S. dependence on their suppliers and markets to their advantage. The section that follows will analyze U.S. reactions to the Toshiba affair in 1987, as well as China's efforts to mobilize American companies to lobbying the U.S. government on its behalf, and Saudi Arabia's efforts to renegotiate payment on a wide range of contracts with U.S. defense industries. The examples demonstrate the ability of foreign governments can influence U.S. companies by exploiting their dependence on foreign suppliers and markets. These examples highlight the reciprocal, though often uneven, nature of dependence.

While dependence is rarely a one-way affair, it is important to remember that dependence is a function of both the value of exchange between actors and the availability of alternate trading partners. Increasing reliance by U.S. firms on foreign suppliers and foreign markets in a particular sector will increase U.S. vulnerability to foreign sanctions primarily when those suppliers of markets are limited to a small number of foreign companies located in a small number of foreign countries.[7] Relying on a diverse set of suppliers and markets will reduce this vulnerability.

American dependence on foreign suppliers. The results of the cases analyzed in the previous chapters indicate that foreign dependence on U.S. suppliers increases the likelihood that the threat of sanctions will succeed in securing corporate compliance with U.S. policies. Conversely, however, increases in U.S. dependence on foreign suppliers will decrease the likelihood that U.S. sanctions will succeed. The case of Toshiba Machine Company demonstrates this effect. Despite the fact that Toshiba was highly dependent on access to both the American market and American technology, the U.S. government was not able to deter Toshiba Machine Company from violating its export embargo, and it was not willing to inflict a substantial penalty on Toshiba following the violation. The failure to secure corporate compliance under these conditions, even with the support of the Japanese government, demonstrates some of the limitations of using sanctions under conditions of mutual dependence.

In 1987, Toshiba Machine Company and Kongsberg-Vapanfabrik of Norway sold computerized milling equipment to the Soviet Union that was capable of producing highly sophisticated propellers for submarines.[8] Kongsberg designed the software used to guide the Toshiba milling equipment. The sale enabled the Soviets to produce larger, quieter, and less detectable propellers than its existing technology. It had dramatic military significance and was in direct violation of multilateral agreements restricting the sale of sensitive technologies to the Soviet Union.

This case demonstrates the importance of securing extraterritorial compliance of private companies rather than focusing exclusively on securing intergovernmental cooperation with U.S. or multilateral rules involving the proliferation of strategic goals. As Beverly Crawford and others have argued, the Toshiba-Kongsberg case is a good example of involuntary defection. Both firms were noncompliant, but it is likely that the Japanese and Norwegian governments were not fully aware of the sale. Once the sale was discovered, both the Japanese and Norwegian governments penalized their firms and dramatically strengthened their export control enforcement efforts. The Japanese government, for example, expanded penalties for export violations under an amendment to its foreign exchange and foreign trade control law, and it accepted U.S. assistance in improving its export monitoring and screening process.

In response to their actions, the U.S. Congress voted (95–2) to penalize Kongsberg and Toshiba by terminating U.S. imports of their products (including purchases by the U.S. government) for three to five years.[9] Senator Jake Garn went so far as to propose a bill that would retroactively ban any company that violated CoCom rules from doing business in the United States.[10] Given Toshiba's overwhelming reliance on the American consumer market with projected losses of over $30 billion in sales over the three-year embargo and the lack of a comparable alternate market, both dominance and dependence hypotheses would predict that these sanctions should have been sufficient to alter corporate policy.[11] Failing to deter Toshiba, the U.S. government should have been able to penalize Toshiba. However, the vast majority of penalties against Toshiba were quickly dropped, leaving only a watered-down three-year ban with exceptions granted for national security and other reasons.[12] A complete ban was applied only to the Toshiba subsidiary, Toshiba Machines, that sold the restricted technology to the Soviets. Instead of cutting off access to lucrative U.S. government and consumer markets for all Toshiba products, the final version of the sanctions embargoed only Toshiba toasters, microwave ovens, and other "low-level" goods. Consequently, despite an initial 100 percent punitive tariff placed on Toshiba goods in April (including laptop computers), less than three months later, the Pentagon placed a $100 million order for laptop computers from Toshiba.[13]

One of the primary reasons that the U.S. government backed away from its original threats was American dependence—both national and corporate—on the supply of computer chips from Toshiba and the supply of sophisticated technology from Japanese firms more generally. Japan was dependent on U.S. suppliers and markets, but the United States was also dependent on Japanese suppliers. In 1987, the United States remained the largest supplier and market for computer products, accounting for 22.8 percent of world exports and 16.4 percent of world imports. Japan, however, was the second largest supplier of computer equipment by a close margin, accounting for 22.5 percent of world exports.[14] Over half of Japanese imports came from, and half of their exports went to the United States. On a scale from 0 to 1, Japanese dependence on U.S. markets was .063 while its dependence on U.S. suppliers was a high .185. (See table 4.1.) At the same time, however, the United States relied heavily on imports of Japanese computer equipment. Japanese exports of computer equipment accounted for 49.2 percent of all American computer equipment imports. On a scale from 0 to 1, American dependence on Japanese computer suppliers was 0.11. One would predict, therefore, both that Japan was dependent on the U.S. suppliers *and* that the United States was dependent on Japanese suppliers in the computer industry.

On the national level, the U.S. government was dependent on the supply of Japanese computer chips as well as continued Japanese cooperation in other areas. The United States military has long pursued a policy of relying primarily on U.S. sources of supply in order to minimize its dependence on others. Following this philosophy, the U.S. military relied heavily on Texas Instruments for its semiconductor and computer needs. Texas Instruments, however, had moved the majority of its production facilities overseas, notably to Japan where it runs a production plant with a subsidiary of Toshiba. As a result, cutting off all government contracts with Toshiba would result in cutting off U.S. military access to a major supplier of its semiconductor and computer chips.

The U.S. Defense Department also perceived itself to be dependent on access to a variety of sophisticated Japanese technologies including radar transmitters, superconductors, software, optical systems, and semiconductors, that it needed for the development of the Strategic Defense Initiative.[15] No comparable alternate supplier of these technologies existed. In addition, the U.S. government needed continued Japanese cooperation on a variety of other trade and financial matters. This broad national dependence on both Japanese suppliers and cooperation from the Japanese government gave Japan a source of leverage, which it used to secure an agreement by the executive branch of the U.S. government to pressure Congress into softening its embargo against Toshiba.[16]

The decision to lighten the sanctions was also strongly motivated by economic concerns at the corporate level. American firms that relied on or sold Toshiba products lobbied strongly against the ban. Corporations argued that high-technology businesses were so complex and intertwined that there would be no way to avoid serious economic damage. As Edward Black, vice president of the Computer and Communications Industries

Association, argued: "There is no major [U.S.] company that would go under because of the sanctions, but we are talking about whole product lines or market areas where a company could be so hobbled that it would be forced to withdraw from the market."[17] These lobbying efforts were headed by large industrial pressure groups including the American Electronics Association, the Computer and Business Equipment Manufacturers Association, the Business Roundtable, the National Association of Manufacturers, and others.[18] As a result of strong criticisms from domestic firms, foreign firms, and foreign governments, the U.S. Commerce Department announced a softening of its rigorous new export policy to stop leaks of high technology to the East bloc.[19]

The Toshiba case is important because it demonstrates that dependence can be reciprocal and the threat or use of sanctions against foreign companies can inflict real costs on the United States. When the United States is dependent on others for certain technologies, capital or other goods it, too, is vulnerable to foreign sanctions. Even though foreign governments and firms may not be able to influence the American policymaking process directly, they *can* directly affect the interests of American firms. The resulting actions taken by these firms, through lobbying efforts or other means, can have a direct impact on the American government. As a result, despite possessing more economic and military resources than any other country a variety of sectors, the United States may not always be able to enforce its policies unilaterally at home or abroad.

American dependence on foreign markets. Restricting or promising additional access to the American consumer market has given the U.S. government a powerful tool to coerce or entice foreign actors. In parallel, restricting or promising access to potentially lucrative non-American markets provides other countries with a powerful stick and carrot to use against the U.S. government and American firms. Recent examples of this phenomenon involve the American arms, computer, and telecommunications industries.

Given cutbacks in the American defense budget, American arms producers are becoming increasingly dependent on access to foreign markets. There are relatively few potential buyers who are both wealthy and uncontroversial enough to purchase the full range of sophisticated defense equipment exported by American producers.[20] At the same time, an increasing number of countries and firms have the capability to provide a full range of weaponry.[21] The combination of an increasing number of potential suppliers and few alternate markets gives high-end arms buyers a source of leverage over foreign producers who are dependent on access to their markets. For instance, in the mid-1990s American military contractors were forced to accept a delay in payment and renegotiation of purchasing agreements with Saudi Arabia. Given the potential loss of $1.5 billion in contracts for 1994,[22] and few comparable alternate markets available to them, the companies involved claimed to have "no alternative" other than to accept the terms dictated by Saudi Arabia. In an effort to minimize dependence on these buyers by opening new markets to American firms, the Clinton administration recently agreed to allow the sale of fighter jets, tanks, and other sophisticated weapons to ten countries of the former East Bloc.[23]

Despite the dominant position of the American consumer market for telecommunications and computer products, the People's Republic of China was similarly able to use promises of access to its large and unique telecommunications market to entice American firms to alter their behavior. China is planning to spend $30 billion to provide basic telephone service.[24] No alternate untapped telecommunications market of similar size exists. By offering an inducement of future access to this immense and unique market, the Chinese effectively altered the baseline against which corporate actors measured the value of their future economic relations with China. Combined with the uniqueness of the Chinese market, the high potential value of market access created a perception of corporate dependence on gaining market access. As a result, China was able to use market access to entice American telecommunications companies to lobby heavily in favor of maintaining China's most favored nation status regardless of its human rights record. Like firms in the telecommunications industry, the Boeing Company, which had hundreds of millions of dollars of orders from Chinese airlines for its planes, was initially one of China's most assertive allies in its fight to maintain Most Favored Nation (MFN) status.[25] It also became one of the biggest losers of U.S. and Chinese sanctions when the Chinese selected Airbus over Boeing in retaliation to later U.S. threats to hold up its membership in the World Trade Organization.

The impact of corporate lobbying was reflected in the unwillingness of the U.S. government to carry out its threat of sanctions against the Chinese government in a series of related events. In August 1993, the Clinton administration imposed sanctions on $1 billion in high-technology trade with the PRC to protest the shipment of M-11 missile technology and equipment from China to Pakistan in violation of U.S. export control policy.[26] Yet, as in the Toshiba case, the sanctions were weakened almost immediately. Despite expressing continued concern over arms transfers and weapons proliferation, the U.S. government allowed seven restricted U.S. satellites and an $8 million supercomputer built by Cray Research, Inc. to be sold.[27] It also lifted existing bans on the export of components related to China's nuclear power plants and generators. And, in May 1994, President Clinton renewed an agreement to extend MFN treatment to

China, despite Secretary of State Warren Christopher's report that, "no Chinese concessions, large or small," had been made.[28] The Chinese threat to deny market access to American firms unless they delinked U.S.-Chinese trade from its human rights policies succeeded, while the U.S. threat to deny China MFN status unless its human rights record improved failed.

The Chinese government was correct to assume that the incentive of preferential access to its huge and unique consumer market would be sufficient to entice foreign firms to lobby against MFN linkage with human rights. It is important to recognize, however, that it was the *net value* of the benefits reflected in gaining access to the Chinese market relative to the costs of not penalizing China for its human rights violations, rather than the absolute size of the Chinese market itself, that gave the Chinese government its leverage over U.S. firms. From a corporate viewpoint, delinking MFN from human rights in 1993 and 1994 was perceived to be relatively cost free when compared to losing access to the future Chinese markets. Thus, the promise to grant access and the threat to deny access to its markets were sufficient to alter corporate behavior.

In 1995 and 1996, the Chinese government again tried to offer market access as a means of securing corporate support for its policies. To date, however, this plan had not succeeded because while the carrot was the same, the net value of the trade-off was not. This time, the Chinese government offered promises of market access in exchange for corporate lobbying to de-link Chinese membership in the World Trade Organization from Chinese compliance with international intellectual property rights regulations. As with the MFN issue, Chinese Trade Minister Wu Yi tried to entice the U.S., European and Japanese governments and their firms by offering them billions of dollars worth of business if they would support Chinese membership.[29] In contrast to the MFN case, however, U.S. firms generally placed a higher value on combating piracy of foreign videos, recordings, and films than gaining access to the Chinese market without a guarantee of intellectual property rights. The general consensus among corporate actors was that long-term gains from market access would be undermined if piracy and intellectual property rights were not secure. Consequently, while U.S. businesses had supported delinking human rights from MFN treatment, they strongly supported efforts by the United States and W.T.O. to secure Chinese compliance with intellectual property rights.

Finally, despite Chinese threats of retaliation, U.S. threats of a 100 percent putative tariff on $1 billion worth of Chinese goods in the spring of 1995, and $2–3 billion of Chinese goods in the spring of 1996, succeeded in securing an agreement by the Chinese government to clamp down on piracy and close a number of offending firms.[30] Despite potential U.S. dependence on Chinese markets in some sections, the U.S. government was ultimately able to succeed in exploiting broader Chinese dependence on U.S. markets. Over 50 percent of PRC exports go to industrialized countries, and over 56 percent of its imports come from industrialized countries.[31] Unless alternates can be found, China will remain dependent on Western markets and suppliers, and thus it will remain vulnerable to the promise or denial of access to them. While it can retaliate by denying specific foreign firms access to its huge domestic market, these threats will affect firms in a limited number of industrial sectors. Overall, less than 2 percent of exports from the United States and industrialized countries go to Chinese markets, and less than 6 percent of U.S. imports and less than 3.2 percent of all imports by industrialized countries come from China.[32] As a result, the utility of such Chinese incentives or threats are undermined by the fact that in most industrial sectors, alternate, albeit smaller and more competitive, markets are available.

Reliability and Competitiveness of American Firms

Even when they are not dependent on access to foreign markets or suppliers and the threat of retaliation is minimal, the use of economic statecraft by the U.S. government can impose short- and long-term costs on American firms conducting businesses overseas. During the trans-Siberian Pipeline crisis, for example, the U.S. government terminated Caterpillar Tractor Company's exports of pipe-laying equipment. In the short term, the costs to Caterpillar were roughly equal to the value of the terminated contracts. The long-term costs, were, however, much larger. Once the U.S. lifted the embargo, Caterpillar was unable to regain the contracts it had lost. A rival Japanese firm, Komatsu, won the contract on the grounds that it could guarantee its ability to fulfill future contract obligations without the fear that the Japanese government would intervene and terminate them at some point in the future. As a spokesperson for Caterpillar later complained: "There is no doubt that during the restrictions the Soviets came to regard us as an unreliable supplier."[33] Reflecting a similar sentiment, a Dresser-France Executive argued: "After the pipeline case we received a lot of feedback from countries friendly to the U.S. about loss of reliability among U.S. firms as suppliers. They wondered what would happen if another embargo was imposed."[34]

The uncertainty of potential government intervention adds costs to business transactions by creating a potential inability to guarantee contracts. Potential clients will try to compensate for these costs. They may do so by demanding safeguards or higher fees as insurance against the potential loss of a contract, or, if the cost of a potential loss is high enough, they may try to avoid U.S. contracts completely.

Even when American exports are not restricted, the time-consuming and costly licensing requirements associated with U.S. export control regulations may undermine the competitive position of American firms operating abroad. For instance, throughout the 1980s Digital Equipment Corporation had to obtain certification for the sale of all of its equipment, and was required to inform the Commerce Department of its products' destination and intended use before a sale in Europe could be completed. European customers expressed frustration and anger about the time delays and requirements to surrender proprietary information when purchasing products from DEC and other American companies.[35] European competitors, such as GEC Computers, PLC of Great Britain, Bull-SEMS SA of France, and Norsk Data A/S of Norway offered products similar to DEC in a more timely, cost-effective manner without requiring personal information from their customers to be sent to the Commerce Department. Consequently, consumers purchased the products they desired, but DEC and other American companies did not profit from the sales.[36]

Given the problems associated with export control limitations on American suppliers and buyers, foreign firms have reduced their reliance on American suppliers since the mid-1980s. The European Airbus consortium, for example, specifically designed its products to minimize reliance on American components.[37] While it had once relied solely on American-made engines, the last three Airbus planes now offer non-U.S. engines.[38] As a result, American firms are placed at an economic disadvantage by not being able to participate as efficiently as possible in the international marketplace. In 1993 alone, one observer estimated that the resulting loss to U.S. businesses from export controls was $24 billion, or roughly 20 percent of the total U.S. merchandise trade deficit for that year.[39] Especially hard hit have been the high-technology and chemical industries. In the long-term, this could hurt the technological competitiveness of U.S. firms in these industries by reducing the number of international strategic partnerships and joint ventures. Indeed, a 1997 survey of European and American companies by the European-American Business Council found the loss of joint venture opportunities was the most frequently cited negative effect of sanctions.[40]

Given these costs, U.S. firms may attempt to insulate themselves from the unexpected contingencies of government intervention. They may be able to do so by moving politically sensitive activities to foreign subsidiaries, thereby increasing the cost to the U.S. government of employing sanctions.[41] In the Toshiba case, for example, the fact that Texas Instruments and Toshiba produced chips under a joint venture undermined the ability of the U.S. government to punish Toshiba using sanctions against its products. While this undermined U.S. leverage, it meant that transactions involving Toshiba chips and computers were largely unaffected by shifts in the politics of U.S.-Japanese relations. Based on the models presented above, however, this approach will only be effective in those industries where the U.S. government perceives itself to be dependent on access to foreign suppliers. If it is not dependent on them, changing legal jurisdictions by locating production in a foreign subsidiary will provide only a minimal degree of protection against the enforcement of U.S. policy as the U.S. government can apply secondary sanctions against foreign subsidiaries or other affiliates of American firms to entice or coerce them.

In response to these problems, the U.S. Congress has gradually been liberalizing a wide range of high-technology exports.[42] Reflecting the perspective of high-technology industries affected by the controls, the Omnibus Export Control Act of 1995 requires the Secretary of Commerce to review export control regulations periodically. If warranted, the Secretary of Commerce may increase specified export control thresholds or remove export controls on computer equipment, computer communications, and networking equipment and software that becomes obsolete.[43] Finally, Congress is currently considering the Sanctions Reform Act of 1998, which would require that sanctions mandated by Congress be focused as narrowly as possible, be tied to a specific foreign policy objective, and protect existing contracts.[44] It would also require the president to report to Congress periodically on its economic cost to the United States and the likely effectiveness of any sanctions imposed.

The 1995 Act also provides favorable licensing treatment for the export of commodities and technology among members of the New Forum or other multilateral export control regimes. Furthermore, efforts have been made within the New Forum to adapt technology restriction lists to meet the rapid technological changes facing the world today. While these changes will not resolve disputes over the restriction of certain dual-use technologies—such as high-end cellular phones with encryption capabilities, fiber-optic equipment, and military-grade data encryption software—substantial progress has been made to minimize the hindrance to nonthreatening trade.[45] The key to the success of the New Forum will be its flexibility in terms of both adaptation to new technology and to new actors that threaten international peace and stability. As one observer of the New Forum notes: "Flexibility and discretion must be the hallmark of a regime dealing with emerging technologies and changing nations."[46]

Indigenous Development of Restricted Resources

If alternate suppliers of restricted products are not available, firms that are denied access to traditional suppliers may try to develop substitutes internally. This option is often difficult and may require a large financial and technological capabilities, but designing products without foreign parts is an effective way of minimizing dependence on foreign suppliers.[47] In the early 1960s, for example, the United States forbad the export of radar equipment to Viscount Aircraft because the British company sold planes to communist China.[48] After failing to alter U.S. policy, the company redesigned its planes to avoid using U.S. equipment. It thus avoided U.S. restrictions and the sales went through.[49] Similarly, in 1987, following the grounding of the U.S. space shuttle fleet, General Motors and General Electric requested and were initially refused export licenses that would allow them to launch their communications satellites on Soviet rockets.[50] Consequently, British Aerospace sent letters notifying U.S. suppliers that it was designing out U.S.-origin components because of the extension of U.S. export controls. To avoid similar constraints, foreign producers of satellite equipment began designing their equipment to avoid using American components.

Restricting the supply of certain goods from American sources may also provide foreign competitors with the motivation necessary to pursue research and development in areas that would not have been pursued had the products been available. It also provides local governments with a justification for redistributing money to research and development at the national level. Therefore, in the long run, the technological lead of the United States will be undermined if access to sophisticated products it now produces is restricted excessively.[51] One of the best incentives for investing in the research and development of new products is the possession of a working model of the final product. In the case of IBM-France and GE-Bull, for example, U.S. restrictions helped motivate the French government to create "national champions" in the French computer industry.

In 1964, the United States government prohibited IBM-France from selling advanced computers to the French government. The action was taken as part of an American attempt to get France to sign the nuclear test-ban treaty and join international restraints on the production of nuclear weapons. It was part of a general ban on the export of sophisticated equipment to France that might be used in the development of its nuclear or space programs. After two years, the French agreed not to use the computers for their nuclear weapons program, and the U.S. approved the sale for use in peaceful nuclear research and development. Unfortunately, however, France did not sign the Non-Proliferation Treaty until 1991.

This case is an example of the potential repercussions of exploiting a dependent relationship. The U.S. was able to exploit French dependence on IBM to secure a compromise from the French. This success, however, had its political and economic costs. Politically, this dispute caused considerable friction between the United States and France across a wide range of issues and reportedly affected France's denial of British entry into the European Common Market.[52] Economically, the denial of sales by the French affiliate emphasized to the French government that it was technologically dependent on American firms in the electronics and computer suppliers. As a result, the French government began an intensive effort to develop indigenous electronics and computer industries, leading to the support of National Champions. It also made later attempts by American companies to acquire French affiliates more difficult. General Electric, for instance, had an extremely difficult time acquiring Machines Bull and was eventually forced to accept a joint-venture arrangement, majority owned by Bull, to do research and development in computers for military purposes.[53] While the continued dependence of the European computer industry on U.S. and Japanese suppliers (discussed in chapter 4) indicates that support for National Champions did not succeed in freeing France from its dependence on foreign suppliers, this case demonstrates the sizeable efforts that national governments, as well as firms, are willing to take to break dependencies on restrictive foreign suppliers.

Internal research and development needed to create local substitutes for restricted products can be extremely costly, particularly if the lead time and cost of developing alternatives is long. However, the increasingly rapid global diffusion of technology suggests that foreign companies will be able to develop restricted goods internally more quickly and at lower cost than in the past. Their ability to do so could potentially undermine both the effectiveness of sanctions and the competitiveness of firms in the sender country by creating new alternate suppliers.[54] Indeed, the fear that U.S. sanctions could give foreign competitors an unfair advantage in emerging markets was one of the principal arguments used by corporate lobbyists in their efforts to change U.S. export control policies in the late 1980s.[55]

SANCTIONS IN AN INCREASINGLY INTERDEPENDENT WORLD

Given the opportunities and constraints of using economic statecraft, it is useful to evaluate the resurgent use of sanctions and incentives to achieve foreign policy objections today. This section will demonstrate in a step-by-step process how the theory of economy statecraft developed in the previous chapters can be used to evaluate the likely effectiveness of the secondary sanctions currently targeted by the United States against foreign companies conducting business in Cuba, Iran, and Libya under the Helms-Burton Act and the Iran-Libya Sanctions Act. Both of these acts are controversial and neither has the support of U.S. trading partners. Consequently, this section concludes by assessing the vulnerability of the United States and its firms to retaliatory sanctions from its Canadian, Mexican, French, and German trading partners.

To use economic statecraft judiciously, policymakers must balance the likelihood of its effectiveness against the potential costs of its use. To do so, policymakers must begin by identifying what they want to accomplish and who in particular they need to influence to achieve their chosen objectives. Having identified the objectives and appropriate target, policymakers must assess the likely effectiveness of economic statecraft. If few alternate suppliers or markets are available for the goods that the sender is planning to offer or deny the target, and the target's trade with the sender accounts for a relatively high proportion of its imports or exports of those goods, then the sender should consider using sanctions to achieve its objectives. In parallel, if few alternate suppliers or markets are available for the goods that the sender is planning to offer of deny the target, and the target's trade with the sender accounts for a relatively low proportion of its imports or exports of those goods, then the sender should consider using incentives. If the costs or benefits of the sanctions or incentives are greater than the target's opportunity and adjustment costs of abiding by the sender's request, then the target will likely comply.

Once policymakers have determined whether sanctions or incentives are likely to achieve their chosen objectives, they must weigh the benefits gained by achieving those goals using economic statecraft against the economic and political costs of doing so. Several of these costs were specified in the previous section. Of those, the most immediate short-term costs for the sender result from the reciprocal nature of dependence. Policymakers must, therefore, assess both the costs imposed on the sender if it were to restrict or expand the target's access to its markets or suppliers (or what ever penalty or reward the sender chooses the use), and the sender's vulnerability to retaliatory sanctions by the target. These costs are a function of the sender's dependence on the target. Finally, the policymakers must assess the broader economic, political and social costs that using economic statecraft may have non-targeted actors in the sender and target country. Once these economic and political analyses are complete, policymakers should use their political judgement to determine whether the capability to use economic statecraft is worth the cost of doing so.

The Helms-Burton Act

U.S. policy towards Cuba in the mid-1990s was encapsulated in the Cuban Democracy Act of 1992 and the Cuban Liberty and Democratic Solidarity (LIBERTAD) Act of 1996, also known as the Helms-Burton Act.[56] The stated goals of these acts include promoting democratic freedom and prosperity for the Cuban people, strengthening international sanctions against the Castro government, providing for U.S. national security in the face of continuing negative sanctions from the Castro government, providing a policy framework for U.S. support of the Cuban transition to democracy, and protecting U.S. nationals against confiscation and the wrongful trafficking in property confiscated by the Castro regime.[57] Both Acts explicitly imposed penalties on the Cuban regime despite minimal Cuban dependence on its existing economic relations with the United States.

The Cuban Democracy Act of 1992 attempted to increase the financial costs imposed on Cuba by closing a loop-hole in the U.S. embargo that had allowed subsidiaries of American companies to conduct business in Cuba. The Cuban Democracy Act (CDA) effectively terminated commercial relations between Cuba and subsidiaries of U.S. companies including Cargill, Dow Chemical, Union Carbide, and United Technologies worth approximately $720 million.[58] The business lost as a result of the CDA, however, accounted for a relatively small proportion of the $5 billion in ongoing commercial relations between Cuba and foreign companies from other countries, the majority of whom are major U.S. trading partners.[59] In 1994, for example, Spain, France, Italy, and other European Union members accounted for 45 percent of Cuba's total trade, while trade with Canada and Mexico made up the bulk of the remainder, mainly in food, tobacco, and minerals.[60] If the United States is to inflict sufficient costs on the Cuban regime to compel it to alter its behavior, then the United States may need to secure the cooperation of the majority of these potential alternate suppliers and markets for the goods cut off by the U.S. embargo. The Helms-Burton Act was designed in part to accomplish this objective.

Goals and targets.   Under the Cuban Liberty and Democratic Solidarity (LIBERTAD) Act of 1996 (PL 104–114), also know as the Helms-Burton Act, the United States is threatening to impose secondary sanctions against foreign firms that conduct business with Cuba in violation of a U.S. embargo.[75] Title III of the Act targets all actors that cause, direct, participate in, or profit from "trafficking" in property that was confiscated or nationalized from American citizens in Cuba after Fidel Castro came to power in 1959. These actors include all those who "act to manage, lease, possess, use or hold an interest in" such property.[62] All such individuals or firms will be considered in violation of U.S. law. Consequently, American companies or citizens whose property was expropriated may sue them in U.S. courts for damages up to the fair market value of the property, or the amount certified to the claimant by the U.S. Foreign Claims Settlement Commission.[63] Furthermore, Title IV of the Act forbids any such actor (including foreign business executives and major shareholders associated with offending companies and their families) from entering the United States. The law formally went into effect on August 1, 1996.

Means of enforcement.   Strengthening the U.S. embargo against Cuba reverses a recent trend toward normalization in U.S. policy toward Cuba and puts the United States at odds with its major trading partners who have continued to follow strategies of "constructive engagement" and open trade with Cuba, Iran, and Libya. With the end of the Cold War, the Bush Administration had increasingly favored the use of incentives rather than negative sanctions as a means of promoting democratization in Cuba. It was also sympathetic to loose coalition of business lobbies that opposed the CDA,[64] though corporate lobbying in favor of normalization of Cuban relations remained minimal until 1994 after the normalization of relations with Vietnam and improvement of relations with China.[65] This limited domestic opposition to increased sanctions countered by a focused group of well-financed supporters of the Cuban Democracy Act led by the Cuban American Federation and the Cuban American National Foundation headed by Jorge Mas Canosa and Congressman Robert Torricelli.[66] In addition, the power of the CDA supporters was enhanced by electoral pressure following a successful fund-raising event in which candidate Clinton courted the Cuban-American community by criticizing the Bush administration for missing an opportunity to clamp down on Fidel Castro and Cuba.[67] Fearing the loss of Florida, President Bush capitulated and signed the CDA into law.

U.S. policy toward Cuba shifted toward normalization between 1992 and 1996. Beginning in 1994, the business lobbies in favor of expanding trade with Cuba grew in size and became better organized.[68] In addition, the Clinton administration, and the State Department in particular, increased their opposition to congressional interference in foreign policy matters through its increased oversight of sanctions in Cuba.[69] Despite growing opposition to sanctions, the CANF continued to lobby Congress in support of the Helms-Burton legislation. The legislation was approved by the House in September and by the Senate in October of 1995, but, in deference to the business community, it did not include Title III. The modified legislation could have enabled the beginning of economic engagement with Cuba if Title III had not been reinstated following the shooting down of two planes belonging to American citizens on 27 February 1996. The shooting down of an American plane focused much broader public attention on Cuba and shifted the goals of U.S. policy from altering Cuban behavior to punishing it for attacking American civilians.[70] In response to the downing of the Brother's-to-the-Rescue plane, Senator Helms and others succeeded in restoring Title III and IV of the Helms-Burton legislation as well as in adding provisions that shifted the authority over the embargo away from the president to Congress.

On 12 March 1996, the president signed the Helms-Burton Act into law. He argued that the United States would not tolerate any act of aggression against its citizens.[71] Furthermore, President Clinton claimed, "the persistent refusal of Cuba to move toward democracy or openness and the particular problems that causes for countries in our hemisphere and for the United States especially justified passage of the bill, which I signed into law."[72] As a Canadian diplomat argued, "Until the tragedy . . . the

White House shared our views. That tragedy turned day into night for us on this issue."[73] The shift in U.S. policy means that, like the rest of the cases analyzed in this book, the United States government would have to get foreign actors to do something they would not otherwise do. As in the previous cases, if the U.S. fails to persuade foreign firms to cooperate, it can use economic statecraft to entice or coerce them into complying with its policies.

The primary penalties embodied in the Helms-Burton Act include the threat of being sued by U.S. companies in U.S. courts for the fair market value of the expropriated property, or the amount certified to the claimant by the U.S. Foreign Claims Settlement Commission. The United States is the only country that has failed to reach a compensation agreement with Cuba, and the amount of outstanding claims regarding expropriated property from American citizens is greater with Cuba than any other country. Prior to the Helms-Burton Act 5,911 corporations and individuals had filed validated claims with the Foreign Claims Settlement Commission worth a total of $1.8 billion.[74] Title III of the Helms-Burton Act greatly expands the number of potential claimants by allowing naturalized citizens who were Cubans at the time of expropriation to file claims in U.S. courts. It permits any current U.S. citizen with claims of at least $50,000 to sue anyone trafficking in their property, with the caveat that they must wait at least two years and until all prior "certified claimants" have been resolved.[75] In addition, Title IV of the law forbids any such actor (including foreign business executives and major shareholders associated with offending companies and their families) from entering the United States.

On 10 July 1996, the State Department announced its first punitive measures under the Helms-Burton Act. As it had during Operation Exodus, the U.S. government sent letters to a limited number of foreign companies threatening to impose sanctions on them if they did not cease

Table 5.1 U.S. Citizen Claims against Expropriated Property

COUNTY CLAIMS	AMOUNT OF CLAIMS (MILLIONS)	AMOUNT SETTLED FOR (MILLIONS)	YEAR SETTLED
Cuba	$1,800	unsettled	unsettled
East Germay	$275	$190	1992
Vietnam	$220	$203	1995
China	$196	$80	1979
Iran	$86	$57	1990
Russia	$60	unsettled	unsettled

Source: Justice Department; Michael Dodds, "Law Allows New Claims against Cuba." *Washington Post,* 16 July 1996, p. A12.

conducting business in Cuba. For example, the Sherritt Company of Toronto Canada received a notice from the State Department that its executives may be barred from the United States.[76] The State Department threatened to bar the director along with eight top officers and their families from entering the United States in six weeks if the company did not terminate its investments in Cuba, worth approximately $250 million.[77] Sherritt had been operating a joint venture with a Cuban state-owned mining company for the past two years. The mine had been expropriated from Freeport-MacMoRan, Inc. of New Orleans in 1959.[78]

U.S. trading partners reacted to the threat of U.S. sanctions by vigorously challenging the extraterritorial application of U.S. law in much the same way as they had during the trans-Siberian Pipeline crisis. For example, European Commission President Jacques Sander argued, "We do not believe it is justifiable or effective for one country to impose its tactics on others and to threaten . . . its friends. If that is done, it is bound to lead to reactions it is in the interests of both to avoid."[79] Similarly, Canada's ambassador in Washington, Raymond Chretien argued, "The Helms-Burton legislation seeks to apply U.S. law outside your borders. This we cannot accept."[80] Mexican President Ernesto Zedillo argued that, "Like Canada, Mexico considers inadmissible any measure . . . that, instead of tearing down barriers, raises them to the detriment of investment and international trade.[81] And, twenty-three of the thirty-four members of the Organization of American States voted, with ten abstaining, to denounce the "blatant interventionist nature" of the law.[82]

In response to the outrage of America's trading partners, President Clinton affirmed the basic premise of the law, but softened its impact by forbidding affected domestic firms from filing lawsuits against foreign firms trafficking in expropriated property for six months beginning on 16 July 1996, and he has done so again every six months since then.[83] Repeatedly suspending the implementation of Title III of the Helms-Burton Act has served three objectives.[84] First, it has increased the likelihood of reaching a negotiated solution to the Cuba problem by allowing six months for negotiations, backed up with a deterrent threat of sanctions if the negotiations fail. Clinton argued, for example, that the delay would allow the U.S. government time to persuade reluctant trading partners to "join us in taking concrete steps to promote democracy in Cuba."[85] According to White House spokesman Michael McCurry, the president "expects to continue suspending the right to file suits as long as America's friends and allies continue their stepped-up efforts to promote transition and democracy."[86] This strategy is far more likely to result in a mutually acceptable outcome than one based on imposing the full force of U.S. sanctions on its trading partners and continuing to do so until they feel compelled to change their behavior. As deterrence theorists have argued, deterrence is more likely to lead to an amicable solution than compellance because it enables targeted actors to justify their behavior on their own terms, rather than as a result of another's influence.[87] This face-saving characteristic of deterrence lessens the rally-around-the-flag effect and makes it less contentious politically than being compelled to comply.

In support of this proposition, Deputy National Security Advisor Samuel Berger argued that this strategy provides the U.S. government with a "lever to promote democracy in Cuba" rather than "a sledgehammer;" though he added that "the threat of liability is real" for more than one hundred foreign firms operating on confiscated property if diplomatic persuasion is unsuccessful.[88] President Clinton argued further that "by working with our allies—not against them—we will avoid a split that the Cuban regime will be sure to exploit."[89] At least initially, this strategy worked. In December 1996, President Clinton was able to convince the European allies to tie their economic concessions to Cuba to Cuban progress on human rights and democracy at every stage.[90] As a result of this concession, President Clinton was able to justify his decision to suspend Title III for a second time in January of 1997 to the U.S. Congress.

Second, the strategy enables both the president and Congress to send a strong political message to Castro that actions taken against U.S. citizens will not be tolerated. Recent U.S. efforts to promote sanctions against Cuba in the United Nations reinforce this message by identifying Cuban actions as unacceptable to the international community.[91] Sending a strong signal by, increasing sanctions against Cuba also bolstered electoral support among Cuban exiles in Florida and New Jersey in the 1996 presidential elections. At the same time, it added to the president's flexibility in the domestic arena making it easier to suspend the sanctions again in January of 1997 once the election was over and domestic pressure had subsided. Suspending the sanctions again enabled the U.S. government to minimize, though not negate, the costs of the sanctions on its trading partners.

If the primary goal of U.S.-Cuban policy symbolic or political in nature, then the U.S. government can achieve its objectives by securing the compliance of a small number of high-profile foreign companies operating in Cuba. If, however, the goal is to inflict sufficient costs on the Cuban regime to force it to alter its behavior, then the secondary sanctions will have to be applied against virtually all firms that could act as alternate suppliers for the goods cut off by the U.S. embargo. Given the over four thousand foreign companies currently conducting business in Cuba, achieving this objective would require dramatically increasing the scope and domain of U.S. secondary sanctions.[92] The broader the secondary sanctions become, the greater the risk of alienating U.S. trading partners and their firms; the greater the risk of reciprocal dependence and retaliation against the United States; the greater the risk to U.S. firms of becoming unreliable trading partners; and the greater the risk that the targeted firms will seek out non-American suppliers or develop restricted goods internally thereby undermining the long-run competitiveness of American companies. Consequently, U.S. businesses from the National Association of Manufactures, the U.S. Chamber of Commerce, and the National Foreign Trade Council have lobbied strongly against the implimentation of Title III of the Helms-Burton Act claiming that it would jeopardize U.S. economic interests abroad, invite retaliation, and fail to accomplish its objective.[93]

Third and most significantly, every time that President Clinton has suspended Title III, he has reaffirmed the law's basic premise that U.S. firms have the right to sue foreign companies for damages. As discussed in the Appendix, there are several legal principles that can be used on which to justify the extraterritorial application of U.S. policy. Most importantly, the Helms-Burton Act applies the objective territoriality principle or "effects doctrine" to domestic companies. The effects doctrine justifies the extraterritorial application of U.S. regulations over foreign actors who have the intent of affecting U.S. citizens whether or not their intentions have been carried out.[94] In this case, the Helms-Burton Act reflects this principle by holding applies firms who use traffic in confiscated property accountable for the benefits denied to U.S. firms as a result of their expropriation by the Cuban government.

In addition to the effects doctrine, the Helms-Burton Act also invokes the "protective principle" which grants the right of a state to exercise jurisdiction over conduct outside its territory if the conduct threatens its security.[95] For example, one of the stated purposes of the Act is to "provide for the continued national security of the United States in the face of continuing threats from the Cuban government."[96] This is significant because it provides a justification for more extensive sanctions than those specified in the Helms-Burton Act itself. These may include the threat of being blacklisted or denied access to the American markets or suppliers. Defining the policy in terms of U.S. national security also enables the United States to take advantage of escape clauses in the World Trade Organization and the North American Free Trade Agreement that allow exceptions to their basic principles of free trade when national security is threatened. While the European Union has threatened to challenge the Helms-Burton sanctions in the W.T.O., and Canada and Mexico have threatened to do the same under NAFTA, the United States is arguably still in compliance with the letter (if not the spirit) of the rules specified by these institutions, though as argued below, claiming an exemption to general W.T.O. protocols is a dangerous strategy. Nonetheless, as a a result of Clinton suspending the implementation of Title III, the E.U. agreed to suspend their complaint in the W.T.O. pending talks with the United States to seek common ground.[97]

The Iran-Libya Sanctions Act

International events conspired to undermine opposition to the Iran-Libya bill (HR 3107) sponsored by Senator Alfonse D'Amato and Representative Benjamin Gilman just as they undermined opposition to the Helms-Burton Act. The Executive Branch had opposed the Iran-Libya sanctions in part because of increased tensions with its European trade partners over the Helms-Burton Act, however, the potential of a terrorist link to the July 17 crash of TWA flight 800 created a groundswell of Executive and Congressional support for it.[98] The House of Representatives approved the Senate's version of the bill on 23 July 1996 and President Clinton agreed to sign the bill into law.[99] The primary European fear is that the Helms-Burton Act has set a precedent that Congress may now use to justify imposing a trade ban against companies that invest in Iran and Libya. The Iran-Libya Sanctions Act could have a much greater impact on Europe than the Helms-Burton Act because European firms do far more business with Iran and Libya than Cuba, and they do so in the profitable and strategically sensitive energy sector.[100]

Goals and targets. The Iran-Libya Sanctions Act is intended to penalize foreign firms that are profiting from Iranian and Libyan oil projects which are off limits to American firms. The stated goal of the legislation is to impose sanctions on persons exporting goods or technology that could enhance Iran's ability to explore for, extract, refine, or transport petroleum resources, and for other related purposes.[101] It requires the president to impose two of six possible sanctions against firms investing more than $40 million in either Iran or Libya's oil industry per year. In particular, the sanctions ban offending foreign companies from U.S. government procurement contracts and deny them access to U.S. markets (although the president can waive this restriction in the national interest). Offending firms may also be denied Export-Import Bank loans, denied export licenses, barred from receiving more than $10 million from U.S. banks in a year, and barred from being primary dealers of U.S. government bonds.[102] The president has the flexibility to waive the sanctions against firms whose governments take steps to punish Iran and Libya or participate in multilateral efforts to isolate those countries.[103] Finally, while the final bill imposes sanctions against firms for investing in either country, it penalizes firms conducting business with Libya more than those conducting business in Iran by imposing additional sanctions on firms that receive any exports from Libya, or that sell petroleum goods, chemical, biological or nuclear weapons, or aviation equipment to Libya in violation of U.N. Security Council resolutions.

While the Iran-Libya legislation is strongly supported by the American Israel Public Affairs Committee and other groups that regard Iran as a threat to regional stability, it is vigorously opposed by both U.S. business lobbies and European, Russian, and South Asian firms. The United States unilaterally terminated its trading relations with Iran in 1995, and has listed both Iran and Libya as sponsors of international terrorism. As a result, U.S. firms are forbidden from conducting business with these countries. In contrast, German, French, and several Asian companies continue to conduct a large amount of business in these countries, particularly in oil exploration and production.[104] Their behavior is part of the strategy of "constructive engagement" that the E.U. has followed with Iran and Libya since 1992.[105] In opposition to the U.S. embargo, Germany Foreign Minister Klaus Kikel argued that, "It is, in our view, better to continue the dialogue with Iran rather than break off all contacts, introduce sanctions and further radicalize Iran by isolating the country."[106] European Union spokesman Paul Guilford argued further that, "We are also determined to combat terrorism, but we don't think this is the right way to go about it. It remains an unacceptable piece of legislation and the European Union will defend its interests."[107] As a consequence, European governments have refused to stop their firms from taking over trade agreements with Iran and Libya dropped by American companies. For example, in the spring of 1995 after the Clinton administration forced an American firm Conoco to remove its bid for an Iranian contract regarding petroleum exploration and production, French, German, and Russian oil companies immediately bid to replace Conoco.[108]

Responding to European criticisms, Representative Lee Hamilton argued: "The ultimate goal of the bill is not to punish foreign firms, but to persuade other governments to adopt measures that squeeze the economies of Iran and Libya."[109] The legislation's sponsors, however, argued that the legislation was intended to give teeth to U.S. policy by directly penalizing firms that did not comply with it. For example, Representative Benjamin Gilman argued that the legislation was intended to force "foreign companies to choose between investing in our market and those of Iran and Libya."[110] Similarly, Senator D'Amato argued, "It's time we take real action against terrorism and the countries that sponsor it. Now the nations of the world will know they can trade with them or trade with us. They have to choose."[111] To lend credibility to this threat, Senator D'Amato recently sent a letter to the French oil company Total SA warning it that proceeding with a $600 million acquisition of two Iranian oil fields from Conoco could threaten Total's ability to conduct business in the Unites States.[112] In response, European governments have issued statements reserving the right to retaliate against the United States.

Fearing economic retaliation, European firms with U.S. subsidiaries, like Siemans AG of Germany, joined General Electric and other U.S. firms with large overseas operations in lobbying against the bill.[113] Foreign Chamber of Commerce Spokesman, Bill Berry argued that, "This is a big mistake. The risk which began with the [anti-Cuba] Helms-Burton bill is going to grow to an enormous extent."[114] Similarly, the European Commission Ambassador to the United States, Hugo Paemen, argued that the bill is "an extreme case of extraterritorial legislation," against which the European Union "is now considering counter-measures to defend its citizens and industry."[115] In retaliation, the European Union threatened to file a complaint with the World Trade Organization, pass domestic legislation banning their own companies from complying with U.S. law, and retaliate by imposing countersanctions against the United States and its firms.

Dominance, Dependence, and the Likelihood of Compliance

Based on the arguments specified above, the likelihood that the United States will be able to compel foreign companies to alter their behavior using secondary sanctions under the Helms-Burton Act and the Iran-Libya Sanctions Act is a function U.S. trade dominance and the net dependence of these firms on U.S. markets and suppliers in the sectors where they are operating.

Securing corporate compliance under the Helms-Burton Act. On 10 July 1996, sanctions were formally implemented against Sherritt International Corporation, a Canadian nickel mining company.[116] Letters threatening sanctions were also sent to Cemex, a Mexican cement company; Societa Finanziaria Telefonica Per Azioni (STET), an Italian telecommunications company; and Grupo Domos, a Mexican telecommunications conglomerate for conducting business in Cuba.[117] In addition, while they had not yet received formal notification from the U.S. government, two Spanish hotel companies announced their withdrawal from Cuba after the value of their stocks plummeted in anticipation of U.S. sanctions.[118]

To minimize the effects of U.S. sanctions on their firms, Canada and Mexico are likely to allow local firms to countersue American companies in local courts so that they can recoup some of their potential losses resulting from being sued in American courts. Consequently, the most potent threat the United States can impose against noncooperative foreign firms is to deny them access to U.S. markets and suppliers. While this threat is not specified in the Helms-Burton Act, the fact that the United States has declared trade with Cuba to be a matter of national security justifies the use of such sanctions if other means fail to secure compliance.

Table 5.2 Foreign Companies with Active Commercial Activities in Cuba

COMPANY	INDUSTRY	HOST COUNTRY
Accor	Tourism	France
BAT	Tobacco	Great Britain
Bayer	Pharmaceuticals	Germany
Benetton	Textiles	Italy
Cemex	Cement	Mexico
Daewoo	Electronics	South Korea
De Beers	Diamonds	South Africa
Deutsche Bank	Banking	Germany
ED & F Man	Sugar	Great Britain
GEC/Alsthom	Electronics	France
Glaxo	Pharmaceuticals	Great Britain
Grupo Domos*	Telecommunications	Mexico
Havana House Cigar and Tobacco	Tobacco	Canada
ING	Banking	The Netherlands
Labatt Breweries	Beer	Canada
Mercedes-Benz	Automobiles	Germany
Mitsubishi	Automobiles	Japan
Pemex	Oil	Mexico
Petrobras	Oil	Brazil
Sherritt*	Nickel	Canada
Sol Melia	Tourism	Spain
Stet*	Telecommunications	Italy
Tate & Lyle	Sugar	Great Britain
Toyota	Automobiles	Japan
Unilever	Soap	Great Britain

Source: U.S.-Cuba Trade and Economic Council and Adam Zagorin, "Punishing Cuba's Partners." *Time* (24 June 1996), p. 54.
*Received letters in May of 1996 from the State Department warning that they may soon be held accountable under the Helms-Burton Act.

Sherritt International Corporation operates nickel mines and is the largest Canadian company doing business in Cuba. Securing its compliance would, thus, be a big victory for U.S. policy. Using 1995 data from the World Bank to estimate trade patterns during the beginning of Helms-Burton, the United States was the world's largest importer and a moderate-sized exporter of nickel.[119] It accounted for 20.8 percent of the world nickel market, and 9.63 percent of world nickel supplies.[120] The U.S. also dominated U.S.-Canadian nickel trade. Its markets absorbed approximately 50 percent of Canada's nickel exports, and U.S. suppliers provided 27.9 percent of Canadian nickel imports. At the same time, the United States may have been vulnerable to countersanctions from the nickel industry. While Canadian markets for nickel were small (only 2.83 percent of world markets), Canada was the world's largest supplier of nickel, accounting for 27.6 percent of world exports in 1995.[121] Furthermore, the United States imported 40.3 percent of its nickel from Canadian suppliers, and 9.98 percent of its exports go west to Canada.

Measuring Canadian dependence on U.S. markets and suppliers, and U.S. dependence on Canadian markets and suppliers, provides a straightforward guide for interpreting these trade patterns. On a scale from 0 to 1, Canadian dependence on U.S. suppliers was 0.03, while its dependence on U.S. markets was 0.10. At the same time, U.S. dependence on Canadian nickel exports was 0.11, while its dependence on Canadian nickel markets was 0.02. This suggests that the Canadian nickel industry was more dependent on access to U.S. markets than U.S. suppliers. However, the benefits of threatening to cut off Canadian access to U.S. markets was undercut by U.S. dependence on access to Canadian nickel suppliers. Finally, while U.S. nickel exporters were not dependent on Canadian markets, threatening to cut off Canadian access to U.S. nickel suppliers would have virtually no effect on the industry's behavior, given that Canada remained the world's largest supplier of nickel.

Cemex of Mexico, a cement company, agreed to suspend its contracts with Cuba under the threat of U.S. sanctions. An analysis of U.S.-Mexican trade in this sector suggests that a moderately dependent and highly asymmetrical relationship between Mexico and the United States can explain Cemex's behavior. The United States dominated the world's cement market accounting for 14.8 percent of world imports, and it accounted for 2.3 percent of world exports in 1995. In addition, U.S. markets absorbed 64.7 percent of Mexican cement exports, and U.S. suppliers provided for 62.2 percent of its cement imports.[122] On a scale from 0 to 1, Mexican dependence on U.S. suppliers was 0.02, while its dependence on U.S. markets was 0.19. In contrast, the United States was not dependent on Mexican cement exports and imports. This suggests Mexico was dependent on U.S. markets and the United States was not vulnerable to countersanctions by the Mexican cement industry. Cemex's net dependence on the United States can explain why it withdrew from Cuba.

The Mexican firm Grupo Domos and the Italian firm Societa Finanziaria Telefonica Per Azioni (STET) are both in the telecommunications industry. In 1995, the United States had the world's largest market in the telecommunications industry, accounting for 19.1 percent of world imports, and it was one of the world's largest suppliers, accounting for 16.1 percent of world exports.[123] U.S. suppliers provided 51.1 percent of

Table 5.3 Dominance and Dependence under the Helms-Burton Act

	DOMINANCE OF U.S. SUPPLIERS	DOMINANCE OF U.S. MARKETS	FOREIGN DEPENDENCE ON U.S. SUPPLIERS	FOREIGN DEPENDENCE ON U.S. MARKETS	U.S. DEPENDENCE ON FOREIGN SUPPLIERS	U.S. DEPENDENCE ON FOREIGN MARKETS
Canada (F) *Sherritt*—Nickel	9.63%	20.8% (World's Largest)	0.03	0.10	0.11	0.02
Mexico (S) *Cemex*—Cement	2.30%	14.8% (World's Largest)	0.03	0.10	0.00	0.01
Mexico (S) *Grupo Domos*—Telecom	16.1% (World's Largest)	19.1% (World's Largest)	0.08	0.19	0.01	0.01
Italy (F) *STET*—Telecom	16.1% (World's Largest)	19.1% (World's Largest)	0.02	0.00	0.00	0.00

Source: Estimates based on World Bank data, 1996.

(S) = Successful Sanctions
(F) = Failed Sanctions

Mexican imports and 11.2 percent of Italian imports, and its markets absorbed 97.0 percent of Mexico's exports and 1.42 percent of Italy's exports in the telecommunications industry.

On a scale from 0 to 1, Mexican dependence on U.S. telecommunications suppliers was 0.19, while Mexican dependence on U.S. telecommunications markets was 0.08. In contrast, Italian dependence on U.S. suppliers and markets in the telecommunications sector was virtually non-existent, at 0.02 and 0.00, respectively. Consequently, sanctions that restricted access to U.S. supplies to Grupo Domos were likely to work, while sanctions against STET were likely to fail. Finally, U.S. dependence on its telecommunications trade with Mexico and Italy was non-existent. Consequently, U.S. firms were not vulnerable to retaliatory threats by foreign telecommunication industries in these countries.

As discussed in chapter 4, the increasing computerization of the telecommunication industry may enable the United States government to exploit American dominance and foreign dependence in the computer industry to increase U.S. leverage over foreign firms in the telecommunications industry. In this case, however, U.S. suppliers accounted for only 0.301 percent of Italian computer imports, while U.S. markets absorbed only 1.73 percent of Italian computer exports.[124] As a result, dependence arguments suggest that U.S. sanctions in the computer industry might help secure compliance by STET. Consistent with this prediction, in 1997 STET side-stepped restrictions under the Helms-Burton Act by paying ITT Corporation $25 million for the rights to use ITT's property in Havana.[125]

Securing corporate compliance under the Iran-Libya Sanctions Act. The Iran-Libya Sanctions Act targets firms in the European energy and petroleum industry that are conducting business with Iran and Libya. A large proportion of European oil imports come from Iran and Libya, with the two countries accounting for 20 percent of French energy imports and 44 percent of Italian imports.[126] Iran also has eleven major petroleum projects under study by European companies, including exploration in the northern part of the Persian Gulf, and the development of Libyan oil fields at Mourzouk and Mabrouk. French, German, and Russian firms, including Total SA of France and Gazprom of Russia, have been singled out because they bid on contracts in Iran that were originally awarded to the American firm Conoco, after Conoco withdrew its bid to conform with American trade restrictions.

While the United States had the world's largest market for refined petroleum, accounting for 15.8 percent of world imports, it is a relatively small supplier, accounting for only 7.78 percent of world exports of refined petroleum in 1994.[127] In parallel, U.S. markets accounted for 15.9 percent of French exports, but only 4.81 percent of German exports of refined

Table 5.4 Dominance and Dependence under the Iran-Libya Sanctions Act

	Dominance of U.S. Suppliers	Dominance of U.S. Markets	Foreign Dependence on U.S. Suppliers	Foreign Dependence on U.S. Markets	U.S. Dependence on Foreign Suppliers	U.S. Dependence on Foreign Markets
France (F) Crude Petroleum	0.035%	24.1% (World's Largest)	0.00	0.00	0.00	0.00
France (F) Refined Petroleum	7.78%	15.8% (World's Largest)	0.00	0.03	0.00	0.00
Germany (F) Crude Petroleum	0.035%	24.1% (World's Largest)	0.00	0.00	0.00	0.00
Germany (F) Refined Petroleum	7.78%	15.1% (World's Largest)	0.00	0.01	0.00	0.01
Russia (F) Mineral Fuels and Related Materials	2.72%	17.6% (World's Largest)	0.00	0.00	0.00	0.00

Source: Except for Russia, estimates are based on World Bank data, 1996. Estimates for Russia are made using the broader SITC classification of mineral fuels and related materials and are based on trade figures between the United States and the former USSR. United Nations, *International Statistics Yearbook*, vol. 2 (New York: United Nations Publishing, 1996).

(S) = Successful Sanctions
(F) = Failed Sanctions

petroleum, and its suppliers only provided 5.56 percent of French imports and 2.28 percent of German imports of refined petroleum. This suggests that restricting French or German access to U.S. markets or suppliers in the refined petroleum industry would have little effect on their behavior. On a scale from 0 to 1, French, German, and Russian dependence on the U.S. in this sector was virtually nonexistent, ranging from only 0.00 to 0.03. This suggests that French, German, and Russian firms in the petroleum industry were not dependent on access to U.S. suppliers or markets and that American threats in these industries will have little effect on their behavior. At the same time, U.S. dependence on French, German, and Russian trade in this sector is was negligeable, suggesting that the United States is not vulnerable to retaliatory threats by firms in this sector.

The United States also had the world's largest market in crude petroleum imports, accounting for 24.1 percent of world markets, but it is a relatively small exporter of crude petroleum, accounting for only 0.035 percent of world exports in 1994.[128] Yet since virtually no French or German exports of crude petroleum went to U.S. markets (they have virtually none to export), and U.S. suppliers provided only a small amount of French and German imports, amounting to 5.17 percent and 7.57 percent of their crude petroleum supplies, respectively. French and German dependence on the U.S. in this sector was virtually nonexistent, suggesting that U.S. leverage over firms in this sector would be minimal. At the same time, U.S. dependence on French or German trade in this sector did not exceed a meager 0.01, suggesting that the United States was not vulnerable to retaliation by firms in this sector.

Given the low level of French and German dependence on U.S. markets and suppliers in the European energy sector, U.S. economic sanctions against firms operating in these sectors are not likely to be successful (at least not unless the U.S. threatened actions that would reduce their access to oil supplies elsewhere). Economic incentives may, however, provide a means of increasing the value of French and German trade with the United States relative to their trade with Iran and Libya. To do this, however, the United States would have to offer the France and Germany an incentive that was greater than that gained by the continuing of their trading relations with Iran and Libya, plus the costs of adjustment incurred by terminating those relations. The cost of such an incentive package to the United States could be substantial. In the German case, for example, continued trade with Iran is motivated by a desire to maintain access to energy suppliers plus a variety of additional economic concerns. While German companies only exported $1.5 billion to Iran in 1995 (mostly in cars, machines, and electronics), they bought about $750 million worth of oil and carpets from Iran and, in June of 1996, Tehran agreed to buy ten long-range passenger jets from the European firm Airbus for $1 billion.[129] Furthermore, Iran owes Germany $8.6 billion from debts incurred during the 1980s and 1990s. Providing an economic incentive package that would compensate German firms for the value of their relations with Iran, plus the costs of adjustment incurred by terminating those relations, will likely be prohibitively expensive for the United States.

This means that economic incentives are not likely to be used, and economic threats are not likely to be effective against French or German firms operating in Iran or Libya. The sanctions may still be implemented for symbolic or political purposes, but given the continued disagreement between the U.S. and its trading partners over the role of the sanctions, and the high value the Europeans place on maintaining their relations with Iran and Libya, doing so would likely have negative political repercussions.

U.S. Vulnerability to Countersanctions

The benefits gained by compelling a private company to alter its behavior using economic sanctions must be balanced against the costs to the sender of restricting its trade with the target as well as the sender's vulnerability to retaliatory sanctions from the targeted firm and the host country in which the firm is operating. The economic component of these costs are primarily a function of the sender's net dependence on trade with the targeted firm and its host country. It is important to recognize that while firms tend to respond to sanctions and incentives on an issue-specific basis, states are more susceptible and prone to issue-linkage. As was done above, U.S. vulnerability to threats by foreign companies to terminate their trade with the United States can be estimated by calculating U.S. dependence on trade with the targeted firm in the sector where they are operating. Estimating U.S. vulnerability to retaliatory sanctions from irate foreign governments is, however, more complex because these sanctions will not necessarily be focused on the same industrial sector as those initially imposed by the United States. Thus, while the U.S. is not dependent on French or German markets and suppliers in the energy sector and, therefore, is not vulnerable to the loss of trade from French or Germany firms in those sectors resulting from the use of secondary sanctions under the Iran-Libya Sanctions Act, it may be vulnerable to retaliatory sanctions in other sectors that are initiated by the French or German governments. Similarly, the U.S. may be vulnerable to retaliatory sanctions from by the Canadian and Mexican governments in sectors other than nickel, cement, and telecommunications.

The first step in determining potential U.S. vulnerability to retaliatory sanctions from other governments is to identify sectors in which trade with the sender of the retaliatory sanctions accounts for a relatively high proportion of U.S. imports or exports. The second step is to determine

U.S. dependence on the sender in each of those sectors. This will provide an estimate U.S. vulnerability to retaliatory sanctions in the sectors in which it is most likely to be susceptible to such threats.

U.S. vulnerabilities to countersanctions under the Helms-Burton Act. Canada and Mexico have both threatened to retaliate if the United States carried out the threats specified in the Helms-Burton Act. Canada provided the largest market for American goods, and it was the largest supplier of goods to American consumers, accounting for 19.0 percent of U.S. imports and 22.5 percent of U.S. exports in 1995.[130] Road motor vehicles were the largest Canadian export to the United States, followed by paper, crude petroleum, shaped wood products, nonelectrical machinery, and natural gas. Canadian suppliers provided over 40 percent of U.S. automobile imports, and over 73 percent of its paper, shaped wood, and natural gas imports. Canada was also the world's largest supplier of paper, shaped wood products, and natural gas, accounting for 30.6 percent, 35.0 percent, and 23.1 percent of world exports in each industry, respectively.[131]

Table 5.5 summarizes U.S. dependence on Canadian exports and its markets. Of the top five import sectors in U.S.-Canadian trade, the United States was most vulnerable to Canadian suppliers of paper and paperboard, shaped wood, and road motor vehicles. Retaliatory threats regarding access to Canadian suppliers were most likely to be effective in those sectors. On the other hand, U.S. markets accounted for 94.6 percent of Canadian auto exports, 79.7 percent of its paper exports, 92.3 percent of its shaped wood exports, and 85.9 percent of its natural gas exports. Furthermore, Canadian firms in all of these sectors were highly dependent on access to the U.S. market. As the dependence estimates indicate, retaliatory Canadian sanctions would, therefore, impose high costs on Canadian firms in that sector.

Of the top five U.S. exports to Canada, the U.S. was most vulnerable to threats regarding access to Canadian markets in the road motor vehicle and nonelectrical power machinery sectors. Again, however, more than 75 percent of Canadian imports in the road motor vehicle, nonelectrical machinery, and nonelectrical power machinery sectors came from American sources, and few alternate suppliers were available in these sectors. Canada was, thus, dependent on access to U.S. suppliers and markets in these sectors. This suggests that retaliatory sanctions by firms in theses sectors were not likely.

Mexico was the third largest market for U.S. exports, and it was the third largest supplier of U.S. imports, accounting for 7.3 percent of U.S. imports, and 10.0 percent of U.S. exports in 1995.[132] Road motor vehicles were the largest Mexican export to the United States, followed by telecommunications equipment, crude petroleum, electrical switch gear, and electrical distributing equipment.[133] Of these exports, the electrical distributing equipment industry was the only one in which Mexican suppliers account

Table 5.5 U.S.-Canada Trade Dependence

	U.S. Dependence on Canadian Exports	U.S. Dependence on Canadian Markets	Canadian Dependence on U.S. Markets	Canadian Dependence on U.S. Exports
Top U.S. Imports from Canada (1995, Decreasing Value)				
Road Motor Vehicles	0.05	0.07	0.29	0.11
Paper and Paperboard	0.17	0.03	0.11	0.21
Crude Petroleum	0.00	0.23	0.22	0.00
Wood, Shaped	0.09	0.01	0.17	0.01
Nonelectrical Machinery	0.02	0.03	0.10	0.11
Top U.S. Exports to Canada (1995, Decreasing Value)				
Road Motor Vehicles	0.05	0.17	0.29	0.11
Nonelectrical Machinery	0.02	0.03	0.10	0.11
Nonelectrical Power Machinery	0.04	0.01	0.04	0.18
Electrical Power Machinery	0.01	0.02	0.09	0.08
Office Machines	0.01	0.04	0.12	0.05

Source: Estimates are based on World Bank data, 1996.

Table 5.6 U.S.-Mexico Trade Dependence

	U.S. Dependence on Mexican Exports	U.S. Dependence on Mexican Markets	Mexican Dependence on U.S. Markets	Mexican Dependence on U.S. Exports
Top U.S. Imports from Mexico (1995, Decreasing Value)				
Road Motor Vehicles	0.01	0.03	0.27	0.13
Telecom	0.03	0.01	0.16	0.04
Crude Petroleum	0.00	0.00	0.18	0.00
Electrical Switchgear	0.03	0.02	0.15	0.04
Electricity Distributing Equipment	0.10	0.08	0.19	0.10
Top U.S. Exports to Mexico (1995, Decreasing Value)				
Road Motor Vehicles	0.01	0.03	0.27	0.13
Electrical Machines	0.01	0.02	0.09	0.07
Electrical Power Machinery	0.00	0.03	0.12	0.11
Nonelectrical Machinery	0.01	0.01	0.11	0.07
Telecom	0.03	0.01	0.16	0.04

Source: Estimates are based on World Bank data, 1996.

for a large proportion of U.S. imports, accounting for 60.0 percent of U.S. imports in 1995. It was also the only sector among the top five in U.S.-Mexican trade in which the United States was potentially dependent on Mexican suppliers or markets. At the same time, Mexico was dependent on access to U.S. markets in all of the top five sectors, and it is dependent on U.S. exports in road motor vehicles. This suggests that the threat of retaliation from Mexican firms is minimal.

While the threat of sector-specific retaliation from foreign firms in response to sanctions under the Helms-Burton Act was and is minimal, the threat of broader, linked sanctions by national governments in Canada, Mexico, and Europe remains much higher. In retaliation, Canada is considering strengthening a law that it used during the trans-Siberian Pipeline crisis that makes such extraterritorial incursions illegal. The legislation would initiate "blocking orders" against judgements handed down under any objectionable foreign law making them unenforceable in Canada.[134] Furthermore, Canada is considering a new "right of recovery law" to give local firms the right to sue U.S. companies in Canadian courts in order to recoup damages suffered under Helms-Burton. Mexico is considering similar countermeasures.[135] Mexican President Ernesto Zedillo and Canadian Prime Minister Jean Chretien argued that, "At best, we can give them a legal resource . . . to fight Helms-Burton. But there is no definite legal answer, simply because Helms-Burton is simply a unilateral action and at the end, there will have to be a unilateral decision on the part of the United States."[136] Similarly, the European Union listed a set of countermeasures it was willing to impose against the United States if President Clinton did not continue to waive enforcement of the Helms-Burton Act. They included the following:

- Take the matter to a W.T.O. dispute panel, since efforts at an amicable settlement have been fruitless.

- Impose national measures, such as requiring visas for American travelers to European Union countries, which would be painful at the height of the travel season.

- Institute European Union and national legislation to provide legal protection for European Union companies hit by the Helms-Burton Act.[137]

Despite Clinton's suspension of the right to sue, the European Union issued a statement saying that it would proceed with plans to retaliate because European Union firms were already suffering the effects of the anti-Cuba law.[138]

As part of their threats and counterthreats, for example, the European Union threatened to submit the dispute for arbitration by the World

Trade Organization.[139] By doing so, E.U. members implicitly threatened to disrupt the multilateral dispute settlement and trade liberalization mechanisms in the W.T.O. U.S. leaders have long promoted these mechanisms as a way to liberalize the world economy.[140] By taking the case to the W.T.O., the E.U. used the value that the United States places in these multilateral mechanisms to increase the costs that the U.S. must bear if it fails to cooperate in negotiations with the E.U. by rescinding the Helms-Burton Act.

As discussed above, the U.S. government has the legal and political capability to defect by refusing to recognize the authority of the W.T.O. in this case. It can do so by claiming a "national security exemption" based on the assertion that Cuba represents a threat to U.S. national security. Consequently, sanctions under the Helms-Burton Act would be considered "security" matter as opposed to "trade" matters. Once this claim is made, the dispute over the Helms-Burton Act would fall outside the trade dispute settlement jurisdiction of the W.T.O. The problem with this strategy is that, by invoking this exemption on one of the very first dispute brought before the W.T.O., the United States would create a precedent that countries can justify breaking with W.T.O. trade guidelines and potentially promote protectionism on national security grounds.[141] National security exemptions, for example, could potentially be used to justify protecting local rice growers in Japan, indigenous computer producers in China and Korea, or regional airline production in Europe.[142] Such practices would undermine both the newly institutionalized capability of the W.T.O. to manage and resolve economic disputes among nations in an increasingly integrated and complex world economy as well as undermine the more basic norms of free trade and economic liberalism it was established to promote.[143] The high value that the United States places on these dispute settlement and trade liberalization mechanisms, combined with the lack of alternatives available to these mechanisms, made it vulnerable to the European threat to disrupt the dispute settlement and trade liberalization mechanisms in the W.T.O.

The European strategy succeeded. Initially, the Clinton administration agreed to press Congress to amend the Helms-Burton Act by waiving the provision in it that bars U.S. visas to directors and executives of companies that traffic in property confiscated by Cuba.[144] In exchange, the E.U. (and Canada) agreed to suspend their W.T.O. case until common "disciplines and principles" protecting the rights of companies and individuals whose property is expropriated were reached.[145] In May of 1998, negotiations on the common disciplines and principles were completed. The United States and the European Union agreed on a compromise in which the Clinton administration agreed to ask Congress for broader power to issue a permanent waiver to visa restrictions under the Helms-Burton Act.[146] Significantly, however, though President Clinton made no commitment to change the threat of lawsuits under the act.

In January of 1999, President Clinton announced a series of initiatives designed to relax U.S. policy toward Cuba. These included the possibility of letting more people and money flow to Cuba, granting some U.S. businesses licenses to operate in Cuba, and promoting U.S.-Cuban military ties. However, rather than welcoming signs of increased U.S. engagement, Fidel Castro responded by enacting a "Law for the Protection of Cuba's National Independence and Economy," which threatens penalties of ten to twenty years in prison for any Cuban citizen who lends himself to the "subversive" proposals of the United States.[147] This response suggests that even if U.S. policy towards Cuba is relaxed, relations between these two countries is likely to remain cool for some time to come.

U.S. vulnerabilities to countersanctions under the Iran-Libya Sanctions Act. In contrast to trade between the United States and its American trading partners, none of the top importing or exporting industries between France and the United States, or Germany and the United States account for a large proportion of trade in that sector for the countries involved. The only partial exception involves the French aircraft industry. U.S. dependence in this sector could give the French government a potential source of leverage over the United States. With the exception of the French aircraft industry, the degree of U.S. or French dependence on one another is low. Consequently, the threat of sanctions and countersanctions will have little effect on firms or governments in either country.

Similarly, U.S. dependence on German exports and markets in the largest sectors of U.S.-German trade is virtually nonexistent. Germany is moderately dependent on access to U.S. markets in the road motor vehicle and nonelectric machinery sectors, but the availability of alternate markets suggests that cutting off German access to U.S. markets will have little effect. As a result, threats and counterthreats on a sector-specific level are not likely to be effective in U.S.-German trade relations.

Lee Hamilton argued that the sanctions "run the risk of causing us more harm than they cause either Iran or Libya."[148] Regardless of the outcome, a brief review of this case suggests that while the effectiveness of secondary sanctions against French and German companies will be low, the economic cost of retaliatory sanctions will also be minimal. As a consequence, the decision to implement the sanctions will ultimately depend on whether the political signal they send is worth the political and economic costs of sending it.

After two years of negotiations between the United States and the E.U. over the Helms-Burton Act and the Iran-Libya Sanctions Act, the U.S. government agreed not to impose economic sanctions on three major foreign energy companies that have signed contracts to develop offshore gas fields in Iran.[149] The three companies—Total SA of France, Gazprom of Russia,

Table 5.7 U.S.-France Trade Dependence

	U.S. DEPENDENCE ON FRENCH EXPORTS	U.S. DEPENDENCE ON FRENCH MARKETS	FRENCH DEPENDENCE ON U.S. MARKETS	FRENCH DEPENDENCE ON U.S. EXPORTS
Top U.S. Imports from France (1995, Decreasing Value)				
Aircraft	0.12	0.00	0.01	0.06
Nonelectrical Power Machinery	0.02	0.00	0.01	0.05
Electrical Machines	0.00	0.00	0.02	0.01
Alcoholic Beverages	0.01	0.00	0.03	0.00
Top U.S. Exports to France (1995, Decreasing Value)				
Automatic Data Processing Equipment	0.00	0.01	0.01	0.03
Nonelectrical Power Machinery	0.02	0.00	0.01	0.05
Nonelectrical Machinery	0.00	0.01	0.01	0.01
Electrical Machinery	0.00	0.00	0.02	0.01

Source: Estimates are based on World Bank data, 1996.

Table 5.8 U.S.-Germany Trade Dependence

	U.S. Dependence on German Exports	U.S. Dependence on German Markets	German Dependence on U.S. Markets	German Dependence on U.S. Exports
Top U.S. Imports from Germany (1995, Decreasing Value)				
Road Motor Vehicles	0.01	0.10	0.05	0.01
Nonelectrical Machinery	0.02	0.01	0.03	0.01
Nonelectrical Power Machinery	0.02	0.00	0.00	0.02
Electrical Machines	0.00	0.01	0.01	0.01
Top U.S. Exports to Germany (1995, Decreasing Value)				
Automatic Data Processing Equipment	0.00	0.02	0.02	0.03
Road Motor Vehicles	0.01	0.01	0.05	0.01
Electrical Machines	0.00	0.01	0.11	0.01
Aircraft	0.03	0.00	0.00	0.06

Source: Estimates are based on World Bank data, 1996.

and Petronas of Malaysia—are currently involved in a $2 billion investment in Iran's South Pars gas field. The U.S. government also agreed not to impose sanctions on future European investments—other than those involved in pipeline projects—as long as the E.U. agreed to tighten its proliferation rules, frustrate Iran's efforts to develop weapons of mass destruction, and deny government assistance to any companies investing in confiscated property in Cuba.[150] These concessions were withheld from Russia, pending improvement in its efforts to restrict the flow of sensitive technology to Iran. In March of 1999, a consortium of French, Italian, and Iranian oil companies signed a $998 million, 10-year contract to develop an oil field in Iran.[151] As predicted, U.S. government officials concluded that in those cases sanctions would have no effect on investments in Iran. Given the likely lack of effectiveness, Secretary of State Madeleine Albright argued that it was more important not to undermine the prospect of European and Russian cooperation on more difficult matters such as broader sanctions on Iraq, the ratification of START II, the Asian financial crisis, and in troubled regions such as the former Yugoslavia. While all sides have expressed a desire to work together, competition over the control of firms operating abroad, particularly in strategic industries like energy and high technology, will continue to be a pressing concern of power politics in the post-cold war era.

CONCLUSION: DOMINANCE, DEPENDENCE, AND POLITICAL POWER

Economic sanctions and incentives are often maligned, misused, and misunderstood, yet they are increasingly the policy tools of choice, particularly against trading partners and foreign firms against whom more coercive instruments of statecraft are of limited practical value. When used appropriately, economic sanctions and incentives can be used to extend political control over foreign companies operating abroad, with or without the support of the local government. This capability is important because private companies are increasingly the principal producers, consumers and merchants of strategic goods and technology. Consequently, their activities can have a significant impact on the exercise and distribution of power in world politics.

The U.S. government has used economic statecraft effectively to extend its control over firms operating abroad by exploiting their dependence on access to American suppliers and markets. The contrasting outcomes of American efforts during Operation Exodus and the trans-Siberian Pipeline embargo, as well as variation within each set of cases, demonstrate the potential scope and domain of this form of political influence. When actors were dependent on access to American markets or

American suppliers, the U.S. government could often compel them to alter their behavior by threatening to cut off this access. U.S. influence, however, was not absolute. As predicted, when firms and states were not dependent on the United States, the threat to cut off access to its market as suppliers did not increase the probability of success. The recent use of sanctions in U.S.-Chinese relations, and the use of secondary sanctions to secure extra-territorial corporate compliance with U.S. policies against Cuba, Iran, and Libya suggest that the dynamics of dominance, dependence, and political power remain as valid and critical today as they have been in the past.

Theories of dependence provide a fruitful addition to traditional arguments linking the distribution of resources and the exercise of power in international politics. In particular, interpreting state and firm actions in terms of their dependence on one another offers three principal insights into the nature and exercise of power. First, dependence arguments demonstrate that the ability of one actor to entice or coerce another in a particular relationship is contingent on both the resources it can offer to provide or threaten to deny the other as well as the availability of those resources outside of that relationship. Consequently, the number and kind of alternatives available to each actor in a relationship are as important in determining its ability to exercize power over others as the physical resources it possesses. This is significant because it suggests that power arguments based on the distribution of economic, political, or military resources between two actors will be imprecise regardless of the degree of precision used to evaluate those resources. Thus while arguments about power relations based on sector-specific dominance are more precise than those based on aggregate indicators of economic or military hegemony, they are often insufficient to explain control over outcomes because they do not consider the options available to each actor. Dependence arguments, on the other hand, emphasize the importance of avilable alternatives on power relations between actors.

Second, by emphasizing the value each actor places on a particular relationship, dependence arguments focus attention on the reciprocal nature of power and vulnerability to economic statescraft. As long as alternate trading partners are available, a high volume of trade with foreign actors in a particular sector does not necessarily imply dependence on them and does not imply local vulnerability to the threat of sanctions. However, as the availability of alternate sources of supply and markets declines, vulnerability to sanctions will increase. This helps to explain the counterintuitive result that, even in sectors where the United States dominates global trade, it may not be able to secure corporate compliance with its policies. As dependence arguments suggest, when American firms are dependent on access to foreign markets or suppliers, the U.S. government may not be able to control their behavior at home or abroad.

Third, rather than decreasing parsimony by using different models for different actors, dependence arguments enable researchers to analyze states, firms, and other nonstate actors using the same theoretical framework. Dependence arguments examine the process of interaction between states, and between states and firms, while maintaining theoretical parsimony. Based on the specific interests or vulnerabilities involved, sanctions and incentives may be targeted against specific states, firms or other nonstate actors operating within other countries. The ability of one state to entice or coerce foreign companies operating within another state's territory to alter their behavior not only decreases the physical resources at target state's disposal, it also undermines the target state's political integrity by challenging its ability to control actors and activities within its territory. Gaining or losing control over local actors, particularly those related to the production or distribution of strategic goods, is a matter of high politics. This makes the use of economic statecraft by any state to extend de facto control over foreign firms operating outside of its national jurisdiction extremely significant for all states. It also means that rather than representing the "end of the state" and a decline of power in world politics, the increasing globalization and privatization of the world economy are altering the relevant sources of power while expanding the scope and domain of competition among states to include actors and activities traditionally considered to be outside of the realm of international power politics.

The policy implication of this book is clear: applied judiciously and under appropriate conditions, economic statecraft can expand the scope and domain of political power by enabling states to influence other states and foreign companies operating in the international arena. The theoretical consequences are also evident: refined and operationalized systematically, theories of dependence can expand the predictive and explanatory capabilites of international relations theories regarding the dynamic interaction between states and firms in world politics. Most important, understanding when and why economic statecraft works provides scholars and practitioners with insights into the nature and exercise of power. These insights will enable them to assess the likely effectiveness and ramifications of using sanctions and incentives before directing them against friends, foes, or firms.

NOTES

1. Eric Pianin, "Clinton Approves Sanctions for Investors in Iran, Libya," *Washington Post* (6 August 1996), p. A8.

2. There are a wide range of political, social, and moral implications of using sanctions that should be evaluated as well, but will not be discussed here. See Cortright and Lopez, eds. (1995).

3. Abbott (1981), pp. 739, 782, 840–49. In response to the taking of American hostages in Iran, the president did exercise his authority under the International Emergency Economic Powers Act to block the movement of Iranian assets possessed or controlled by all persons subject to the jurisdiction of the United States. With the exception of nonbanking entities organized in foreign countries, the United States applied the legislation across international borders.

4. Moran (1993), p. 69.

5. The President's Export Council, "Unilateral Economic Sanctions: A Review of Existing Sanctions and Their Impacts on U.S. Economic Interests with Recommendations for Policy and Process Improvement," (June 1997), p. 2.

6. Moran (1993), p. 63.

7. For further discussion of this point, see Moran (1990, 1993).

8. See Crawford (1993), pp. 139–50 for a detailed discussion of the Toshiba case.

9. Crawford (1993), p. 142.

10. The ban was part of a series of legislation including the Multilateral Export Control Sanctions Act of 1987 that amends the Export Administration Act of 1979 and the Export Administration Amendments Act of 1985.

11. Stuart Auerbach, "Toshiba Spends Millions to Blunt U.S. Sanctions," *International Herald Tribune* (14 October 1988), p. 1.

12. Exemptions were granted for goods under contract before May 1, 1987, goods necessary for national defense, and components and spare parts. Ibid., p. 1; Crawford (1993), p. 258.

13. Ian Rodger, "Toshiba Sees Prospect of U.S. Sale," *Financial Times* (15 July 1987), p. I; Ian Rodger, "Toshiba Chases Pentagon Order," *Financial Times* (23 July 1987), Section I, p. 4.

14. United Nations, *International Trade Statistics Yearbook* (1989).

15. Crawford (1993), p. 146–47.

16. Tim Carrington, "Japan to Take Part in SDI: Toshiba Barred for a While," *Wall Street Journal* (22 July 1987), p. 5. Also see Crawford (1993), pp. 147–48.

17. Susan F. Rasky, "Firms Want U.S. to Spare Toshiba," *International Herald Tribune* (15 September 1987), p. 9.

18. Toshiba America corporation spent in excess of $9 million in support of these lobbying efforts. Thomas Olmstead, "Selling Off America," in Jeffrey A. Frieden and David A. Lake, eds., *International Political Economy: Perspectives on Global Power and Wealth,* 3rd Edition (New York: St. Martin's, 1995), p. 197.

19. "U.S. Eases Rules on High-Tech Exports," *International Herald Tribune* (12 September 1984).

20. Klare, "Adding Fuel to the Fires: The Conventional Arms Trade in the 1990s," in Klare and Thomas (1994), pp. 141–2.

21. Ibid., pp. 139–42.

22. The companies involved included: McDonnell-Douglas, Raytheon, Hughes, General Dynamics, and FMC Corporation. E. Schmidt, "Saudis Near an Accord to Slow Arms Payments," *New York Times* (18 January 1994), p. A8.

23. D. Priest and D. Williams, "U.S. Allows Arms Sales to 10 in Ex-East Bloc," *Washington Post* (18 February 1995), p. A1.

24. A. Ramirez, "Move to Liberalize U.S. High-Tech Exports Gains," *New York Times* (21 September 1993), p. D3.

25. S. Engelberg and M. Tolchin. "Foreigners Find New Allies in U.S. Industry," *New York Times* (2 November 1994), p. A1.

26. Elaine Sciolino, "U.S. Will Allow Computer Sale to Court China," *New York Times* (19 November 1993), pp. A1, A6.

27. Ibid.

28. R. W. Apply, Jr. "No Progress as Clinton Meets with China's Chief," *New York Times* (20 November 1993), p. A1. When Commerce Secretary Ronald Brown visited the People's Republic of China in August 1994 (the first U.S. Cabinet member to visit the P.R.C. since the renewal of MFN status), he promoted American business, but mentioned human rights violations only once. Steven Mufson, "U.S., China Act to Boost Trade Ties," *Washington Post* (30 August 1994), p. A1.

29. P. Behr, "China Failing to Sway U.S. in GATT Entry Dispute," *International Herald Tribune* (6 November 1994). See also George Shambaugh, "Threatening Friends and Enticing Enemies in an Uncertain World," in *Enforcing Cooperation: "Risky" States and the Intergovernmental Management of Conflict*, Gerald Schneider and Patricia Weitsman, eds. (New York: Macmillan, 1996).

30. T. Walker, "U.S. Agreement with China Averting Trade War over Copyright Piracy," *Financial Times* (27 February 1995), p. 18.

31. International Monetary Fund, (1994, 1995).

32. Ibid.

33. *Mini-Micro Systems* (July 1984), p. 84.

34. Cited in Jacobson, Lenway, and Ring (1993), pp. 471–72.

35. Recent changes in legislation require that the license processing time be shorter than 120 days, but the average processing time for licenses is over one year. Cahill (1986), p. 177.

36. Ibid.

37. Mastanduno (1992), p. 298.

38. National Association of Manufacturers, "A Catalog of New U.S. Economic Sanctions for Foreign Policy Purposes 1993–1996," (March 1997), available on the World Wide Web at http://usaengage.org/studies/name2.html#catelog.

39. James Aley, "The Cost of Export Controls," *Fortune* (3 October 1994), p. 29.

40. European-American Business Council, "Is the Price Too High? The Cost of U.S. Sanctions," (Washington, DC: European-American Business Council Publication, October 1997).

41. Jacobson, Lenway, and Ring (1993), p. 458.

42. Ramirez (21 September 1993), p. D3.

43. *1995 Bill Tracking Report,* House of Representatives 361, "Omnibus Export Administration Act of 1995" (4 January 1995), p. 141.

44. Tom Carter, "Lugar Bill Defines Criteria, Eliminates Punitive Measures," *The Washington Times* (15 December 1997), p. A15; Thomas Lippman, "U.S. Rethinking Economic Sanctions: State Department Teams Weighs Costs, Impact of Trade Restriction," *Washington Post* (26 January 1998), p. A6.

45. Draft Interim Report, Sub-Committee on the Proliferation of Military Technology, Hon. Sherwood I. Boehlert, NATO International Secretariat (May 1994); "Post-CoCom Regime Could be Set Up by End of Year, U.S. Official Says," *International Trade Reporter,* BNA Inc. (7 June 1995); and "The New CoCom and Old Concerns," *East European & Former Telecom Report* (1 January 1995).

46. Andrew J. Pierre, "The Missing Link in Global Stability," *Christian Science Monitor* (30 June 1995).

47. W. J. Broad, "Industries Fight Ban on Using Soviet Rockets," *New York Times* (13 December 1987), p. 2; Crawford (1993), pp. 33–34; and Mastanduno (1990), (1992).

48. Behrman (1970), p. 102.

49. In contrast, in response to the Carter administration revoking an export license to the Sperry Corporation, the British government criticized the United States for revoking Sperry's license, but side-stepped the issue by claiming that no British firm was willing to supply the Soviets with the computers they desired. Mastanduno (1992), p. 155. Similarly, the German government denied the German firm Siemens the right to bid on the contract in order to avoid a confrontation with the United States. See *The Guardian* (17 August 1979); and Angela Stent, *East-West Technology Transfer: European Perspectives* (Beverly Hills: Sage, 1980), p. 33; Mastanduno (1992), p. 154.

50. Broad (1987); Crawford (1993), pp. 33–34.

51. Mastanduno makes a similar argument that excessive use of export controls may undermine the power on which their enforcement is based. Mastanduno, in Baldwin and Milner (1990), pp. 208–209.

52. Behrman (1970), p. 105.

53. Behrman (1970), p. 102.

54. Mastanduno (1990); Shambaugh (1993).

55. K. Cahill, *Trade Wars: High-Technology Scandals of the 1980s* (London: W. H. Allen, 1986), p. 177; Mastanduno (1992), p. 298; and Ramirez, (21 September 1993), p. D3.

56. Cuban Liberty and Democratic Solidarity Act of 1996, 22 USC 6021, Public Law 104–114 (12 March 1996), 110 Stat. 185–824.

57. Cuban Liberty and Democratic Solidarity Act of 1996, 22 USC 6021, Public Law 104–114 (12 March 1996), Section 3, 110 Stat 788–789.

58. Cyndee Miller, "Cuba Looks for Investors: U.S. Firms Would be Glad to Oblige," *Marketing News* (6 July 1992), p. 2.

59. Ibid. and Adam Zagorin, "Punishing Cuba's Partners," *Time* (24 June 1996), p. 54.

60. Jeffrey Ulbrich, "EU Strikes at U.S. on Cuba," *Associated Press Release* (12 July 1995), 12:54 pm, p. 1.

61. Cuban Liberty and Democratic Solidarity Act of 1996, 22 USC 6021, Public Law 104–14 (12 March 1996), 110 Stat. 185–824.

62. Ibid.; see also "A Helms-Burton Waiver . . . ," *Washington Post* (17 July 1996), p. A18; David Sanger, "U.S. to Punish Canadians under Cuban Law," *The New York Times* (11 July 1996), p. A1.

63. Plus interest, court costs, and attorney fees.

64. Caroll Doherty, "House Joins Senate in Backing Bills to Tighten Embargo," *Congressional Quarterly* (26 September 1992), p. 2964; Patrick Kiger, *Squeeze Play: The United States, Cuba, and the Helms-Burton Act* (Washington, D.C.: Center to Public Integrity, 1997); William LeoGrande, "From Havana to Miami: U.S. Cuba Policy as a Two-Level Game," *Journal of Interamerican Studies and World Affairs* (Spring 1998), p. 73; and Miller (6 July 1992), p. 2. For a thorough review of the domestic politics of U.S.-Cuban policy, see Daniel Miller, "The Domestic Politics of U.S. Cuba Policy," Honors Thesis, Georgetown University (6 May 1998).

65. Gail De George, "U.S. Business Isn't Afraid to Shout Cuba Si," *Business Week* (6 November 1995), p. 39.

66. While the Cuban American community was divided in its political views regarding U.S.-Cuban relations, CANF was better organized, better financed, and more politically sophisticated than its competitors. Carla Anne Robbins, "Dateline Washington: Cuban American Clout," *Foreign Policy* (Fall 1992), p. 165.

67. Kiger (1997), p. 35.

68. Kiger (1997), p. 53; Mimi Whitefield, "Stakes High in Cuba Claims Bill," *Miami Herald* (2 October 1995), Business Magazine, p. 13.

69. Christopher Marquis, "New Voices Join Call to End Cuba Embargo," *Miami Herald* (14 June 1995), p. A1.

70. Caroll Doherty, "Congress Ignores Objections in Push to Punish Castro," *Congressional Quarterly* (9 March 1996), p. 633.

71. Stanley Meisler, "Clinton Gets Scolding by E.U. on Cuba Curbs," *Los Angeles Times* (13 June 1996), p. A11.

72. Ibid.

73. Charles Trueheart, "Neighbors Slam U.S. on Cuba," *Washington Post* (14 June 1996), p. A38.

74. Prior to the passage of the Helms-Burton Act, only individuals who were U.S. citizens at the time of the Cuban revolution who had documented and registered a request with the Department of Justice by 1967 could seek compensation for damages from expropriation. Michael Dodds, "Law Allows New Claims against Cuba: President Could Waive Controversial Parts," *Washington Post* (16 July 1996), p. A12.

75. Dodds, (16 July 1996), p. A12.

76. Trueheart (14 June 1996), p. A38.

77. Michael Dodds, "U.S. Announces Measures against Canadian Firm," *Washington Post* (11 July 1996), p. A14.

78. Dodds, (11 July 1996), p. A14.

79. Thomas Lippman, "Europeans Assail U.S. Trade Curbs," *Washington Post* (13 June 1996), p. A20.

80. Trueheart (14 June 1996), p. A38.

81. "International Flap on Cuba Law," *Los Angeles Times* (13 June 1996), p. B-8.

82. "The Helms-Burton Law: Biter Bitten," *The Economist* (8 June 1996), p. 45.

83. Lorraine Woellert, "Clinton Suspends Cuba Sanctions Again," *The Washington Times* (17 January 1998), p. D7.

84. Despite criticism of this strategy, it was a very insightful tactic. "Deft Move on Cuba," *Washington Post* (5 January 1997), p. C6. For a criticism of this policy, see Charles Krauthammer, "Clintonism: Split, Waffle and Wait," *Washington Post* (19 July 1996), p. A27.

85. John F. Harris, "Clinton Delays Effect of Cuba Lawsuit Act: Battle with Trade Partners Averted," *Washington Post* (17 July 1986), p. A1.

86. Woellert, (17 January 1998), p. D7.

87. Robert Art, "To What Ends Military Power," *International Security* 4 (spring 1980), pp. 4–35.

88. George Gredda, "Clinton Walks the Cuba Fence," *Associated Press Release* (17 July 1996), 1:42 A.M., p. 1.

89. Ibid.

90. "Deft Move on Cuba," *Washington Post* (5 January 1997), p. C6.

91. The request for U.N. sanctions was in response to "the use of weapons against civil aircraft in flight as being incompatible with elementary considerations of humanity." "U.S. Asks U.N. to Condemn Cuba," *Associated Press Release* (19 July 1996), 11:18 P.M., p. 1.

92. Zagorin (24 June 1996), p. 54.

93. Thomas Lippman, "Business Groups Urge Clinton to Disallow Suits over Seized Property in Cuba," *Washington Post* (6 July 1996), p. A24.

94. *United States v. Aluminum Company of America*, 148 F. 2d 416, 443 (2d Cir. 1945).

95. Buergenthal (1990), p. 172.

96. Cuban Liberty and Democratic Solidarity act of 1996, 22 USC 6021, Public Law 104–14 (12 March 1996), Section 401, 110 Stat. 788. This justification is also reflected in earlier legislation against Cuba including the Trading with the Enemy Act and the Cuban Assets Control Regulations.

97. Woellert (17 January 1998), p. D7.

98. Paul Blustein, "House Passes Measure against Foreign Firms Investing in Iranian, Libyan Oil," *Washington Post* (24 June 1996), p. A25.

99. James Abrams, "Congress Passes Sanctions Bill," *Associated Press Release* (23 July 1996), 7:19 P.M., p. 1.

100. "The Helms-Burton Law: Biter Bitten," *The Economist* (8 June 1996), p. 45.

101. 104th Congress, 2d Session, H.R. 3107, Report No. 104–523, Union Calendar No. 308, p. 1B.

102. "House Votes Iran, Libya Sanctions," *Washington Post* (20 June 1996), p. A8.

103. Carol Doherty, "Panel Approves Softer Version of Sanctions on Iran Trade," *Congressional Quarterly* (15 June 1996): 1669.

104. Alissa Rubin, "House Passes Curbs on Trade with Iran and Libya," *Congressional Quarterly* (22 June 1996): 1775.

105. Tyler Marshall, "E.U. Leaders React to U.S. Threat of Sanctions to Limit Trade," *Los Angeles Times* (23 June 1996), p. 4.

106. Rick Atkinson, "Divergent Policies toward Iran Strain U.S.-German Relations," *Washington Post* (27 June 1996), p. A21.

107. Abrams (23 June 1996), p. 1.

108. "Iran and Conoco," *Washington Post* (16 March 1995), p. A20.

109. Rubin, (22 June 1996), p. 1775.

110. Ibid.

111. Abrams (23 July 1996), p. 1.

112. Craig Whitney, "Europe Attacks U.S. Bid to Bar Investments in Cuba and Iran," *New York Times* (23 June 1996), p. 12.

113. Doherty, (15 June 1996), p. 1669.

114. Paul Blustein, "House Passes Measure against Foreign Firms Investing in Iranian, Libyan Oil," *Washington Post* (24 June 1996), p. A25.

115. Ibid.

116. David Sanger, "U.S. to Punish Canadians under Cuba Law," *New York Times* (11 July 1996), p. A1.

117. "The Helms-Burton Law: Biter Bitten," *The Economist* (8 June 1996), p. 45; Whitney (23 June 1996), p. 12.

118. Karen Schwartz, "Anti-Cuba Law Defended," *Associated Press Release* (12 July 1996), 5:34 P.M., p. 1.

119. United Nations, *International Trade Statistics Yearbook,* vol. 2 (1995).

120. Using SITC 683, Nickel. United Nations, *International Trade Statistics Yearbook,* vol. 2 (1995).

121. Ibid.

122. Using SITC 661, Lime/Cement/Construction Material. Data are collected United Nations, *International Trade Statistics Yearbook,* vol. 2 (1995).

123. 1994 data, using SITC 764, Telecommunications Equipment. United Nations, *International Trade Statistics Yearbook,* vol. 2 (1995).

124. Using SITC 752, Computer Equipment. United Nations, *International Trade Statistics Yearbook,* vol. 2 (1995).

125. Woellert (17 January 1998), p. D7.

126. Andrew Borowiec, "Europeans Uncertain about Next Move Amid Anger over U.S. Sanctions Threat," *The Washington Times* (9 August 1996), p. A15.

127. Using SITC 334 Refined Petroleum Products. United Nations, *International Trade Statistics Yearbook,* vol. 2. (1995).

128. Using SITC 333, Crude Petroleum/Oil. United Nations, *International Trade Statistics Yearbook,* vol. 2. (1995).

129. Rick Atkinson, "Divergent Policies toward Iran Strain U.S.-German Relations," *Washington Post* (27 June 1996), p. A21.

130. United Nations, *International Trade Statistics Yearbook,* vol. 2. (1995).

131. Using SITC 641 Paper and Paperboard; SITC 243, Wood Shaped; and SITC 341, Natural Gas. Data are for fiscal year 1995.

132. United Nations, *International Trade Statistics Yearbook,* vol. 2. (1995).

133. Using SITC 732, Road Motor Vehicles; SITC 724, Telecommunications Equipment; SITC 333, Crude Petroleum/Oil; SITC 722, Electric Power Switch Gear; SITC 723 Electrical Distributing Machinery.

134. From Reuters, "Canada, Mexico Lash Out at U.S. Law on Cuba," *Los Angeles Times* (18 June 1996), p. A4.

135. "The Helms-Burton Law: Biter Bitten," *The Economist* (8 June 1996), p. 45.

136. John Rice, "Protest of U.S. Cuba Embargo Law," *Associated Press Release* (17 June 1996), 6:48 P.M., p. 2.

137. Ulbrich (12 July 1995), p. 1.

138. "Clinton Compromises on Cuba Sanctions Bill," *Reuters Press Release* (16 July 1996), 4:17 p.m., p. 1.

139. David Sanger, "Europe Delays Challenge to U.S. Law Barring Cuba Business Deals," *New York Times* (13 February 1997); "W.T.O. Names Panel in E.U.-U.S. Dispute over Cuba," *Reuters Press Release* (20 February 1997), 1:42 P.M.; "E.U. May Press U.S. on Cuba Law," *Associated Press Release* (25 February 1997), 2:40 A.M.

140. Joan Spero and Jeffrey Hart, *The Politics of International Economic Relations,* 5th ed. (New York: St. Martin's, 1987), p. 52.

141. Sanger (13 February 1997), p. A1.

142. Ibid.

143. Ibid.

144. Paul Blustein and Thomas Lippman, "Administration Offers Compromise to Europeans over Helms-Burton Act," *Washington Post* (11 April 1997), p. A23; Paul Blustein and Thomas Lippman, "Trade Clash on Cuba Is Averted," *Washington Post* (12 April 1997), p. A1.

145. Blustein and Lippman (12 April 1997), p. A1.

146. Dan Balz, "U.S. Eases Stand on Cuba, Iran Sanctions: Helms Condemns, Europe Hails Move," *Washington Post* (19 May 1998), p. A15.

147. "Cuba Crackdown," *The Washington Post* (24 February 1999), p. A20.

148. Abrams (23 July 1996), p. 1.

149. Balz (19 May 1998), A15.

150. Thomas Lippman, "Politicians at Odds on Sanctions as Policy: The Administration Says Tool Can Be Costly," *The Washington Post* (19 May 1998), p. A17.

151. "French Defy U.S. and Join Iranian Oil Plan," *The New York Times* (2 March 1999), p. A4.

Appendix: Legal Bases of U.S. Export Control Policy

This appendix examines the legal basis of U.S. export control policy and the legal justifications for extending U.S. regulations over actors and resources outside of its territorial boundaries.

DOMESTIC SOURCES OF U.S. EXPORT CONTROL POLICY

The legal authority to monitor and enforce U.S. export control policy rests primarily within the Executive Branch of the U.S. government. This is important because Congress has historically been much more aggressive in its use of sanctions than the president. Given this tendency, it is ironic that when President Bill Clinton signed the Cuban Liberty and Democratic Solidarity (LIBERTAD) Act of 1996 and the Iran and Libya Sanctions Act of 1996 into law, he significantly limited Executive Branch authority and increased Congressional oversight of this policy tool.[1] Nonetheless, most of the cases analyzed in this book fall under the jurisdiction of the Department of the Treasury, the Department of Commerce, and the Department of Defense under the statutory authority of the Trading with the Enemy Act, the International Emergency Economic Powers Act, and the Export Administration Act (formerly the Export Control Act).[2] (See table 2.3.)

The Trading with the Enemy Act of 1917 provides the president with broad powers to investigate, regulate, or prohibit all commercial and financial transactions by anyone subject to U.S. jurisdiction with foreign countries and their nationals during times of war or national emergency.[3] The regulation applies to "any citizen or resident of the United States, any corporation organized under the laws of the United States, or any partnership, association, corporation, or other organization wheresoever organized or doing business which is owned or controlled by an American citizen, resident or corporation without a specific licence from the Secretary of the Treasury."[4] This policy was implemented through the Foreign Assets Control Regulations (FACRs) to restrict trade with the People's Republic of China, North Korea, North Vietnam, and Cambodia in 1950, and beginning in 1963, it was used to support an ongoing U.S. embargo against Cuba through the Cuban Assets Control Regulations (CACRs).

The Trading with the Enemy Act was amended in 1977 to limit presidential authority during wartime, but it also authorized the continuation of existing trade relations.[5] While the Trading with the Enemy Act remains a powerful tool of U.S. foreign policy, the normalization of relations has led to a reduction in restrictions under the FACRs and CACRs regarding the sale of nonstrategic goods as well as an increase in the degree of "ownership" or percentage of U.S.-made components required before a foreign business is considered "American."[6]

The International Emergency Economic Powers Act (IEEPA) was created under Section 5(b) of the Trading with the Enemy Act in 1977.[7] While it expands the president's authority to apply sanctions against other countries in peacetime, it also imposes greater procedural and substantive constraints on presidential discretion than the Trading with the Enemy Act.[8] If, however, the president declares a national emergency due to threats to national security, foreign policy, or the U.S. economy, he can restrict imports and financial transactions without any specific statutory authority, regardless of legislative efforts to restrict the executive's authority. U.S. regulations extend to foreign companies that are either subsidiaries or U.S. firms or possess goods that contain a certain percentage of U.S. components.[9] In November of 1979, for example, these controls were used to block Iranian assets in U.S. banks and their overseas branches and subsidiaries. In the first ten years after its creation, the IEEPA was invoked seven times in six distinct foreign policy situations.[10] The Office of Foreign Assets Control is currently administering IEEPA restrictions against Iran,[11] Libya,[12] Iraq,[13] and the Federal Republic of Yugoslavia and Bosnian Serb-controlled areas of the Republic of Bosnia and Herzegovina.

The Export Administration Act (EAA) of 1969, which superseded the Export Control Act of 1947, emphasizes the nonemergency control of goods and technology for reasons of national security, foreign policy, short supply, and nuclear nonproliferation.[14] It authorizes the president to curtail or prohibit the export and reexport of dual-use goods and technology in order to "further the foreign policy of the United States and to aid in fulfilling its international responsibilities."[15] It also allows the president "to exercise the necessary vigilance over exports from the standpoint of their significance to national security of the United States."[16] This includes the authority "to stop or limit the export of any goods and technology subject to U.S. jurisdiction, or exported by any person subject to the jurisdiction of the United States."[17] The Department of Commerce is primarily responsible for administering and enforcing these controls. Licenses issued by the Department of Commerce apply to the export and re-export of goods and technology containing U.S. components (except those shipped to Canada for Canadian consumption), regardless of how many times the goods have been bought and sold outside of the United States. The Export Administration Act was reauthorized in 1979, but lapsed in August of 1994. The day before it lapsed, the president invoked his authority—under Executive Order No. 12924 under authority of the International Emergency Economic Power Act—to continue the system of controls that the U.S. had maintained under the EAA.[18] The EAA is currently under revision. The U.S. government has used restrictions under this authority to forbid exports and reexports of goods and technology to a wide range of countries including Iran, Iraq, Libya, South Africa, Syria, and the Soviet Union.[19] Despite intense opposition from the French, British, and Italian governments, these regulations were also invoked to deny export privileges to six European firms involved in the construction of the trans-Siberian Pipeline (see chapter 4).

Since the end of the Cold War, the U.S. government has attempted to streamline its export control process to eliminate unnecessary trade restrictions. Under the Omnibus Export Control Act of 1995, the Secretary of Commerce is required to establish a U.S. Commodity Control Index identifying all commodities and technology on which controls are imposed, to specify license requirements for such items, and to designate countries and end users to which exports of commodities and technology are controlled.[20] It also requires the Secretary of Commerce to review national export control regulations periodically and, if warranted, to increase specified export control thresholds or remove export controls on computer equipment, computer communications and networking equipment, and other technology that may become obsolete. The 1995 act provides for favorable licensing treatment for the export of commodities and technology among members of the New Forum and other multilateral export control regimes.

In 1996, Congress completed a comprehensive revision and reorganization of the Export Administration Regulations which implement the Export Administration Act. The Export Administration Regulations (EARs) are currently issued by the Bureau of Export Administration in the U.S. Department of Commerce. The Bureau of Export Administration (BXA) is responsible for developing export control policies, issuing export licenses, and prosecuting violators, as well as enforcing the EAA's antiboycott provisions. In order to increase compliance with these regulations, the BXA has expanded its licensing review procedures and the postshipment verification of exports, and it has institutionalized a variety of programs like the Strategic and Nonproliferation Training sessions (SNET) to promote interagency collaboration and cooperation, and the Business Executives Enforcement Team (BEET) Program to promote public awareness and increase cooperation of the business community.[21] It also publishes annual reports that summarize changes in export control regulations and export control enforcement activities, and maintains a World Wide Web page to provide interested parties with up-to-date information on U.S. export regulations and activities.[22] Despite continued criticism that the EARs are still based on Cold War era strategic concerns and place excessive costs on American business,[23] these and other efforts have reduced the value of goods requiring an export license from $6.1 billion per quarter in 1993 to $2.7 billion per quarter in 1998.[24]

Congress is currently considering the Sanctions Reform Act, which was introduced by Representatives Philip Crane and Lee Hamilton in the House Ways and Means Committee in October 1997, and by Senator Richard Lugar in January 1998.[25] The Act would require that sanctions mandated by Congress be focused as narrowly as possible and be tied to a specific foreign policy objective, and that existing contracts would be protected. It would also require the president to report to Congress periodically on its economic cost to the United States and its likely effectiveness.

EXTENDING U.S. REGULATIONS ABROAD

The U.S. government has justified extending its authority abroad based on a variety of legal grounds including the nationality principle, the territoriality principle, the objective territoriality principle, the protective principle, and the universality principle.[26] The most common justification used to promote the extraterritorial application of U.S. export control policy has been the nationality principle of international law. While the nationality principle is widely accepted under certain circumstances, it often clashes with the territoriality principle, which grants absolute and exclusive jurisdiction to the state over actions, actors, and resources within a specified territory regardless of their national origin.[27]

Based on the nationality principle, a state's jurisdiction extends to its citizens independent of their location.[28] The U.S. government has used this principle to justify controlling the re-export of goods and technology that either originate in the United States, have entered into the U.S. economy, are direct products of U.S. technology, or contain at least a certain percentage of U.S. parts and components.[29] "Re-export" refers to the sale of a good by a firm or country that originally purchased it from a third party. The problem of re-exporting is that even with effective enforcement of domestic regulations, an intermediary in a friendly country who legally acquired a restricted good could sell that good to a destination or an end-user forbidden by the export regulations of the country where the good originated. While the intermediary's actions may fully comply with the laws of his or her country, they may undercut the export restrictions imposed by the country of origin. To avoid this problem, the United States government uses the nationality principle to justify indicting foreign companies that re-export restricted goods to forbidden end-users under the Export Administration Act and International Emergency Economic Powers Act.

The United States has also used the nationality principle to justify applying its laws directly to businesses in other countries that are associated with American individuals or corporations. Under the Trading with the Enemy Act, this policy is justified on the grounds that a foreign incorporated subsidiary assumes the nationality of its United States parent.[30] As such, they are "United States persons," subject to the jurisdiction of the United States. American firms are often required to contain "consent orders" that obligate the seller and buyer to abide by U.S. export control regulations. Violating American export control policy carries penalties of indictment under U.S. law, including imprisonment for executives and fines of up to $100,000 per offense. If the fine is not paid, the U.S. government can issue a "writ of attachment" and confiscate and sell the property to a foreign company within the United States.[31] While many countries require "end-use" or "end-user" certificates for the sale of arms and other strategic technology, the United States is one of only a few countries that has frequently required these certificates during peacetime.

In addition, the U.S. has asserted its authority overseas based on the objective territoriality principle, the protective principle, and the universality principle. The "objective territoriality principle" is also known as the "effects doctrine."[32] The objective territoriality principle has evolved from the 1945 ruling of Judge Learned Han who argued that U.S. law could be applied to foreign actors that intended to, or did, affect the United States. The *Restatement of the Revised Foreign Relations Law of the United States* has taken a very expansive view of this ruling. It argues that foreign actors who have the intent of affecting U.S. citizens are subject to U.S. jurisdiction regardless of whether or not their intentions have been carried out and regardless of whether or not their actions had any actual effect on U.S. citizens.[33]

The protective principle grants U.S. courts their broadest powers, but it has been used less often than the territoriality and nationality principles. Under Section 402 (3) of the *Restatement*, the protective principle permits a state "to exercise jurisdiction over conduct outside its territory that threatens its security, as long as the conduct is generally recognized as criminal by states in the international community."[34] This justification is being used by the United States to justify the extraterritorial application of sanctions against foreign companies conducting business in Cuba under the Helms-Burton Law. By justifying its policy in terms of national security, the U.S. government can take advantage of escape clauses in the World Trade Organization and the North American Free Trade Agreement that allow exceptions to their basic principles of free trade when national security is threatened. While the European Union threatened to challenge this justification in the World Trade Organization, and Canada and Mexico threatened to do the same under NAFTA, the United States is arguably still in compliance with the letter (if not the spirit) of the law as specified by these institutions.

Finally, the universality principle recognizes the authority of all members of the international community to punish acts (like piracy on the high seas or crimes against humanity) that are recognized to be universally dangerous to all states and their subjects. The nationality, territoriality, objective territoriality, protective, and universality principles have all been accepted to varying degrees by the international community. The primary issue has been the question of which principle takes precedence when conflicts of jurisdiction arise between two or more states.

CONFLICTS OF CONCURRENT JURISDICTION

The United States has provoked numerous international controversies by extending its domestic regulations abroad. Several of the most prominent cases include the freezing of all official Iranian financial assets in the United States and overseas on 14 November 1979 in response to the seizure of American hostages, the banning of exports of oil and gas equipment to the Soviet Union following the imposition of martial law in Poland (see chapter 4), and the current threats to terminate relations with firms conducting business in Cuba, Iran, and Libya (see chapter 6). At the same time, however, the United States has also joined other countries in implementing legislation against the use of secondary sanctions to compel foreign firms to comply with domestic legislation. For example, the antiboycott provision of the Export Administration Act forbids American companies and their subsidiaries from furthering or supporting boycotts fostered or imposed against a country friendly to the United States.[35] These contradictions send mixed signals to foreign companies and governments about the U.S. position regarding conflicts of jurisdiction.

American legal opinion regarding conflicts of jurisdiction between states can generally be divided into two groups. One group emphasizes the balancing of respective national interests as discussed in the *Restatement of the Revised Foreign Relations Law of the United States*. Proponents of this approach argue that the primary jurisdiction over a multinational corporation rests with the state where a corporation is doing business, with the caveat that if a conflict of jurisdiction arises, the conflict must be resolved by exercising reasonableness and comity, balancing the respective interests of the states involved.[36] Section 40 of the *Restatement* identifies several factors—including the vital national interest of each state, the extent and nature of the hardship that inconsistent command would impose on parties subject to conflicting national decisions, the extent to which any required conduct would take place within the territory of another state, the nationality of the persons in question, and the degree of enforcement each state could apply—that are to be weighed in order to determine which state's interests are more vital and, based on the principles of comity and reciprocity, which state should therefore be awarded jurisdiction.[37] This balancing-of-national-interests test was used by U.S. courts throughout the 1970s and 1980s to determine whether jurisdictional claims made under the territoriality, nationality, or protective principle should take precedence.[38]

A second approach to conflicts of jurisdiction is reflected in the Act of State Doctrine from the 1964 *Sabbatino* case, and the ruling of Judge Malcom Wilkey in the 1984 *Laker Airways* case.[39] The 1964 Act of State Doctrine dictates that U.S. courts will not pass judgment on acts committed by foreign governments in their territories if the government is recognized and extant at the time of the conflict, even if it alleged that the act of the foreign government violates international law.[40] In the *Sabbatino* case, Justice John Harlan based the Act of State Doctrine on the separation of powers principle articulated in the U.S. constitution. He argued that applying judicial rulings overseas in the absence of a treaty interfered with the Executive's right to conduct foreign policy. Despite this claim, the U.S. Congress narrowed the Act of State doctrine by requiring U.S. courts to adjudicate claims regarding property that was expropriated without full, adequate, and prompt compensation in violation of international law. The Sabbatino Amendment to the Foreign Assistant Act of 1964 limited the Act of State Doctrine in cases of expropriation, but it left the basic principle of the Act of State doctrine intact. Furthermore, it set the precedent that specific legislation would be necessary to keep the Act of State Doctrine from being applied. The 1996 Helms-Burton Law regarding foreign use of expropriated property in Cuba is a good contemporary example of this issue.

Beyond the Act of State Doctrine, Judge Malcolm Wilkey argued in his 1984 ruling in the *Laker Airways Ltd. V. Sabena, Belgian World Airlines* case, that in situations of concurrent jurisdiction, the balance of interests between two states could not be effectively resolved in a judicial forum.[41] He argued that international law "clearly prohibits unreasonable assertions of jurisdiction. It does not, however, additionally require that only the state with the most reasonable relationship to the situation has the legal right to regulate it."[42] Therefore, U.S. courts were not qualified to apply a balance of interest test between competing national jurisdictions because such a decision rested on an assessment of political factors beyond the court's expertise. This means that situations involving conflicts of jurisdiction must ultimately be resolved through the political interaction between states. Consequently, this ruling supports the assertion in this volume that a legal interpretation of de jure bounds of sovereign authority is not sufficient to understand or resolve conflicts involving competition among states over the de facto control over actors operating across national borders.

The American use of the nationality principle to justify the extension of national regulations into other states' territories remains a matter of dispute, as does the more fundamental question of how the "nationality" of a multinational corporation should be determined.[43] These questions have been debated at length in numerous law reviews, legal briefs, and judicial opinions.[44] Most of this legal literature addresses the issue of extraterritoriality by testing the "validity" of American export control policy against accepted rules of international law and tries to promote "reasonableness" in interpreting competing bases of jurisdiction based on the territorial and nationality principles in international law.[45] These debates help to clarify some of the issues as well as the legal positions of the states involved. Legal analyses of sovereignty, however, do not reveal the sources of international disputes over extraterritoriality nor do they explain the varying reactions of states in these disputes. The reason for this is that the nationality of a subsidiary and the jurisdiction to which it is subject is determined, in large part, by international power politics rather than by international law.[46] International law increasingly recognizes that sovereign authority is concurrent with sovereign control under certain circumstances, but it also recognizes a continuum of jurisdiction in which sovereign jurisdiction of any one state is less than absolute. When conflicts of jurisdiction occur under these circumstances, international law may serve as a guide and justification for state action, but the ultimate determination of sovereign control and sovereign authority is often political rather than legal in nature.

NOTES

1. Wynn H. Segall, "Export Controls and Economic Sanctions," *The International Lawyer* 31, 2 (summer 1997): 393–401.

2. For a discussion of the legal and political debate surrounding these regulations, see Kenneth Abbott, "Collective Goods, Mobile Resources, and Extraterritorial Trade Controls,"*Law and Contemporary Problems* 50 (1987): 117–52; Andreas Lowenfeld, *International Economic Law: Trade Controls for Political Ends.* 2d ed. (New York: Matthew Bender, 1983); and Alan Lowe, *Extraterritorial Jurisdiction: An Annotated Collection of Legal Material* (Cambridge: Grotius Publications, 1983).

3. Trading with the Enemy Act, act of October 1917, c. 106, 40 Stat. 415, as amended 50 U.S.C.A. App. §§ 1–44 (Est 1990 & Supp. 1996). For specific country policies, see 15 C.F.R. pt. 385 (1988). Other unilateral U.S. sanctions include the Iraq Sanctions Act of 1990, the Iran-Iraq Arms Non-Proliferation Act of 1992, the Cuba Democracy Act of 1992, the Cuba Liberty and Democratic solidarity (LIBERTAD) Act of 1996, the Iran and Libya Sanctions Act of 1996), the Foreign Relations Authorization Act of 1990–91, and the Foreign Operations, Export Financing, and Related Programs At of 1996. For a discussion of U.S. unilateral sanctions as of January 1997, see The President's Export Council, *Unilateral Economic Sanctions: A Review of Existing Sanctions and Their Impacts on U.S. Economic Interests with Recommendations for Policy and Process Improvement* (Washington, D.C.: The White House, June 1997). Also available on the World Wide Web, at http://www.usaengage.org/studies/unilat1.html.

4. David Leyton-Brown "Extraterritoriality in Trade Sanctions," in David Leyton-Brown, ed. *The Utility of International Economic Sanctions* (London: Croom Helm, 1987), p. 256.

5. The President's Export Council, *Unilateral Economic Sanctions* (June 1997).

6. Leyton-Brown (1987), p. 256.

7. International Emergency Economic Powers Act, Pub. L. 95–223, Title II, 91 Stat. 1626 (28 October 1977), as amended, 50 U.S.C.§§ 1701–06 (West 1991 & Supp. 1996).

8. See Barry Carter, *International Economic Sanctions: Improving the Haphazard U.s. International Legal Regime* (New York: Cambridge University Press, 1988).

9. Marian Nash Leich, "U.S. Practice," *American Journal of International Law* 76 (October 1982), p. 836.

10. See Carter (1988).

11. Under Executive Order No. 12957 (15 March 1995), U.S. persons are prohibited from engaging in certain activities related to the development of petroleum resources in Iran. Executive Order No. 12959 (6 May 1995), forbids activity related to the trade in Iranian goods and services, as well as the export and re-export of certain of goods, technology, and services from the United States. Investments by U.S. persons are prohibited and, while it has been modified, Executive Order No. 12170 (14 November 1979) has been used to block Iranian assets in the United States.

12. Executive Order No. 12543 (7 January 1986) and Executive Order No. 12544 (8 January 1986) prohibit exports of goods and technology as well as transportation and travel to Libya, and the extension of credit to the Libyan government.

13. In accordance with United Nations Security Council Resolution 661 (6 August 1990), Executive Order No. 12722 (2 August 1990) restricts exports, re-export and imports of goods, services, and technology from Iraq, as well as financial transactions with the Iraqi government.

14. The Export Control Act, 50 U.S.C. app.§§ 2021–32 (1964) (expired in 1969); The Export Administration Act, 50 U.S.C. app.§§ 2401–20. See Dallmeyer (1989), pp. 570–75.

15. The Export Control Act, 50 U.S.C. app.§§ 2021; see also Jack N. Behrman, *National Interests and Multinational Enterprises* (Englewood Cliffs, N.J.: Prentice Hall, 1970), p. 103.

16. The purpose of the act is to secure the supply of resources at home and abroad that could affect the welfare and foreign policy of the United States. See Behrman (1970), p. 103.

17. Leyton-Brown, (1987), p. 258.

18. Nonproliferation controls under the EAA are also maintained under the Nuclear Nonproliferation Act of 1978. Bureau of Export Administration, "History of Export Controls," World Wide Web, http://bxa.fedworld.gov/mission/html.

19. Dorinda G. Dallmeyer, "Foreign Policy and Export Controls: How Will the Canada-United States Free Trade Agreement Accommodate the Extraterritorial Application of United States Laws to Canadian Exports of Goods and Technology?" *Georgia Journal of International and Comparative Law* 19, 3 (1989): 572–75.

20. *1995 Bill Tracking Report,* House of Representatives 361, "Omnibus Export Administration Act of 1995" (4 January 1995), p. 141.

21. U.S. Department of Commerce, Bureau of Export Administration, *Export Administration Annual Report 1995 and 1996 Report on Foreign Policy Export Controls* (Washington, D.C.: Government Printing Office, 1996), pp. II–54–II–57.

22. The World Wide Web page of the Bureau of Export Administration at the Department of Commerce is located at http://www.bxa.doc.gov/.

23. Richard N. Haass, ed., *Economic Sanctions and American Diplomacy* (New York: Council of Foreign Relations Press, 1998), and "Sanctioning Madness," *Foreign Affairs* (November/December 1997).

24. Bureau of Export Administration, "History of Export Controls," World Wide Web, http://bxa.fedworld.gov/mission/html.

25. Tom Carter, "Lugar Bill Defines Criteria, Eliminates Punitive Measures," *The Washington Times* (15 December 1997); Jareer Elass, "Administration Tries to Cool Sanctions Fever," *The Oil Daily* (10 November 1997); Thomas Lippman, "U.S. Rethinking Economic Sanctions: State Department Teams Weighs Costs, Impact of Trade Restriction," *Washington Post* (26 January 1998).

26. While similar issues have been debated in a variety of issue areas including antitrust and extradition policy, the following sources provide a general background of the debate regarding the extraterritorial control of strategic goods and technology: Kenneth Abbot, "Defining the Extraterritorial Reach of American Export Controls: Congress as Catalyst," *Cornell International Law Journal* 79 (winter 1984): 79–158; Linda Andros, "Chemical Weapons Proliferation: Extraterritorial Controls: When Too Much Is Not Enough," *New York Law School Journal of International and Comparative Law* 13, 3 (1992); David Matthews, "Controlling the Exportation of Strategically Sensitive Technology: The Extraterritorial Jurisdiction of the Multilateral Export Control Enhancement Amendments Act of 1988, *Columbia Journal of Transnational Law* 28, 3 (1990): 747–74; Armand L. C. de Mestral, T.

Gruchalla-Wesierski, *Extraterritorial Application of Export Control Legislation: Canada and the U.S.A.* (London: Martinus Nijhoff, 1990); Dorinda G. Dallmeyer, "Foreign Policy and Export Controls: How Will the Canada-United States Free Trade Agreement Accommodate the Extraterritorial Application of United States Laws to Canadian Exports of Goods and Technology?" *Georgia Journal of International and Comparative Law* 19, 3 (1989): 565–88; David Koplow, "Long Arms and Chemical Arm: Extraterritoriality and the Draft Chemical Weapons Convention," *Yale Journal of International Law* 15, 1 (winter 1990): 1–83; Homer E. Moyer and Linda A. Mabry, *Export Controls as Instruments of Foreign Policy: The History, Legal Issues, and Policy Lessons of Three Recent Cases.* (Washington, D.C.: University of America Press, 1983); Harold Maier, "Resolving Extraterritorial Conflicts, or 'There and Back Again,' " *Virginia Journal of International Law* 25, 1 (1984) 7–48; Neale and Stephens (1988); Cecil J. Olmstead, ed., *Extraterritorial Application of Laws and Responses Thereto* (Oxford: ESC Publishing, 1984); Peter Oettinger, "National Discretion: Choosing CoCom's Successor and the New Export Administration Act," *The American University Journal of International Law and Policy* 9, 2 (winter 1994): 559–95; and Thomas Schoenbaum and Dorinda Dallmeyer, "The Extraterritorial Application of United States Laws Affecting Trade between Nations," in *Dynamics of Japanese-United States Trade Relations,* Thomas Schoenbaum, Mitsuo Matsushita, and Dorinda Dallmeyer, eds. (Athens, Ga.: Dean Rusk Center for International and Comparative Law, University of Georgia School of Law, 1986); and Jay L. Westbrook, "Extraterritoriality, Conflict of Laws, and the Regulation of Transnational Business," *Texas International Law Journal* 25, 1 (winter 1990): 71–97. For a summary of U.S. and E.C. policies regarding extraterritoriality and antitrust policy, see Joseph P. Griffin, "E.C. and U.S. Extraterritoriality: Activism and Cooperation." *Fordham International Law Journal* 17:2 (1994): 353–88.

27. Robert Bledsoe, and Bloeslaw Boczek, *The International Law Dictionary* (Oxford: Clio Press, 1987), pp. 105–106.

28. Bledsoe and Boczek (1987), pp. 103–104.

29. Laura Carlson Chen, "Chapter 204: Export Licensing Checklist," *Business Laws, Inc.,* Supplement (June 1994), p. 118.

30. The United States government invoked both of these arguments to prohibit trade with North Korea, Vietnam, Cambodia, Cuba, and the Soviet Union following its crackdown in Poland. In response to the Arab boycott of Israel and the seizure of hostages in Iran, the United States justified the extraterritorial extension of its regulations on the basis of corporate association with American individuals or American corporations. U.S. actions against Libya were applied against all firms trading in American-origin goods and technology regardless of their affiliation with American firms. See Douglas Rosenthal and William Knighton, *National Laws and International Commerce: The Problem of Extraterritoriality,* Chatham House Papers #17 (London: Routledge & Kegan Paul, 1982), pp. 58–59.

31. The United States v. Bank of Nova Scotia, United States Court of Appeals, Eleventh Circuit, 1982. 691 F. 2d 1384, denied 462 U.S. 1119, 102 S. Ct. 3086, 77,

L.Ed. 1384 (1983). Summarized in Louis Henkin, *International Law: Cases and Materials*, 2d ed. (St. Paul, Minn.: West Publishing, 1987), pp. 872–74.

32. *United States v. Aluminum Company of America*, 148 F. 2d 416, 443 (2d Cir. 1945).

33. American Law Institute, *Rest. 3d, Restatement of Foreign Relations Law of the United States (revised)*. (St. Paul, Minn.: American Law Institute Publishers, 1987).

34. Thomas Buergenthal and Harold Maier, *Public International Law* (St. Paul, Minn.: West Publishing, 1990), p. 172.

35. Aaron J. Sarna, *Boycott and Blacklist: A History of Arab Economic Warfare against Israel* (Totowa, N.J.: Roman & Littlefield, 1986), pp. 111–18.

36. American Law Institute, *Restatement of the Law (Revised) 1980 to Present*, Draft No. 2 § 403 (St. Paul, Minn.: American Law Institute Publishers, 1987); Griffin (1994): 353–88.

37. Thomas Buergenthal and Harold Maier, *Public International Law* (St. Paul, Minn.: West Publishing, 1990), p. 179.

38. Harold Maier, "Resolving Extraterritorial Conflicts, or "There and Back Again, "*Virginia Journal of International Law* 25, 1 (1984): 16. See *United States v. Bank of Nova Scotia*, 691 F. 2d 1384 (11th Circ. 1982), cert. Denied, 103 S Ct. 3086 (1983).

39. *Banco Nacional de Cuba v. Sabbatino*, 376 U.S. 398, 425 (1964); *Laker Airways, Ltd. v. Sabena, Belgian World Airways*, 731 F. 2d 909 (D.C. Circ. 1984).

40. Buergenthal (1990), p. 236; American Law Institute (1987) *Restatement of the Law (Revised)* § 443.

41. Maier (1984), pp. 33–41.

42. Maier (1984), p. 38.

43. Andreas Lowenfeld, *International Economic Law: Trade Controls for Political Ends*. 2d ed. (New York: Matthew Bender, 1983); and Alan Lowe, "Public International Law and the Conflict of Laws," *International and Comparative Law Quarterly* 33 (1984), p. 515.

44. See for example Abbott (1987); Lowenfeld (1983); and Lowe (1984).

45. See for example the Symposium on the Restatement of Foreign Relations Law of the United States (Revised) *Virginia Journal of International Law* 25, 1 (1984).

46. Stephen Kobrin, "Enforcing Export Embargoes through Multinational Corporations: Why Doesn't It Work Anymore?" *Business in the Contemporary World* 1, 2 (1989): 31–42.

SELECTED BIBLIOGRAPHY

Abbott, Kenneth, W. "Linking Trade and Political Goals: Foreign Policy Export Controls in the 1970s and 1980s." *Minnesota Law Review* 65 (1981): 739–889.
———. "Defining Extraterritorial Reach of American Export Controls." *Cornell International Law Journal* 79 (1984): 79–158.
———. "Collective Goods, Mobile Resources, and Extraterritorial Trade Controls." *Law and Contemporary Problems* 50 (1987): 117–52.
Adler-Karlsson, Gunnar. *Western Economic Warfare, 1947–1967.* Stockholm: Almquist and Wiksell, 1968.
Alan, James. *Sovereign Statehood: The Basis of International Society.* London: Allen and Unwin, 1986.
Albright, David. "Iraq's Shop-Till-You-Drop Nuclear Program." *Bulletin of the Atomic Scientists* 48 (1992): 7–37.
Aldrich, John H., and Forest D. Nelson. *Linear Probability, LOGIT, and PROBIT Models.* Beverly Hills: Sage, 1984.
Allison, Graham, T. *The Essence of Decision.* Boston: Little, Brown, 1971.
American Law Institute. *Restatement of the Law (Revised) 1980 to Present.* St. Paul, Minn.: American Law Institute Publishers, 1987.
Andros, Linda. "Chemical Weapons Proliferation: Extraterritorial Controls: When Too Much Is Not Enough." *New York Law School Journal of International and Comparative Law* 13, 3 (1992): 257–314.
Appleton, Arthur. "Dresser Industries: The Failure of Foreign Policy Trade Controls under the Export Administration Act." *Maryland Journal of International Law and Trade,* 8, 1 (1984): 122–43.
Arend, Anthony Clark. 1999. *Legal Rules and International Society.* New York: Oxford University Press.
Art, Robert. "To What Ends Military Power?" *International Security* 4 (1980): 3–35.
Ashley, Richard. "The Poverty of Neorealism." *International Organization* 38 (1984): 225–86.
Astori, Gianfranco, et al. *The State of the Alliance, 1987–88.* Boulder, Colo.: Westview, 1988.
Axelrod, Robert. *The Evolution of Cooperation.* New York: Basic Books, 1984.
Bachrach, P., and M. Baratz. "The Two Faces of Power." *American Political Science Review* 56 (1962): 947–52.
———. "Decisions and Nondecisions: An Analytical Framework." *American Political Science Review* 57 (1963): 632–42.

————. *Power and Plenty: Theory and Practice.* New York: Oxford University Press, 1970.

Baldwin, David A. "Power and Money." *Journal of Politics* 33 (1971a): 578–614.

————. "The Costs of Power." *Journal of Conflict Resolution* 15 (1971b): 145–55.

————. "The Power of Positive Sanctions." *World Politics* 24 (1971c): 19–38.

————. "Power and Social Exchange." *American Political Science Review* 72 (1978): 1229–42.

————. "Power Analysis and World Politics: New Trends Versus Old Tendencies." *World Politics* 31, 2 (1979): 161–94.

————. "Interdependence and Power: A Conceptual Analysis," *International Organization* 34, 4 (1980): 471–506.

————. *Economic Statecraft.* Princeton, N.J.: Princeton University Press, 1985.

————, ed. *Neorealism and Neoliberalism: The Contemporary Debate.* New York: Columbia University Press, 1993.

Baldwin, David A., and Helen V. Milner, eds. *East-West Trade and the Atlantic Alliance.* New York: St. Martin's, 1990.

Baldwin, David A., and Robert Pape. "Evaluating Economic Sanctions." *International Security* 32, 2 (1998): 189–98.

Baldwin, Robert E. *The Political Economy of U.S. Import Policy.* Cambridge: MIT Press, 1985.

Baranson, Jack. *Technology and the Multinationals.* Lexington, Ky.: Lexington Books, 1978.

Barkin, J. Samuel, and Bruce Cronin. "The State and the Nation: Changing Norms and the Rules of Sovereignty in International Relations," *International Organizations* 48, 1 (1994): 107–30.

Barkin, J. Samuel, and George Shambaugh, eds. *Anarchy and the Environment: The International Relations of Common Pool Resources.* Albany, N.Y.: State University of New York Press, 1999.

Barry, Brian. *Power and Political Authority.* New York: John Wiley, 1976.

Behrman, Jack N. *National Interests and Multinational Enterprises.* Englewood Cliffs, N.J.: Prentice Hall, 1970.

Bergsten, C. Fred, and Lawrence B. Krause, eds. *World Politics and International Economics.* Washington, D.C.: Brookings Institution, 1975.

Bergsten, C. Fred, Thomas Horst, and Theodore Moran. *American Multinationals and American Interests.* Washington, D.C.: Brookings Institution, 1978.

Berkman, Herold, and Ivan Vernon. *Contemporary Perspectives in International Business.* Chicago: Rand McNally, 1979.

Bertsch, Gary, ed. *East-West Strategic Trade, CoCom and the Atlantic Alliance.* Paris: Atlantic Institute, 1983.

————. *Controlling East-West Trade and Technology Transfer.* Durham, N.C.: Duke University Press, 1988.

Bethlen, S., and I. Volgyes. *Europe and the Superpowers.* Boulder, Colo.: Westview, 1985.

Bill Tracking Report. House of Representatives 361. "Omnibus Export Administration Act of 1995" (4 January 1995).

Blau, P. M. "Critical Remarks on Weber's Theory of Authority." *American Political Science Review* 57 (1963): 305–16.

Bledsoe, Robert, and Bloeslaw Boczek. *The International Law Dictionary.* Oxford: Clio Press, 1987.

Blinken, Antony J. *Ally Versus Ally: America, Europe, and the Siberian Pipeline Crisis.* New York: Praeger, 1987.

BNA Washington Insider.

Boulding, Kenneth. *Conflict and Defense: A General Theory.* New York: Harper, 1962.

Brewster, Kingman, Jr. *Law and United States Business in Canada.* Ottawa, Ont.: Canadian-American Committee, 1960.

Buchanan, David, and James McCalman. *High Performance Work Systems: The Digital Experience.* New York: Routledge, 1989.

Bucy, Fred. "Technology Transfer and East-East Trade: A Reappraisal." *International Security* 5, 3 (1980/1981): 132–51.

Bueno de Mesquita, Bruce. "Risk, Power Distribution and the Likelihood of War." *International Studies Quarterly* 25 (1981): 541–68.

Buergenthal, Thomas, and Harold Maier. *Public International Law.* St. Paul, Minn.: West Publishing, 1990.

Bull, Hedley. *The Anarchical Society: A Study of Order in World Politics.* New York: Columbia University Press, 1977.

Bull, Hedley, and Adam Watson, eds. *The Expansion of International Society.* Oxford: Clarendon Press, 1984.

Business Laws, Inc.

Buzan, Barry. "Economic Structure and International Security." *International Organization* 38, 4 (1984): 597–624.

———. *People, States, and Fear: An Agenda for International Security Studies for the Post–Cold War Era.* Boulder, Colo.: Lynne Rienner, 1991.

Cahill, Kevin. *Trade Wars: The High-Technology Scandal of the 1980s.* London: W. H. Allen, 1986.

Campbell, David. *Politics Without Principle: Sovereignty, Ethics, and Narratives of the Gulf War.* Boulder: Lynne Rienner Publishers, 1993.

Campbell-Kelly, Martin. *ICL: A Business and Technical History.* Oxford: Clarendon, 1989.

Carr, E. H. *The Twenty Years' Crisis.* New York: St. Martin's, 1970.

Carrick, R. J. *East-West Technology Transfer in Perspective.* Berkeley: University of California Press, 1978.

Carter, Barry, E. *International Economic Sanctions: Improving the Haphazard U.S. International Legal Regime.* New York: Cambridge University Press, 1988.

Castel, J. G. *Extraterritoriality in International Trade.* Toronto, Ont.: Butterworths, 1988.

Caves, Richard. *Multinational Enterprise and Economic Analysis.* New York: Cambridge University Press, 1982.

Chen, Laura Carlson. "Chapter 204: Export Licensing Checklist." *Business Laws, Inc.*, 1994.

Christian Science Monitor.

Clark, Duncan L. *Send Guns and Money: Security Assistance and U.S. Foreign Policy.* Westport, Conn.: Greenwood Publishing Group, 1997.

Claude, Inis. *Power and International Relations.* New York: Random House, 1962.

Commission of the European Communities. *Towards a Dynamic European Economy: Green Paper on the Development of the Common Market for Telecommunications Services and Equipment.* Brussels: COM (87) 290 final (June 1987).

Congressional Quarterly, Inc. *Traded: U.S. Policy Since 1945.* Washington, D.C.: Congressional Quarterly, 1984.

Conybeare, John. "Public Goods, Prisoners' Dilemmas and the International Political Economy." *International Studies Quarterly* 28 (1984): 5–22.

———. *Trade Wars: The Theory and Practice of International Commercial Rivalry.* New York: Columbia University Press, 1994.

Cooper, Richard. "Economic Interdependence and Foreign Policy in the Seventies." *World Politics* 24 (1972): 159–81.

Cortright, David, and George A. Lopez, eds. *Economic Sanctions: Panacea or Peacebuilding in a Post–Cold War World?* Boulder, Colo.: Westview, 1995.

Cortright, David, ed. *The Price of Peace: Incentives and International Conflict Prevention.* New York: Rowman & Littlefield, 1997.

Cowhey, Peter, and Jonathan Aronson. "A New Trade Order." *Foreign Affairs* 72, 1 (1993): 183–95.

Crandall, Robert. *After the Breakup: U.S. Telecommunications in a More CompetitiveEra.* Washington, D.C.: Brookings Institution, 1991.

Crawford, Beverly. *Economic Vulnerability in International Relations: East-West Trade, Investment, and Finance.* New York: Columbia University Press, 1993.

Crawford, Beverly, and Stephanie Lenway. "Decision Modes and International Regime Change: Western Collaboration and East-West Trade." *World Politics* 37, 3 (1985): 375–402.

Cziempiel, E., and James Rosenau, eds. *Global Changes and Theoretical Challenges: Approaches to World Politics for the 1990s.* Lexington, Mass.: Lexington Books, 1989.

Czinkota, Michael R., ed. *Export Controls: Building Reasonable Commercial Ties with Political Adversaries.* New York: Praeger, 1984.

Dahl, Robert A. "The Concept of Power." *Behavioral Science* 52 (1958): 201–15.

———. *Who Governs? Democracy and Power in an American City.* New Haven, Conn.: Yale University Press, 1961.

———. *Modern Political Analysis.* 4th ed. Englewood, N.J.: Prentice-Hall, 1984.

Daily Telegraph, 1984.

Dallmeyer, Dorinda G. "Foreign Policy and Export Controls: How Will the Canada-United States Free Trade Agreement Accommodate the Extraterritorial Application of United States Laws to Canadian Exports of Goods and

Technology?" *Georgia Journal of International and Comparative Law* 19, 3 (1989): 565–88.

Datamation.

Daoudi, M. S., and M. S. Dajani. *Economic Sanctions: Ideals and Experience* Boston: Routledge & Kegan Paul, 1983.

Deutsch, Karl et al. *Political Community in the North Atlantic Area.* Princeton, N.J.: Princeton University Press, 1957.

Deutsch, Karl. *The Analysis of International Relations.* 2d ed. Englewood Cliffs, N.J.: Prentice Hall, 1978.

Doran, Charles, and Wes Parsons. "War and the Cycle of Relative Power." *American Political Science Review* 74 (1980): 947–65.

Doxey, Margaret. *Economic Sanctions and International Enforcement.* 2d ed. New York: Oxford University Press, 1980.

———. *International Sanctions in Contemporary Perspective,* 2d ed. New York: St. Martin's, 1987.

Dresser Industries v. Baldridge. Motion for Temporary Restraining Order. No. 82–2385. D.D.C. (filed 23 August 1982).

Dyson, Kenneth. *European Detente: Case Studies of the Politics of East-West Relations.* London: Frances Pinter, 1986.

Earle, E. M., ed. *Makers of Modern Strategy: Military Thought from Machiavelli to Hitler.* Princeton, N.J.: Princeton University Press, 1943.

East European & Former Telecom Report.

"East-West Economic Issues: Questions and Answers." *State Department Background Paper.* Williamsburg Summit (26 May 1983), Section IV, Question 1.

Easton, David, ed. *Varieties of Political Theory.* Englewood Cliffs, N.J.: Prentice Hall, 1966.

Ellings, Richard. *Embargoes and World Powers.* Boulder, Colo.: Westview, 1985.

Evans, Peter B., Dietrich Rueschemeyer, and Theda Skocpol, eds. *Bringing the State Back In.* Cambridge: Cambridge University Press, 1985.

Financial Times.

Flamm, Kenneth. *Targeting the Computer: Government Support and International Competition.* Washington, D.C.: Brookings Institution, 1987.

Freedman, Lawrence, ed. *The Troubled Alliance: Atlantic Relations in the 1980s.* London: Heinemann, 1983.

Frey, Frederick W. "Comment: On Issues and Nonissues in the Study of Power." *American Political Science Review* 65 (1971): 1081–1101.

Friedman, J., C. Bladen, and S. Rosen. *Alliance in International Politics.* Boston: Allen and Bacon, 1970.

Frieden, Jeffry A., and David A. Lake, eds. *International Political Economy: Perspectives on Global Power and Wealth.* 2d ed. New York: St. Martin's, 1995.

Frost, Ellen, and Angela Stent. "NATO's Troubles with East-West Trade." *International Security* 8, 1 (1983): 179–200.

Gee, Jack. "A New Era in Global Telecom." *IW Electronics and Technology* (17 July 1992): 42–47.

Gee, Sherman. *Technology Transfer, Innovation and International Competition.* New York: John Wiley, 1981.

General Accounting Office. *U.S. Business Access to Certain Foreign State-of-the-Art Technologies.* Washington, D.C.: U.S. Government Printing Office (September 1991).

George, Alexander. "Case Studies and Theory Development: The Method of Structured, Focused Comparison," in Paul Gordon Lauren, ed. *Diplomacy: New Approaches in History, Theory and Policy.* New York: Free Press, 1979.

Gilpin, Robert. *U.S. Power and the Multinational Corporation.* New York: Basic Books, 1975.

———. *War and Change in World Politics.* New York: Cambridge University Press, 1981.

———. *The Political Economy of International Relations.* Princeton, N.J.: Princeton University Press, 1987.

Gladwin, Thomas, and Ingo Walter. *Multinationals under Fire.* New York: Wiley, 1980.

Gordon, Lincoln, ed. *Eroding Empire.* Washington, D.C.: Brookings Institution, 1987.

Gourevitch, Peter A. *Politics in Hard Times.* Ithaca, N.Y.: Cornell University Press, 1986.

Gowa, Joanne. *Allies, Adversaries, and International Trade.* Princeton, N.Y.: Princeton University Press, 1994.

———. *Closing the Gold Window: Domestic Politics and the End of Bretton Woods.* Ithaca: Cornell University Press, N.Y., 1983.

———. "Hegemons, IOs, and Markets, the Case of the Substitution Account." *International Organization* 38, 4 (1984): 661–83.

———. "Economic Policy Making." *International Organization* 41, 1 (1988): 15–32.

Gramsci, Antonio. *Selections from the Prison Notebooks of Antonio Gramsci.* Ed. and trans. Quintman Hoare and Geoffrey Nowell-Smith. London: Random House, 1970.

Grande, Edgar. "The New Role of the State in Telecommunications: An International Comparison." *West European Politics* 17, 3 (1994): 138–57.

Granger, John V. *Technology and International Relations.* San Francisco: W. H. Freeman, 1979.

Griffin, Joseph P. "E.C. and U.S. Extraterritoriality: Activism and Cooperation." *Fordham International Law Journal* 17, 2 (1994): 353–88.

The Guardian.

Gustafson, Thane. *Selling the Russians the Rope? Soviet Technology Policy and U.S. Export Controls.* Santa Monica: Rand, 1981.

Haas, Ernst. *The Uniting of Europe.* Stanford: Stanford University Press, 1958.

———. "Why Collaborate? Issue-Linkage and International Regimes." *World Politics* 32 (1980a).

————. *When Knowledge Is Power.* Berkeley: University of California Press, 1990.

Haas, Peter. "Do Regimes Matter: Epistemic Communities and the Med." *International Organization* 43 (1989): 377–404.

Haass, Richard N., ed. *Economic Sanctions and American Diplomacy.* New York: Council of Foreign Relations Press, 1998.

————. "Sanctioning Madness." *Foreign Affairs* (November/December 1997): 74–85.

Haggard, Stephan, and Beth Simmons. "Theories of International Regimes." *International Organization* 41, 3 (1987): 491–517.

Haig, Alexander. *Caveat: Reagan, Realism, and Foreign Policy.* New York: Macmillan, 1984.

Hanrieder, Woifram, ed. *Economic Issues and the Atlantic Community.* New York: Praeger, 1982.

Hanson, Philip. *RIIA Discussion Papers 1, Soviet Industrial Espionage: Some New Information.* London: Royal Institute of International Affairs, 1987.

Harding, Christopher. *European Community Investigations and Sanctions: The Supranational Control of Business Delinquency.* New York: St. Martin's, 1993.

Hassner, Pierre. "The View from Paris." In Lincoln Gordon, ed. *Eroding Empire.* Washington, D.C.: Brookings Institution, 1987.

Heckscher, Eli F. *Mercantilism.* Trans. Mendel Shapiro. London: Allen and Unwin, 1955.

Henderson, Jeffrey. *The Globalization of High-Technology Production.* New York: Routledge, 1981.

Herman, A. H. *Conflict of National Laws with International Business Activity: Issues of Extraterritoriality.* London: British-North American Committee, 1982.

Henkin, Louis. *International Law: Cases and Materials,* 2d ed. St. Paul, Minn.: West Publishing, 1987.

Hewett, Ed A. "The Pipeline Connection: Issues for the Alliance." *The Brookings Review,* 1981.

Hills, Jill. *Deregulating Telecoms: Competition and Control in the United States, Japan, and Britain.* London: Pinter, 1986.

Hippler, Jochen. "Iraq's Military Power: The German Connection." *Middle East Report* 21 (1991): 27–31.

Hirschman, Albert. *National Power and the Structure of Foreign Trade.* Berkeley: University of California Press, 1980.

Hoffman, Stanley. "Review of the *Handbook on Political Science.*" *American Political Science Review* 71 (1977): 1621–23.

Holsti, K. J. *Change in the International System.* Boulder, Colo.: Westview Press, 1980.

————. *The Dividing Discipline.* New York: Allen and Irwin, 1985.

Holsti, K. J., P. Terrence Hopmann, and John Sullivan. *Unity and Disintegration in International Alliances.* New York: John Wiley, 1973.

Hopmann, P. Terrence. "Asymmetrical Bargaining in the Conference on Security and Cooperation in Europe." *International Organization* 32, 1 (1978): 141–78.

House of Commons Debates. 1959. Volume I.

Hufbauer, Gary C., and Jeffrey J. Schott. *Economic Sanctions Reconsidered.* Washington, D.C.: Institute for International Economics, 1985.

Huth, Paul K. *Extended Deterrence and the Prevention of War.* New Haven, Conn.: Yale University Press, 1988.

Hymer, Stephen. *The International Operations of National Firms.* Cambridge: University Press of America, 1976.

Ikenberry, John, ed. *The State and American Foreign Economic Policy.* Cambridge: MIT Press, 1988.

The Independent.

International Chamber of Commerce, Committee on Extraterritorial Application of National Laws. *The Extraterritorial Application of National Laws.* New York: ICC Publishing, 1987.

International Herald Tribune.

International Legal Materials.

International Trade Reporter.

Jackson, Robert and Carl Rosberg. "What Africa's Weak States Persist: The Empirical and Juridical in Statehood." *World Politics* 35, 3 (1982): 1–24.

Jacobson, Carol, Stephanie Lenway, and Peter Ring. "The Political Embeddedness of Private Economic Transactions." *Journal of Management Studies* 30, 3 (1993): 453–78.

Jane's Defense Weekly.

Jenks, Clarence Wilfred. *Law in the World Community.* New York: D. McKay, 1967.

Jentleson, Bruce, W. "From Consensus to Conflict: The Domestic Political Economy of East-West Energy Trade Policy." *International Organization* 38, 4 (1984): 625–60.

———. *Pipeline Politics.* Ithaca, N.Y.: Cornell University Press, 1986.

Jervis, Robert. *Perception and Misperception in International Politics.* Princeton, N.J.: Princeton University Press, 1978.

———. "Cooperation under the Security Dilemma." *World Politics* 30 (1978): 167–214.

———. "Systems Theory." In Lauren, Paul G., ed. *Diplomacy: New Approaches in History, Theory, and Policy.* New York: Free Press, 1979.

———. "Realism, Game Theory, and Cooperation." *World Politics* 40 (1988): 317–49.

Jiji Ticker Press Service.

Jones, R. J. Barry, and Peter Willets, eds. *Interdependence on Trial.* London: Frances Pinter, 1984.

Joyner, Christopher. "Sanctions, Compliance, and International Law: Reflections on the U.N. Experience against Iraq." *Virginia Journal of International Law* 32, 1 (1991): 1–46.

Kaempfer, William H., and Anton D. Lowenberg. *International Economic Sanctions: A Public Choice Perspective.* Boulder, Colo.: Westview Press, 1992.

Kann, Robert. "Alliances Versus Ententes." *World Politics* 28 (1976): 611–21.

Katzenstein, Peter J. *Between Power and Plenty.* Madison: University of Wisconsin Press, 1978.

————. *Small States in World Markets.* Ithaca, N.Y.: Cornell University Press, 1985.

Kelly, Tim. *The British Computer Industry: Crisis and Development.* New York: Croom Helm, 1987.

Kemme, David M., cd. *Technology Markets and Export Controls in the 1990s.* New York: New York University Press, 1991.

Keohane, Robert O. *After Hegemony: Cooperation and Discord in the World Political Economy.* Princeton, N.J.: Princeton University Press, 1984.

————. *Neorealism and Its Critics.* New York: Columbia University Press, 1986a.

————. "Reciprocity in International Relations." *International Organization* 40 (1986b): 1–27.

————. "International Institutions: Two Approaches." *International Studies Quarterly* 32 (1988): 379–96.

Keohane, Robert O., and Joseph S. Nye. *Power and Interdependence.* Boston: Little Brown, 1977.

Kindleberger, Charles. *The World in Depression, 1929–39.* Berkeley: University of California Press, 1986.

————. *The International Corporation.* Cambridge: Harvard University Press, 1970.

Klare, Michael. *Rogue States and Nuclear Outlaws: America's Search for a New Foreign Policy.* New York: Hill and Wang, 1995.

Klare, Michael, and Daniel Thomas, eds. *World Security: Challenges for a New Century.* 2d ed. New York: St. Martin's, 1994.

Knorr, Klaus. *The Power of Nations.* New York: Basic Books, 1975.

Knorr, Klaus, and Frank N. Trager, eds. *Economic Issues and National Security.* Lawrence, Ks.: Allen Press, 1977.

Kobrin, Stephen. "Enforcing Export Embargoes through Multinational Corporations: Why Doesn't It Work Anymore?" *Business in the Contemporary World* 1, 2 (1989): 31–42.

————. "Testing the Bargaining Hypothesis in the Manufacturing Sector in Developing Countries." *International Organization* 41, 4 (1987): 609–38.

Krasner, Stephen. "State Power and the Structure of the International Trading System." *World Politics* 28, 3 (1976): 317–47.

————. *Defending the National Interest.* Princeton: Princeton University Press, 1978.

————. ed. *International Regimes.* Ithaca, N.Y.: Cornell University Press, 1983.

————. *Structural Conflict.* Berkeley: University of California Press, 1985.

————. "Sovereignty: An Institutional Perspective." *Comparative Political Studies* 21, 1 (1988): 66–94.

————. "Compromising Westphalia." *International Security* 30, 3 (1995/96): 115–51.

Kratochwil, Friedrich. "The Force of Prescriptions." *International Organization* 38, 4 (1984): 685–708.

————. *Rules, Norms, and Decisions.* New York: Cambridge University Press, 1989.

Kratochwil, Friedrich, and John G. Ruggie. "International Organization: A State of the Art on the Art of the State." *International Organization* 40 (1986): 753–776.

Kroll, John. "The Complexity of Interdependence." *International Studies Quarterly* 37 (1993): 321–47.

Krugman, Paul. "A Mode of Innovation, Technology Transfer and the World Distribution of Income." *Journal of Political Economy* 87 (1979): 253–66.

Kupchan, Charles. "NATO and the Persian Gulf: Examining Intra-Alliance Behavior." *International Organization* 42 (1988): 317–46.

Lacey, John, R., ed. *Act of State and Extraterritorial Reach.* Chicago: American Bar Association (1983).

Lachaux, Claude, Denis Lacorn, and Christian Lamoureux, eds. *De L'Arme Economique.* Paris: Foundation pour les Etudes de Dèfense Nationale, 1987.

Lakatos, Imre, and Alan Musgrave, eds. *Criticism and the Growth of Knowledge.* Cambridge: Cambridge University Press, 1970.

Lake, David. "International Economic Structures and American Foreign Policy." *World Politics* 35, 4 (1983): 517–43.

———. "The State and American Trade Strategy in the Pre-Hegemonic Era." *International Organization* 42, 1 (1988): 33–58.

Lake, David and James, Scott. "The Second Face of Hegemony." *International Organization* 43, 1 (1989): 1–29.

Lasswell, Harold D., and Kaplan, Abraham. *Power and Society.* New Haven, Conn.: Yale University Press, 1986.

Lauren, Paul G., ed. *Diplomacy: New Approaches in History, Theory, and Policy.* New York: Free Press, 1979.

Lenway, Stephanie, and Crawford, Beverly. "When Business Becomes Politics: Risk and Uncertainty in East-West Trade," *Research in Corporate Social Performance and Policy: A Research Annual* 8 (1986): 29–53.

Lepgold, Joseph. *The Declining Hegemon.* New York: Greenwood Press, 1990.

Leyton-Brown, David, ed. *The Utility of Economic Sanctions.* London: Croom Melm, 1987.

Lieber, Robert J. *The Oil Decade: Conflict and Cooperation in the West.* New York: Praeger, 1983.

Line, Richard. *The International Electronics Industry, Special Report No. 2050.* London: Economist Intelligence Unit, 1990.

Lipson, Charles. "International Cooperation in Economic and Security Affairs." *World Politics* 37 (1984): 495–538.

———. *Standing Guard.* Berkeley: University of California Press, 1985.

Liska, George. *Nations in Alliance: The Limits of Interdependence.* Baltimore, Md.: Johns Hopkins Press, 1962.

Long, William. *Economic Incentives and Bilateral Cooperation.* Ann Arbor: University of Michigan Press, 1996.

————. "Trade and Technology Incentives and Bilateral Cooperation," *International Studies Quarterly* 40, 1 (1996): 77–106.

————. *U.S. Export Control Policy.* New York: Columbia University Press, 1989.

Losman, Donald L. *International Economic Sanctions: The Cases of Cuba, Israel, and Rhodesia.* Albuquerque: University of New Mexico Press, 1979.

Lowenfeld, Andreas. *International Economic Law: Trade Controls for Political Ends.* 2d ed. New York: Matthew Bender, 1983.

Lowe, Alan V. *Extraterritorial Jurisdiction: An Annotated Collection of Legal Material.* Cambridge: Grotius, 1983.

————. "Public International Law and the Conflict of Laws." *International and Comparative Law Quarterly* 33 (1984): 515–30.

Lukes, Steven, ed. *Power.* Oxford: Basil Blackwell, 1986.

————. *Power: A Radical View.* New York: Macmillan, 1974.

Lunine, Janet. "High-Technology Warfare: The Export Administration Act Amendments of 1985 and the Problem of Foreign Reexport." *New York University Journal of International Law and Politics* 18, 2 (1985/86): 663–702.

Macdonald, Stuart. *Technology and the Tyranny of Export Controls.* London: Macmillan, 1990.

Mackintosh, Ian. *Sunrise Europe: The Dynamics of Information Technology.* New York: Basil Blackwell, 1986.

Maier, Harold. "Resolving Extraterritorial Conflicts, or 'There and Back Again,' " *Virginia Journal of International Law* 25, 1 (1984): 7–48.

Malerba, Franco. *The Semiconductor Business: The Economics of Rapid Growth and Decline.* Madison: University of Wisconsin Press, 1985.

Malloy, Michael, P. *Economic Sanctions and U.S. Trade.* Boston: Little, Brown, 1990.

Mansfield, Edward. *Power, Trade and War.* Princeton, N.J.: Princeton University Press, 1994.

————. "The Concentration of Capabilities and International Trade." *International Organization* 46 (1992): 105–28.

Mansfield, Edwin. *Technology Transfer, Productivity, and Economic Policy.* New York: W. W. Norton, 1982.

Morrow, James. "Signaling Difficulties with Linkage in Crisis Bargaining." *International Studies Quarterly* 36 (1992): 153–72.

Martin, Lisa. *Coercive Cooperation.* Princeton, N.J.: Princeton University Press, 1992.

Mastanduno, Michael. "Strategies of Economic Containment: United States Trade Relations with the Soviet Union." *World Politics* 37, 4 (1985).

————. *Economic Containment: CoCom and the Politics of East-West Trade.* Ithaca, N.Y.: Cornell University Press, 1992.

Matthews, David. "Controlling the Exportation of Strategically Sensitive Technology: The Extraterritorial Jurisdiction of the Multilateral Export Control Enhancement Amendments Act of 1988." *Columbia Journal of Transnational Law* 28, 3 (1988): 747–774.

McCalman, James. *The Electronics Industry in Britain: Coping with Change.* London: Routledge, 1988.

McClellan, Stephen T. *The Coming Computer Industry Shakeout.* New York: John Wiley and Sons, 1984.

McDougal, Myres, and W. Michael Reisman. *International Law Essays.* Mineola, N.Y.: Foundation Press, 1981.

McIntyre, J., and Cupitt, Richard. "East West Strategic Trade Control: Crumbling Consensus?" *Survey* (1980): 81–108.

McKeown, Timothy J. "Hegemonic Stability Theory and Nineteenth-Century Tariff Levels in Europe." *International Organization* 37 (1983): 73–91.

de Mestral, Armand L. C., and Gruchalla-Wesierski, T. *Extraterritorial Application of Export Control Legislation: Canada and the U.S.A.* London: Martinus Nijhoff, 1990.

Metcalfe, Robyn S. *The New Wizard War: How the Soviets Steal U.S. High Technology— And How We Give It Away.* Redmond, Wash.: Tempus Books, 1988.

Michaely, Michael. *Theory of Commercial Policy: Trade and Protection.* Chicago: University of Chicago Press, 1977.

Milner, Helen. *Resisting Protectionism.* Princeton, N.J.: Princeton University Press, 1988.

———. "The Assumption of Anarchy in International Relations Theory." *Review of International Studies* (1991): 67–86.

Mitchell, T. "The Limits of the State: Beyond Statist Approaches and Their Critics." *Review of International Studies* 12 (1991): 77–96.

Modelski, George, and William Thompson. *Sea Power and Global Politics: 1494– 1983.* Seattle: University of Washington, 1987.

Le Monde.

Moore, John Norton. "Prolegomenon to the Jurisprudence of Myres McDougal and Harold Lasswell," *Virginia Law Review* 54, 4 (1968): 662–88.

Moran, Theodore H. *American Economic Policy and National Security.* New York: Council on Foreign Relations, 1993.

———. "Foreign Acquisition of Critical U.S. Industries: Where Should the United States Draw the Line?" *Washington Quarterly* 16, 3 (1993): 61–71.

———. "Grand Strategy: The Pursuit of Power and the Pursuit of Plenty." *International Organization* 50, 1 (1996): 175–205.

———. "The Globalization of America's Defense Industries: Managing the Threat of Foreign Dependence." *International Security* 15 (1990): 57–100.

Morgenthau, Hans J. *Politics among Nations.* New York: Knopf, 1966.

Morici, Peter. *The Global Competitive Struggle: Challenges to the U.S. and Canada.* Washington, D.C.: National Planning Association, 1984.

Moyer, Homer E., and Linda A. Mabry. *Export Controls as Instruments of Foreign Policy: The History, Legal Issues, and Policy Lessons of Three Recent Cases.* Washington, D.C.: University of America Press, 1983.

Mytelka, Lynn, ed. *Strategic Partnerships: States, Firms, and International* Competition. Rutherford, N.J.: Farleigh Dickinson University, 1991.

Neale, Alan D., and M. L. Stephens. *International Business and National Jurisdiction.* Oxford: Clarendon, 1988.

Nelson, Richard. *High-Technology Politics: A Five-Nation Comparison.* Washington, D.C.: American Enterprise Institute, 1984.

New York Times.

Nincic, Miroslav, and Peter Wallensteen. *The Dilemmas of Economic Coercion: Sanctions in World Politics.* New York: Praeger Publishers, 1983.

North Atlantic Treaty Organization. Draft Interim Report. Sub-Committee on the Proliferation of Military Technology. Hon. Sherwood I. Boehlert, NATO International Secretariat (May 1994).

Organization for Economic Cooperation and Development. 1982–1987. *Foreign Trade by Commodity, Series C.* Paris: OECD Publishing.

———. *The Semiconductor Industry: Trade Related Issues.* Paris: OECD Publishing, 1985.

Olmstead, Cecil J., ed. *Extraterritorial Application of Laws and Responses Thereto.* Oxford: ESC Publishing, 1984.

Olson, Mancur. *The Logic of Collective Action.* Cambridge: Harvard University Press, 1971.

Organski, A. F. K., and Jacek Kugler. *The War Ledger.* Chicago: University of Chicago Press, 1980.

Oye, Kenneth, ed. *Cooperation under Anarchy.* Princeton, N.J.: Princeton University Press, 1986.

Pape, Robert. "Why Economic Sanctions Still Don't Work." *International Security* 22 (1997): 90–136.

Paquet, Gilles. *The Multinational Firm and the Nation State.* New York: Macmillan, 1972.

Paret, Peter, ed. *Makers of Modern Strategy.* Princeton, N.J.: Princeton University Press, 1986.

Paul, J. K., ed. *High-Technology International Trade and Competition.* Park Ridge, N.J.: Noyes, 1984.

Pisar, Samuel. *Coexistence and Commerce.* New York: McGraw Hill, 1970.

Pollins, Brian. "Does Trade Still Follow the Flag?" *American Political Science Review* 83 (1989): 465–80.

Putnam, Robert, and Nicholas Bayne. *Hanging Together.* London: Royal Institute of International Affairs, 1987.

Putnam, Robert. "Diplomacy and Domestic Politics." *International Organization* 42, 3 (1988): 427–60.

Rapoport, Anatol. *Two-Person Game Theory: The Essential Ideas.* Ann Arbor: University of Michigan Press, 1969.

Reich, Robert. *The Work of Nations.* New York: A. A. Knopf, 1991.

Renwick, Robin. *Economic Sanctions.* Cambridge: Center for International Affairs, Harvard University, 1981.

Report of the National Critical Technologies Panel. Washington, D.C.: U.S. Government Printing Office (March 1991).

Reuter European Business Report.

Riker, William H. "Some Ambiguities in the Notion of Power." *American Political Science Review* 58 (1964): 341–49.

Rioux, Jean-Francois. *Limiting the Proliferation of Weapons: The Role of Supply-Side Strategies.* Ottawa, Ont.: Carleton University Press, 1992.

Rode, Reinhard, and Hanns D. Jacobsen, eds. *Economic Warfare or Detente: Assessment of East-West Relations in the 1980s.* London: Westview, 1985.

Rogowski, Ronald. *Commerce and Coalitions: How Trade Affects Domestic Alignments.* Princeton, N.J.: Princeton University Press, 1989.

Rosecrance, Richard. "International Theory Revisited." *International Organization* 35 (1981): 691–714.

Rosenau, James, Kenneth W. Thompson, and Gavin Boyd, eds. *World Politics.* New York: Free Press, 1976.

Rosenberg, Justin. "A Neo-Realist Theory of Sovereignty? Giddens's *The Nation-State and Violence,*" *Millennium* 19 (1991): 249–60.

Rosenthal, Douglas, and Knighton, William. *Chatham House Papers #17: National Laws and International Commerce: The Problem of Extraterritoriality.* London: Routledge & Kegan Paul, 1982.

Rothstein, Robert. "Consensual Knowledge and International Collaboration." *International Organization* 38 (1984): 733–62.

Rowe, David M. *The Domestic Political Economy of International Economic Sanctions.* Harvard University Working Paper Series, Paper No. 93–1. Cambridge: Center for International Affairs, Harvard University, 1993.

Ruggie, John G. 1983. *The Antinomies of Interdependence: National Welfare and the International Division of Labor.* New York: Columbia University Press, 1983.

Russett, Bruce, ed. *Peace, War, and Numbers.* Beverly Hills: Sage, 1972.

———. "The Mysterious Case of Vanishing Hegemony; or, Is Mark Twain Really Dead?" *International Organization* 29, 2 (1985): 207–31.

Sabrosky, Alan Ned, ed. *Polarity and War: The Changing Structure of International Conflict.* Boulder, Colo.: Westview Press, 1985.

Sagafi-nejad, Tagi, Richard W. Moxon, and Howard V. Perlmutter. *Controlling International Technology Transfer: Issues, Perspectives, and Implications.* New York: Pergamon Press, 1981.

Sandholtz, Wayne. *High-Tech Europe: The Politics of International Cooperation.* Berkeley: University of California Press, 1992.

Sarna, Aaron, J. *Boycott and Blacklist: A History of Arab Economic Warfare against Israel.* Totowa, N.J.: Roman & Littlefield, 1986.

Sauvant, Karl P. *Trade and Foreign Direct Investment in Data Services.* Boulder, Colo.: Westview, 1986.

Seward, Bernard, Jr., ed. *Technology Control, Competition, and National Security.* New York: University Press of America, 1987.

Schelling, Thomas C. *Arms and Influence.* Westport, Conn.: Greenwood, 1976.

———. *The Strategy of Conflict.* Cambridge: Harvard University Press, 1980.

Schneider, Gerald, and Patricia Weitsman, eds. *Enforcing Cooperation: "Risky" States and the Intergovernmental Management of Conflict.* New York: Macmillan, 1996.

Schoenbaum, Thomas, Mitsuo Matsushita, and Dorinda Dallmeyer, eds. *Dynamics of Japanese-United States Trade Relations.* Athens, Ga.: Dean Rusk Center for International and Comparative Law, University of Georgia School of Law, 1986.

Schwarzenberger, Georg. *The Inductive Approach to International Law.* Ferry, N.Y.: Oceana Publications, 1965.

Schweller, Randall. "Tripolarity and the Second World War." *International Studies Quarterly* 37, 1 (1992): 73–103.

Sedaitis, Judith, ed. *Commercializing High-Technology: East and West.* Stanford: Stanford University Center for International Security and Arms Control, 1996.

Segall, Wynn H. "Export Controls and Economic Sanctions." *The International Lawyer* 31, 2 (1997): 393–401.

Shaffer, Mark E., ed. *Technology Transfer and East-West Relations.* London: Croom Helm (1985).

Shambaugh, George E. "Cooperation under Structural Asymmetry." Seminar Paper. Columbia University (1988).

———. "Sanctions and Sovereignty in the Cold War Era and Today." Panel Presentation. Annual Meeting of the American Political Science Association. Washington, D.C. (1993).

———. "Dominance, Dependence, and Political Power: Tethering Technology in the 1990s and Today." *International Studies Quarterly* 40, 4 (1996): 559–88.

Shambaugh, George E., and Patricia A. Weitsman. "First, Second and Third Wave Approaches to the Study of Institutions in International Politics: Is Progress Ever Possible without Reinventing the Wheel?" Presented at the Annual Meeting of the American Political Science Association (September 1992).

Sills, David, ed. *International Encyclopedia of the Social Sciences.* New York: Macmillan, 1968.

Simon, G. A. *Models of Man, Social and Rational: Mathematical Essays on Rational and Human Behavior in a Social Setting.* New York: Wiley, 1957.

Smith, Gordon, ed. *The Politics of East-West Trade.* Boulder, Colo.: Westview, 1984.

Snidal, Duncan. "Coordination Versus Prisoners' Dilemma." *American Political Science Review* 79 (1985a): 923–42.

———. "The Limits of Hegemonic Stability Theory." *International Organization* 39, 4 (1985b): 579–614.

Snyder, Glenn, and Diesing, Paul. *Conflict among Nations.* Princeton, N.J.: Princeton University Press, 1977.

"Soviet Involvement in Poland." Statement on U.S. Measures Taken against the Soviet Union 29 December 1981. *Weekly Compilation of Presidential Documents* 1429 (4 January 1982): 17.

Spruyt, Hendrik. *The Sovereign State and Its Competitors: An Analysis of Systems Change.* Princeton, N.J.: Princeton University Press, 1994.

Stein, Arthur. "The Hegemon's Dilemma." *International Organization* 38, 2 (1984): 355–86.

Stent, Angela. *East-West Technology Transfer: European Perspectives.* Beverly Hills: Sage, 1980.

————. *From Embargo to Ostpolitik: The Political Economy of the West German-Soviet Relations, 1955–1980.* New York: Cambridge University Press, 1981.

Stern, Jonathan. *East European Energy and East-West Trade in Energy.* British Institutes' Joint Energy Policy Programme, Energy Paper Number 1. London: Policy Studies Institute, 1982.

Strange, Susan. *Paths to International Political Economy.* London: George Allen and Unwin, 1984.

————. *States and Markets.* New York: Basil Balckwell, 1988.

————. "The Persistent Myth of Lost Hegemony." *International Organization* 41, 4 (1987): 551–71.

Sunkel, Osvaldo. "Big Business and Dependencia: A Latin American View." *Foreign Affairs* 50, 3 (1972): 517–31.

Thomson, Janice E. "State Sovereignty in International Relations: Bridging the Gap between Theory and Empirical Research." *International Studies Quarterly* 39, 2 (1995): 213–33.

The Times.

Timmerman, Kenneth. *The Death Lobby: How the West Armed Iraq.* Boston: Houghton Mifflin, 1991.

Todd, Daniel. *The World Electronics Industry.* London: Routledge, 1990.

Tyson, Laura d'Andrea. *Who's Bashing Whom? Trade Conflict in High-Technology Industries.* Washington, D.C.: Institute for International Economics, 1992.

United Nations. United Nations Center on Transnational Corporations. *Transnational Corporations in the Semiconductor Industry.* New York: United Nations Publishing, 1986.

————. Economic Commission for Europe. *The Telecommunication Industry: Growth and Structural Change.* New York: United Nations, 1987.

————. *International Statistics Yearbook.* Vol. 2. New York: United Nations (1983–1995).

U.S. Congress. Panel on the Impact of National Security Controls on International Technology Transfer. Committee on Science, Engineering, and Public Policy, National Academy of Sciences. *Balancing the National Interest: U.S. National Security Export Controls and Global Competition.* Washington, D.C.: National Academy Press, 1987.

————. House Committee on Foreign Affairs. Subcommittee on International Economic Policy and Trade. *United States Exports of Sensitive Technology to Iraq: Hearings* (8 April 1991 and 22 May 1991).

U.S. Department of Commerce. International Trade Administration. *High-Technology Industries: Profiles and Outlooks—The Computer Industry.* Washington, D.C.: U.S. Government Printing Office (April 1983).

———. International Trade Administration. *High-Technology Industries: Profiles and Outlooks—The Telecommunications Industry.* Washington, D.C.: U.S. Government Printing Office (April 1983).

———. International Trade Administration. *Country Market Survey: Computers and Peripheral Equipment, United Kingdom.* Washington, D.C.: U.S. Government Printing Office, 1984.

———. International Trade Administration. *Country Market Survey: Telecommunications Equipment, France.* Washington, D.C.: U.S. Government Printing Office (June 1987).

U.S. Department of Defense. *An Analysis of Export Control of U.S. Technology—A DoD Perspective.* Washington, D.C.: Office of Defense Research and Engineering, 1976.

———. Directive 2040.2. "International Transfers of Technology, Goods, Services, and Munitions." Section D. (17 January 1984).

———. *The Military Critical Technology List.* Washington, D.C.: Department of Defense, Office of the Undersecretary of Defense, Defense Research and Engineering (October 1984).

———. *The Technology Transfer Program: A Report to the 98th Congress.* Washington, D.C.: U.S. Department of Defense, 1984.

U.S. Department of State. *U.S. Department of State Bulletin* 309:39. Statement of 9 July 1958 (4 August 1958).

U.S. Export Weekly (2 March 1982).

U.S. Office of Technology Assessment. *Technology and East-West Trade.* Washington D.C.: U.S. Government Printing Office, 1979.

U.S. National Academy of Sciences. Panel on the Future Design and Implementation of U.S. National Security Export Controls. Committee on Science, Engineering, and Public Policy. *Finding Common Ground: U.S. Export Controls in a Changed Global Environment.* Washington, D.C.: National Academy Press, 1991.

University of Virginia. Center for Law and National Security. *Technology Control, Competition, and National Security: Conflict and Consensus.* Lanham: University Press of America, 1987.

Vernon, Raymond. *Big Business and the States: Changes Relations in Western Europe* Cambridge: Harvard University Press, 1974.

———. *Sovereignty at Bay.* New York: Basic Books, 1971.

———. *Storm over Multinationals.* Cambridge: University Press of America, 1977.

———. *Exploring the Global Economy.* Cambridge: University Press of America, 1985.

Vernon, Raymond, and Deborah Spar. *Beyond Globalism: Remaking American Foreign Economic Policy.* New York: Free Press, 1989.

Viner, Jacob. "Power Versus Plenty as Objectives of Foreign Policy in the Seventeenth and Eighteenth Centuries." *World Politics* 1, 1 (1948): 1–29.

Wagner, Harisson. "The Theory of Games and the Problem of International Cooperation." *American Political Science Review* 77 (1983): 546–76.

———. "Economic Interdependence, Bargaining, Power, and Political Influence." *International Organization* 42, 3 (1988): 461–83.

Walt, Stephen. *The Origins of Alliances.* Ithaca, N.Y.: Cornell University Press, 1987.

———. "Testing Theories of Alliance Formation." *International Organization* 42, 2 (1988): 275–316.

Waltz, Kenneth N. *Man, the State, and War: A Theoretical Analysis.* New York: Columbia University Press, 1959.

———. *Theory of International Politics.* Reading: Addison-Wesley, 1979.

———. "The Emerging Structure of International Politics." *International Security* 18, 2 (1993): 44–79.

Ward, Michael Don. "Research Gaps in Alliance Dynamics." *Monograph Series in World Affairs.* University of Denver. 19, 1 (1982).

Washington Post.

The Washington Times.

Weber, Max. *Economy and Society: An Outline of Interpretive Sociology.* New York: Bedminster, 1968.

Weekly Compilation of Presidential Documents 17 (13 November 1982).

Weil, Prosper. *The Law of Maritime Delimitation: Reflections.* Cambridge: Grotius, 1989.

Wendt, Alexander. "Anarchy Is What States Make of It: The Social Construction of State Politics." *International Organization* 46, 2 (1992): 391–425.

Westbrook, Jay L. "Extraterritoriality, Conflict of Laws, and the Regulation of Transnational Business." *Texas International Law Journal* 25, 1 (1990): 71–97.

Whitman, Marina von Numan. *Reflections of Interdependence: Issues for Economic Theory and U.S. Policy.* Pittsburgh: University of Pittsburgh Press, 1979.

Wiles, Peter. *Communist International Economics.* Oxford: Basil Blackwell, 1968.

Wolfers, Arnold. *Discord and Collaboration.* Baltimore, Md.: Johns Hopkins Press, 1962.

Woods, Stanley. *Atlantic Paper No. 63, Western Europe: Technology and the Future.* Paris: Croom Helm, 1987.

Woolcock, Stephen. *Western Policies on East-West Trade.* Chatham House Papers #15. London: Royal Institute of International Affairs, 1982.

Yarbrough, Beth, and Yarbrough, Robert. "Cooperation in the Liberalization of International Trade: After Hegemony, What?" *International Organization* 41, 1 (1987): 1–26.

Young, Oran. "Anarchy and Social Choice." *World Politics* 30, 2 (1978): 241–63.

———. *International Cooperation: Building Regimes for Natural Resources and the Environment.* Ithaca, N.Y.: Cornell University Press, 1989.

INDEX